CW00819108

The Bavarian Army has been overshadowed by those of Gustavus Adolphus and Wallenstein, but it was one of only a few armies to have fought throughout the Thirty Years War, first as part of the Catholic League and then an independent army after the Peace of Prague. Among the generals of the Bavarian Army were Count Johann von Tilly and Gottfried von Pappenheim, who are two of the most famous generals of the war. This book covers not only the Bavarian Army's organisation, but also has chapters on recruitment, officers, clothing, weaponry, pay and rations of a soldier during the Thirty Years War. As well as life and death in the army, this book also looks at the women who accompanied it. The chapter on 'civilians and soldiers' looks at the impact of the war on the civilian population, their reaction to it and the infamous sack of Magdeburg which sent shockwaves across Europe. This chapter also looks at the impact on Bavaria by having Swedish, Spanish and Imperialist troops quartered upon it and how this affected the country's war effort. In addition there are chapters on regimental colours and a detailed look into the tactics of the time, including those of Spain, Sweden and the Dutch. As well as using archival and archaeological evidence to throw new light on the subject the author has used several memoirs written by those who served in the army during the war, including Peter Hagendorf who served in Pappenheim's Regiment of Foot from 1627 until the regiment was disbanded after the war. Hagendorf's vivid account is unique because not only is it a full account of the life of a common soldier during the war, but it also records the human side of campaign, including the death of his two wives and all but two of his children. This book is essential reading to anyone interested in the wars of the early seventeenth century, not just the Thirty Years War.

Laurence Spring studied at the Universities of London and Aberystwyth. He is also a qualified archivist, and has worked for many years at the Surrey History Centre. He has researched the early seventeenth century for many years and has written on various aspects of the English Civil War, including the campaigns of Sir William Waller and the armies of Sir William Waller and the Earl of Manchester. He has also written many books on the Russian Army during the Napoleonic Wars. Since he has an archival background he prefers to search through archives looking for interesting facts for his books that give a vivid insight into the subject, and which are usually not mentioned in secondary sources or contradict the established facts. His first book for Helion, *The First British Army, 1624–1628: The Army of the Duke of Buckingham*, was published in 2016.

Mark Allen (illustrator, front cover image)
An industry professional in publishing and book sales, Mark Allen has worked for WH Smith, PSL, Blandford Press and Cassell, before becoming Sales Director at Photobook Information Services which seemed to involve playing lots of cricket for West Malvern and not a lot else. Since 1991 Mark has spent most of his time painting model soldiers for a living, with a brief return, to a proper job, with Waterstones.

The Bavarian Army during the Thirty Years War 1618–1648

The Backbone of the Catholic League

Laurence Spring

Helion & Company Limited
26 Willow Road
Solihull
West Midlands
B91 1UE
England
Tel. 0121 705 3393
Fax 0121 711 4075
Email: info@helion.co.uk
Website: www.helion.co.uk
Twitter: @helionbooks
Visit our blog http://blog.helion.co.uk/

Published by Helion & Company 2017
Designed and typeset by Serena Jones
Cover designed by by Paul Hewitt, Battlefield Design (www.battlefield-design.co.uk)
Printed by Short Run Press, Exeter, Devon

Front cover: ensign with infantry colours, Bavarian Army *c*.1630s. Painting by Mark Allen © Helion & Company 2017
Rear cover: the sacking of Magdeburg, 1631

ISBN 978-1-911512-39-4

British Library Cataloguing-in-Publication Data.
A catalogue record for this book is available from the British Library.

For details of other military history titles published by Helion & Company Limited contact the above address, or visit our website: http://www.helion.co.uk.

We always welcome receiving book proposals from prospective authors.

Contents

List of Illustrations

Maps

Illustrations

Acknowledgements

I would like to thank the staff of the Bavarian State Archives, the Bavarian State Library, the Bavarian Army Museum, the British Library, the National Archives at Kew, England, the staff of the Swedish Army Museum in Stockholm, and the French National Library.

My thanks also go to Dr Langbrandtner of the LVR-Archivberatungs- und Fortbildungszentrum who sent me copies of the Hatzfeld Archives, and Cordula Kasper who wrote *Die Bayerische Kriegsorganisation in der zweiten Hälfte des Dreissigjährigen Krieges, 1635–1649* which examined many of the archives at the Bavarian State Archives. Not forgetting Eva Turek of the Swedish Army Museum who I corresponded with in the late 1980s and early 1990s about the regimental colours in the museum's collection.

Many thanks also to Serena Jones for proofreading the text.

Finally, my thanks to Stephen Ede-Borrett for supplying the illustrations to the Bavarian flags and colours, and Dr Lesley Prince for the artist rendering and reconstruction of the flags and colours.

Chronology

Bohemian War 1618–1621

1618	**23 May,** Defenestration of Prague, insurrection of Bohemia and setting up of a government of 30 directors
	August, Imperial troops under Bucquoy and Dampierre invade Bohemia to suppress insurrection
	21 November, Bohemian army under General Ernst von Mansfeld captures Pilsen
1619	**20 March,** Emperor Matthias dies, and is succeeded by Ferdinand I
	May, Bohemian troops invade Moravia
	June, a Bohemian army under General Thurn besieges Vienna
	16 June, Mansfeld is defeated by Bucquoy at the Battle of Zablat
	5 July, Dampierre is defeated at Dolni
	26 August, Frederick V, Elector of the Palatinate, elected king of Bohemia
	8 October, Maximilian of Bavaria agrees to help Ferdinand II crush the Bohemian insurrection
	November, Bohemian army again besieges Vienna
1620	**September,** joint offensive by the Imperial and Catholic League armies under Tilly forces the Bohemian army to return to Bohemia
	8 November, Tilly defeats the Bohemian army at the Battle of the White Mountains near Prague
1621	**21 June,** 21 representatives of the Bohemian estates are beheaded in Prague

Palatinate War 1621–1623

1621	**28 July,** an Imperialist force is defeated at Neutitschein in Moravia
1622	**January,** Pressburg Peace between Ferdinand II and Bethlen Gabor
	27 April, Tilly is defeated by Mansfeld at Wiesloch
	6 May, Tilly defeats George Frederick of Baden-Durlach's Army at Wimpfen
	20 June, Tilly defeats Christian of Brunswick's army at Höchst
	6 August, Tilly again defeats Christian of Brunswick's army, at Stadtlohn

Danish War 1625–1629

1625	**25 July,** Wallenstein raises an army for the Emperor
1626	**26 April,** Wallenstein defeats Mansfeld's army at Dessau
1627	**27 August,** Tilly and Wallenstein defeat Christian of Brunswick's army at Lutter
1628	**23 May–3 August,** Wallenstein fails to capture Stralsund
	2 September, part of Wallenstein's army defeats Christian IV of Denmark's army at Wolgast
1629	**6 March,** Ferdinand II issues the Edict of Restitution, ordering that all church property confiscated after the Peace of Augsburg be restored to the Catholic Church
	22 May, peace signed between Christian IV of Denmark and Ferdinand II
1630	**13 August,** Wallenstein dismissed as commander-in-chief of Imperialist forces

Swedish War 1630–1635

1630	**24 June,** King Gustavus Adolphus of Sweden lands in Pomerania
1631	**20 May,** Tilly's troops storm the city of Magdeburg
	17 September, a Swedish-Saxon army defeats Tilly at the Battle of Breitenfeld
	December, Wallenstein reappointed Imperialist commander-in-chief
1632	**4–14 April,** Tilly is defeated while trying to prevent Gustavus Adolphus' army crossing the river Lech near Rain
	3 September, Gustavus Adolphus is repulsed by Wallenstein near Nuremberg
	16 November, the Battle of Lützen, between the forces of Wallenstein and Gustavus Adolphus, where the latter is killed
1633	Wallenstein allegedly begins negotiating for peace
1634	**25 February,** Wallenstein is assassinated at Eger
	6 September, a Bavarian-Imperialist army defeats the Swedish army at Nördlingen
1635	**30 May,** Peace of Prague concluded between the Emperor and Elector of Saxony and several other Protestant princes

French–Swedish War 1635–1648

1636	**4 October,** a Swedish army defeated at Wittstock by an Imperialist-Saxon army
1637	Emperor Ferdinand II dies and is succeeded by his son Ferdinand III
1638	**28 February,** a Bavarian army is defeated by Prince Bernard of Saxe-Weimar at the Battle of Rheinfelden

1642	**2 November,** a Swedish army beats the Imperialist Army at the Second Battle of Breitenfeld
1643	Denmark reenters the war, this time on the side of the Emperor
	5 May, a Bavarian army defeats the French at the Battle of Tuttlingen
1645	**23 February,** a Swedish army beats the Imperialists at the Battle of Jankau
	3 August, a Bavarian army is defeated by the Prince of Condé's army at Allerheim
1646	A Franco-Swedish force invades Bavaria
1647	Bavaria is forced to conclude peace with France and Sweden
1648	**16 May,** a Franco-Swedish force defeats a Bavarian-Imperialist army at Augsburg
	24 October, after three years of negotiations peace is finally declared at Münster and Osnabruck

Introduction

There were many states that formed Germany during the early seventeenth century; one of the largest was Bavaria. Its origins dated back to Roman times as the province of Noricum. In the fifth century this province was ruled by the Ostrogoth king, Theodoric the Great (*c.*454–526), and from 1180 by the Wittelsbach dynasty, a position they enjoyed until Germany became a republic in 1918.

In 800 when Charles the Great (Charlemagne) was crowned Emperor of the Holy Roman Empire he ruled much of Europe. However when it was divided in two, the western part became France and the eastern part was formed from various Germanic states, including Bavaria. Although these states were part of the Empire they enjoyed a semi-autonomous existence and were able to discuss their grievances in one of the Imperial courts. For more important matters the emperor could call an Imperial Diet, which the state rulers, including the Duke of Bavaria and the various free cities within the empire, could cast their vote.

However it was just the seven electors of the empire – the Electors Palatinate, Saxony, and Brandenburg, the King of Bohemia and the Archbishops of Mainz, Trier and Cologne – who could elect a new emperor, although this had become a formality, with the throne going to a member of the Habsburg family. The Palatinate was ruled by a branch of the Wittelsbach family; it would not be until 1623 that the Bavarian branch would enjoy this status, when Holy Roman Emperor Ferdinand II secretly transferred power from Fredrick V, Elector of Palatinate to Maximilian of Bavaria. He also gave Maximilian part of the Palatinate as payment for recovering Bohemia and defeating Frederick's armies. Bohemia itself was important to the emperor, not only because since the sixteenth century it had been ruled by the Habsburgs, but also because its king was traditionally the emperor-elect.

Maximilian had come to the Bavarian throne aged 24, when his father abdicated leaving the country almost bankrupt. However, Maximilian not only managed to turn the economy around but made Bavaria a wealthy country within 20 years. He was devoutly religious, rising at about 3:00 a.m., and after an hour's prayer he set to work, breaking off to attend Vespers two or three times in a morning, and for an hour in the afternoon. He worked late into the evening and said more prayers before he went to sleep. Despite being a Catholic he had some very 'Puritan' values, disliking the excesses of pleasure, drinking and eating. After his death in 1651 it was found that he travelled with a hair shirt and utensils for self-flagellation. However, although he had his own Jesuit confessor he only followed his advice when he agreed with it.[1]

It is estimated that the population of Bavaria was about one million at the beginning of the seventeenth century. Although there were 34 cities, 93 market towns and 4,700 towns, and 104 monasteries, more than 80 percent of Bavaria was agricultural or common land. In 1606 there were 30,565 farms in the Upper Palatinate housing 118,000 families.[2]

The Reformation during the sixteenth century split the Empire into Lutheran and Catholic States. Among the latter was Bavaria, while the former included the Palatinate. Finally, after a bloody war between the two religions, the Peace of Augsburg was signed in 1555. True, this Peace was not perfect, since neither side could predict a new form of Protestantism – Calvinism – appearing; nor was it strictly adhered to, since those that converted after this date did not give up their lands as the Peace required. However, while the Netherlands and France erupted into civil war over religion (among other issues), the Peace did bring peace within the Empire for the next 63 years. In fact the Empire was not directly involved in a war until 1593, with the outbreak of war with the Ottoman Empire which lasted until 1606.

This is not to say that there was not tension within the Empire, especially in Austria where Emperor Rudolf II tried to impose the Counter-Reformation more aggressively, which resulted in open revolt at the turn of the seventeenth century. His Protestant subjects in Bohemia were also in open revolt, demanding greater religious liberty, and in 1609 Rudolf was forced to grant the Letter of Majesty. His brother Matthias had sided with the rebels, and on 11 March 1611 Rudolf was forced to abdicate as King of Bohemia in favour of his brother. Rudolf was stripped of all his titles except Emperor of the Holy Roman Empire, died on 20 January 1612 and was succeeded by Matthias. However, if the Protestants of Bohemia thought they would be able to enjoy their religious freedom they were sadly mistaken, as Matthias immediately began to undermine the Letter of Majesty by appointing Catholics to all the important positions. By now Matthias was 55 and childless, so he appointed Archduke Ferdinand as his successor, who was crowned King of Bohemia in 1617. Ferdinand was even more of a fanatical Catholic than either Rudolf or Matthias and soon began to impose his will on the Bohemian nobility.

Meanwhile Ferdinand's cousin, Maximilian of Bavaria, was also trying to impose the Counter-Reformation in the Germanic States, annexing Donauwörth in December 1607 after a religious dispute resulted in it receiving an Imperial Ban. In 1608 some of the Protestant States formed the Protestant Union, although apart from the Palatinate its membership only included a few states within the Empire and the Lutheran John George, Elector of Saxony, did not join. In response the Catholic League was formed the following year, although like its counterpart only a few states

1 Geoffrey Mortimer, *The Origins of the Thirty Years War and the revolt in Bohemia, 1618* (Basingstoke: Palgrave MacMillan, 2015), pp.190–191.

2 Andreas Kraus, *Geschichte Bayerns: von den Anfängen bis zur Gegenwart* (Munich: C. H. Beck, 1983), pp.227–228, 253.

joined. Nevertheless, both the League and the Union were commanded by branches of the Wittelsbach family. Neither were the Catholics united as some backed the Emperor, fearing that Maximilian of Bavaria was becoming too powerful, while others did not want him interfering in the running of their states.

With tensions still running high over Bavaria's annexation of Donauwörth, in 1609 a new crisis arose over who would succeed the ruler of the Duchy of Cleves-Jülich. Both sides began to arm and there were a few clashes, but after the assassination of King Henry IV of France, who had supported the Protestants' claim, neither side was willing to be involved in a full scale war; therefore the 'Cleves-Jülich Affair' was settled diplomatically and with the conversion of one of the claimants to Catholicism. Therefore, in 1614 with the Affair over the Empire once more settled down into a state of peace.

However, each of the Germanic states now not only practised its own religion but also from 1582 the Catholic states introduced the Gregorian calendar: it celebrated the new year on 1 January and was 10 days in front of the Julian calendar still adhered to by the Protestant states, and which celebrated New Year's Day on 25 March. It would not be until 1700 that all Germanic states followed the Julian Calendar. Money was also different, although most states recognised the *gulden*, which was often abbreviated to 'fl' in documents, having its origins in the florin. There were 60 *kreuzers* in a *gulden*.

On 23 May 1618 a meeting was held in Prague's new city hall over Protestant rights of worship. The debate became heated and the two Imperial delegates, Jaroslav Martinitz and Wilhelm Slavata, were thrown from the town hall window along with their servant, Phillip Fabricius. Amazingly all three survived, although Slavata had serious head injuries having hit a window sill during his fall. Whether this 'Defenestration of Prague' was pre-planned or a spur-of-the-moment event, it marks the beginning of the Thirty Years War. The Bohemian nobles appointed 36 Directors to administer the country, who set about raising an army. Sweden and Denmark recognised the new regime but it was only the Dutch, along with Bethlen Gabor Prince of Transylvania and Charles Emmanuel of Savoy, who were willing to give military support. The latter sent an army under the command of General Count Ernst von Mansfeld.

However, on 20 March 1619 Emperor Matthias died, and it was clear that Archduke Ferdinand would succeed him and press forward with the Counter-Reformation. This prompted the provinces of Moravia, Lusatia and Silesia to support the Bohemian Rebels and in July 1619 they established the Act of Confederation, although it would not be until 22 August that Ferdinand was deposed as King of Bohemia. After much thought on the part of the Bohemians and little thought by Frederick of the Palatinate, he accepted the crown on 26 August 1619, which in theory gave him two votes at the Electoral meetings. However, on 28 August 1619 a meeting was held at Frankfurt am Main to elect the new Emperor, where curiously the delegate from Bohemia was refused entry and that from the Palatinate voted for Ferdinand.

Despite this setback at Frankfurt, in a superstitious age the signs for Frederick were good. He had been elected king of Bohemia on his birthday and on the day of his coronation his army defeated an Imperialist army. If this was not enough, a swarm

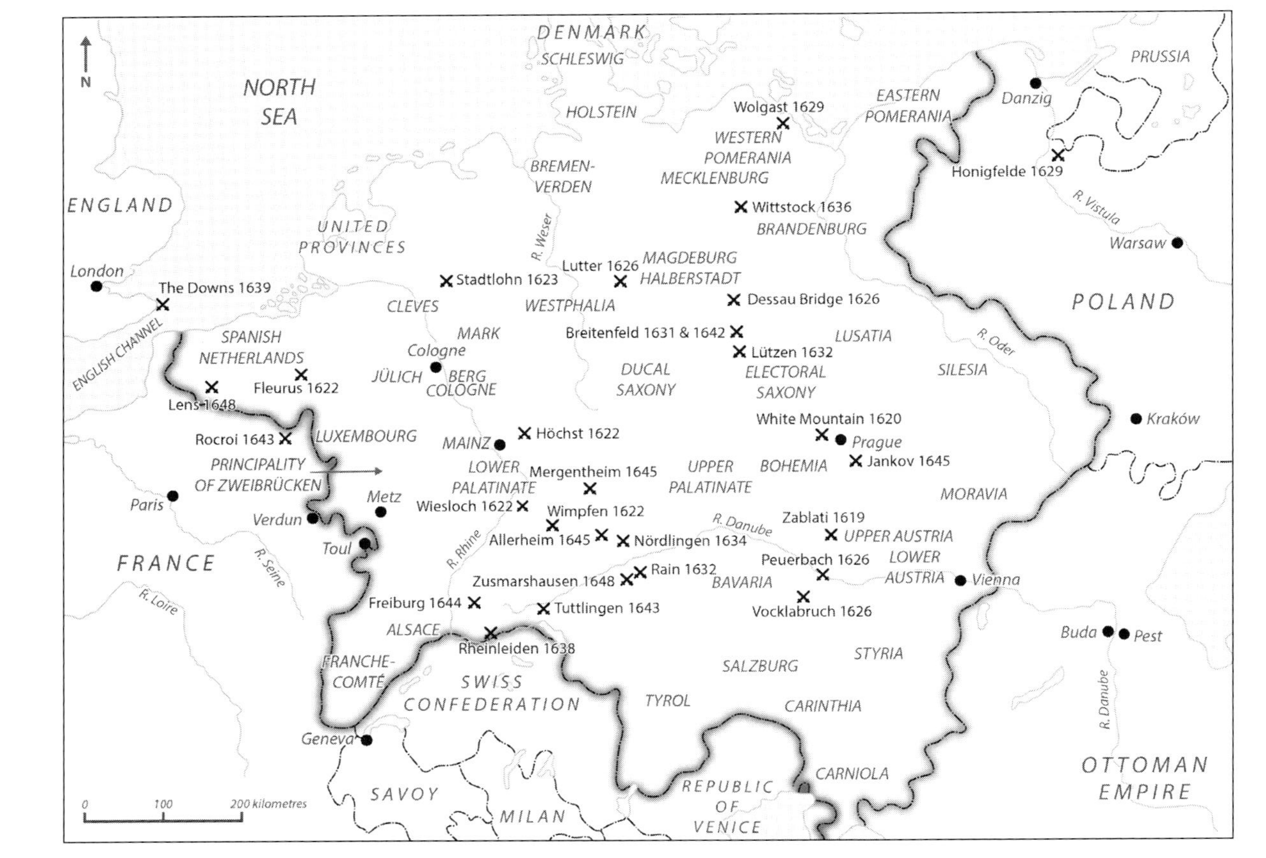

Central Europe during the Thirty Years War

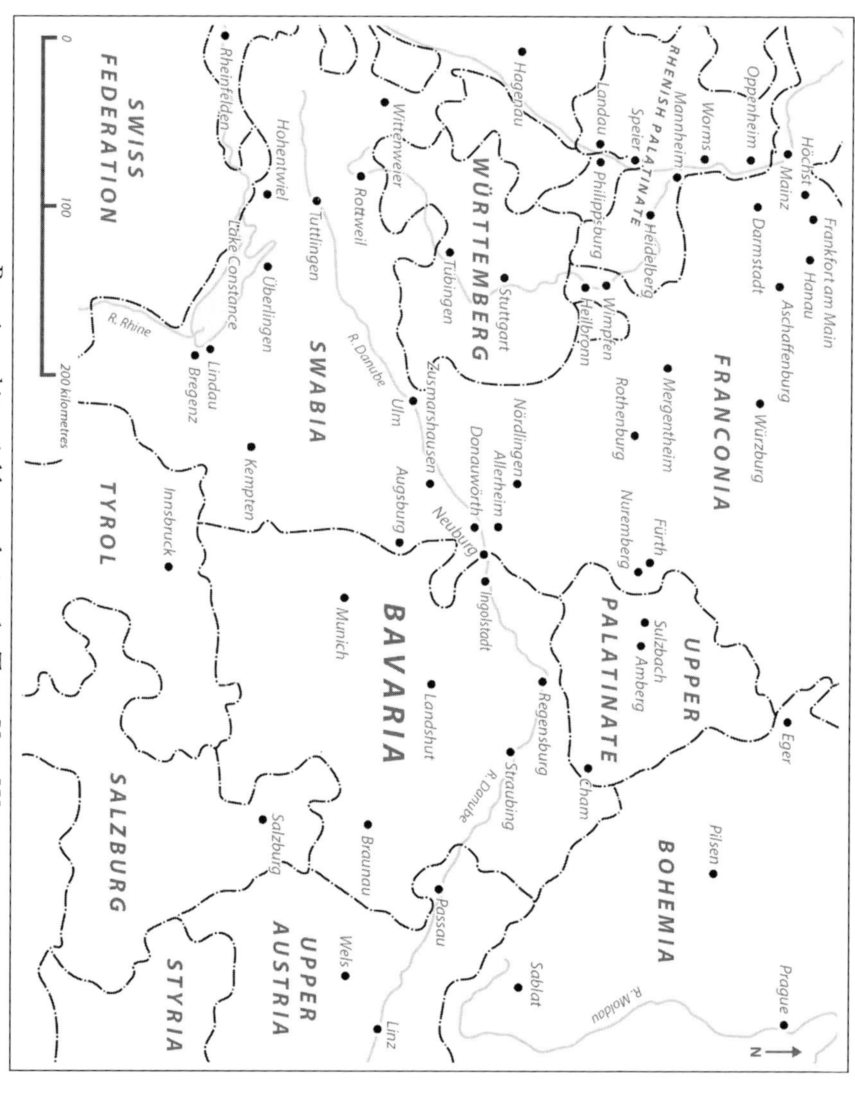

Bavaria and its neighbours during the Thirty Years War

of bees was said to have followed his army and 'hived by them' and Prague had been suffering from plague until the day he entered the city. Moreover when Frederick's army marched on Vienna, Jesus was said to have spoken to him via his crucifix saying that his enemies would be defeated.[3]

Therefore Ferdinand needed an army to crush the rebellion, so on 8 October 1619 the 'Munich Agreement' was signed in which Maximilian of Bavaria agreed to raise 18,000 infantry and 2,600 horse. In return he was to have overall command, although he left the command of the army to Johann von Tilly. In return Ferdinand agreed to finance the army, and until Maximilian received payment he could hold any recaptured land. Since Ferdinand was as extravagant as Maximilian was spendthrift it was likely that this land would remain in Bavarian hands for years to come. Furthermore if Bavaria did lose any land then the Emperor would compensate Maximilian with a part of the Habsburg lands. Spain also agreed to subsidise 1,000 horse.[4]

The Catholic League's army, composed mainly of Bavarian regiments, would invade Bohemia, while a Spanish army sent from the Netherlands to quell the Palatinate. Ferdinand needed a quick war because Spain was preparing for the end to the Twelve Years Truce in 1621 with the Dutch. Meanwhile an army led by the Lutheran Elector John George of Saxony would invade Lusatia and Silesia on the understanding that Saxony could annex Lusatia.

However, the Battle of White Mountain, fought on 8 November 1620, did not end the war, because Frederick would try to regain the Palatinate with Mansfeld's and Bethlen Gabor's armies. The Bavarian Army replaced the Spanish troops in the Palatinate and Ferdinand gave the Upper Palatinate to Maximilian who also held Upper Austria as gratuity until the emperor paid him the money he owed. It was not until 1628 that Ferdinand regained Upper Austria, while Maximilian sent Jesuits into his new province to convert the population to Catholicism, who took a sympathetic approach.

In April 1623 it was reported that 200 monks, or Jesuits, were at Munich to be sent to the Palatinate as part of the Counter-Reformation and by May 1625 the Protestants in the state were forced to go to an assigned church each day to be instructed in Catholicism by the Jesuits.[5] Thousands of white sticks, the traditional sign of safe conduct, were made and issued to those who refused to convert and wished to emigrate to another province. Many could not afford to do so or had nowhere to go, but in years to come the Upper Palatinate was one of the most ardent areas of Catholicism in Germany.

Meanwhile, the conflict continued. In 1625 Christian IV, who was the Duke of Holstein as well as King of Denmark, entered the war followed in 1630 by Sweden under Gustavus Adolphus. Finally in 1635 Catholic France entered the fray on the

3 The National Archives (TNA): SP 9/201, f.218.

4 'Münchener Vertrag zwischen Maximilian I. und Kaiser Ferdinand II, vom 8 Oktober 1619', in *Die Politik Maximilians I von Bayern und seiner Verbündeten, 1618–1651*, part I vol. 1, Jan 1618–Dec 1620 (Vienna: R. Oldenbourg, 1966), ed. Karl Mayr-Deisinger and Georg Franz, p.239.

5 TNA: SP 101/28 f.291; SP 101/42 f.243.

Protestants' side, and much of Germany was plunged into war until the final peace was signed in 1648.

All this time Bavarian forces continued to fight until exhausted by constant war; Bavaria made peace in 1647. This peace was short-lived, however, and fighting broke out again until the following year. Its army was disbanded in 1649.

It is often said that until Wallenstein offered to raise an army for the Emperor in 1625, Ferdinand had to rely on the army of the Catholic League. However, this was not so: Ferdinand had raised his own army in 1619, first under the command of General Charles Bonaventure de Longueville, Count Bucquoy, who drowned in 1621, followed by Hieronymus Caraffa, the Marquis de Montenegro. Montenegro had joined the Spanish Army in 1587 aged 23, fighting in the Dutch Revolt and the Franco-Spanish War of 1595–1598. In 1620 Caraffa entered Imperial service and prevented Bethlen Gabor from joining the Bohemian Army before the Battle of White Mountain. However, in December 1623 his army was defeated by Gabor, which resulted in 'all the Italians, Spanish and Walloons' being put to the sword. Gabor's army is said to have only shown mercy to the Germans. Caraffa was captured along with most of his officers.[6]

This defeat forced Ferdinand to make peace with Bethlen Gabor in 1624, and following his release Caraffa returned to Spain, being appointed viceroy and captain general of Aragon. In 1633 he was recalled to the Netherlands, but fell ill and died on the journey. At the beginning of 1624 Caraffa's Imperialist army composed nine regiments of horse and 11 regiments of foot, or about the size of the League's army, which in February 1623 mustered 14 regiments of foot and six regiments of horse. However, according to Tilly, at this time his infantry mustered only about 15,000 men and his cavalry 3,000–3,500 horse. Despite its name the Catholic League's army was composed almost entirely of regiments raised by Bavaria.[7]

When Caraffa retired from the Imperialist service, this gave Wallenstein, who was already a senior commander within Ferdinand's army, the chance to offer to raise new regiments for the Emperor. On 7 April 1625, Wallenstein was appointed commander in chief of 'all his [the emperor's] troops currently in the Holy Roman Empire and the Netherlands, as well as those that may be sent to him.' Wallenstein promised to raise 50,000 men, although this was initially reduced to 20,000. Ferdinand needed a larger army because the war was spreading within the Empire. Early in 1625 Christian IV entered the war on Frederick's side. Although 1625 to 1629 would be known as the 'Danish period' of the war, it was as the Duke of Holstein rather than the King of Denmark, that Christian initially entered the fray; even so he could still command great resources in his war effort.[8]

6 TNA: SP 101/46 f.205; *News from the Hague*, 14 December 1623.

7 Alphons von Wrede, *Geschichte der k. und k. Wehrmacht: die Regimenter, Corps, Branchen und Anstalten von 1618 bis Ende des XIX. Jahrhunderts* (Vienna: L. W. Seidal and Son, 1898–1905), vol. 2, pp.12, 96; Goetz, *Brief und Akten Zur Geschichte Des Dreissigjährigen Krieges*, vol. 2, part 1, p.87. In 1620 the Imperialist Army had 18 regiments of horse and 14 regiments of foot and increased the following year to 25 and 22 respectively, although several regiments were disbanded in the next two years.

8 Peter Wilson, *The Thirty Years War: A Sourcebook* (Basingstoke: Palgrave Macmillan, 2010), p.103; Wrede, pp.12, 96.

Despite there being foreign interventions by Denmark, Sweden and France it was the deposing of Frederick from his Palatinate that would be a running sore during the war. Although Frederick died in 1632, his children – Charles Louis, Rupert, and Maurice – would continue the fight, which on 28 May 1638 prompted the Venetian Ambassador to England, Francesco Zonca, to write to the Doge and Senate, 'the elector of Mayence has written to the Emperor that if no means is found of arranging the differences between the Bavarian and Palatinate houses they can never hope for peace in Germany.'[9]

Moreover Ferdinand needed a larger army because he needed to control larger and larger areas of his empire. The size of the Imperialist Army steadily increased, having a staggering 101 regiments of horse and 47 regiment of foot in 1636, although this had fallen to 46 and 40 respectively in 1648. These figures do not include the armies of Bavaria and Saxony which, from the Peace of Prague in 1635, officially came under the command of the Emperor but remained separate armies.[10]

Bavaria could not afford to raise such a large army since it only received a fraction of the subsidies of the Emperor or other nations such as Sweden, but it only needed to protect Maximilian's interests. This was fine while his army was successful, but if it were defeated then he could not easily afford to replace it. Fortunately after the first Battle of Breitenfeld enough of Tilly's army remained so that it could be rebuilt. Maximilian once wrote that 'what we lack in quantity must be made up in quality' and indeed the Bavarian Army was respected by its enemies.[11]

9 Hinds, Allen B. (ed.) *Calendar of State Papers Relating To English Affairs in the Archives and Collections of Venice*, vol. 24, 1636–1639 (London: His Majesty's Stationery Office, 1923)

10 Wrede, vol. 2, pp.12, 96.

11 Derek Croxton, *Peacemaking in Early Modern Europe: Cardinal Mazarin and the Congress of Westphalia, 1643–648* (Selinsgrove, New Jersey: Susquehanna University Press, 1999), p.88.

1

The Officer Corps

At the beginning of the Thirty Years War there were no standing armies: instead countries and states had to rely on civic guards or local militias which were called out in emergencies such as periods of unrest. Therefore when the war the broke out few had any experience of fighting or commanding troops. Although the Thirty Years War officially began on 23 May 1618 with the Defenestration of Prague, it was not until 8 October 1619 that Elector Maximilian of Bavaria, as head of the Catholic League, agreed to raise an army of 30,000 men by the spring of the following year. Commissions were sent out to the nobility and the gentry bestowing their military position and detailing, how many men they were expected to raise, and the number of companies or troops that would make up the regiment. A typical infantry regiment usually consisted of 3,000 men; although commissions for 1,000 and 2,000 men were also known, when Levin von Mortaigne was appointed colonel he was commissioned to raise 3,250. Cavalry regiments varied greatly in strength but on average were about 500 strong. Once the colonels had been appointed then they would, in theory, send out commissions appointing men to command the various troops or companies within their regiments. In practice a head of state might 'suggest' an officer they could appoint to a position.[1]

Moreover when a colonelcy of a regiment became vacant there was no guarantee that the lieutenant colonel would be chosen to command it: Lieutenant Colonel Hans Wolf von Salis petitioned Maximilian three times before he became a colonel. Sometimes Maximilian's candidate was not always accepted by the regiment, for example when the colonelcy of the Würzburg Regiment of Foot became vacant in 1621 Maximilian appointed Count George Ernst von Hohenzollern-Sigmaringen as its colonel. However, the regiment mutinied because they wanted Wolf Dietrich Truchsess von Wetzhausen, their lieutenant colonel, to be appointed to that position. Both officers and men petitioned Johan Bishop of Würzburg, who had raised the regiment, and when he sided with them Maximilian was forced to back down and Count George Ernst was given a commission to raise a new regiment instead. The

1 Arno Duch, *Die Politik Maximilians I von Bayern und seiner Verbündeten, 1618–1651* (Munich: R. Oldenbourg, 1970), pp.75–76.

Elector may have held a grudge against the Würzburg Regiment as it was almost always the last to be paid.[2]

1. Johann von Tilly, one of the chief commanders of the Imperial forces in the initial half of the Thirty Years War.

It has been estimated that a colonel needed between 400,000 and 450,000 *fl* per year to maintain a regiment of foot 3,000 strong, and 260,000 to 300,000 *fl* for a regiment of 1,200 cavalry. Fortunately for the colonels very few regiments mustered this strength so the outlay was much smaller, with a regiment of horse rarely mustering more than 500 strong, particularly during the latter part of the war. Nevertheless when Otto Heinrich Fugger raised a regiment for the Spanish service at the beginning of the war it cost him 50,000 guilders. Despite coming from a wealthy Augsburg banking family, he had to borrow much of the money from them and obtain loans of between 1,000 and 15,000 guilders at 5–6 percent interest per annum. He was still paying back the money for this regiment when he died in 1644. When he entered Bavarian service in 1631 he commanded another regiment, as well as taking over Johann von Tilly's Regiment of Foot on 30 December 1632. He would still have had to pay for the upkeep of these regiments until he was reimbursed by Maximilian, although this might be some time coming.

Apart from the 'Long War' with the Ottoman Empire, and the Dutch Revolt, which from 1609 was enjoying a 12 year truce, many officers had little or no experience in warfare, but being part of the nobility they were expected to serve. This was alright if they were cut out for a military life, but others, like the Imperialist General Federico Savelli, were forced into soldiering: Savelli by his father, Duke Bernard de Savelli. True, Federico had served in the Long War and had been the commander of the Papal forces, but in February 1631 when he surrendered Demmin to Gustavus Adolphus after a brief siege, Gustavus advised him to serve the Emperor at court rather than in the army. Nevertheless, Savelli went on to serve at the siege of Magdeburg and at the battle of Breitenfeld, after which Ferdinand sent him to assist Pope Urban VIII. Despite never being happy when he was soldiering, he returned to army life in 1635 and became a Field Marshal in 1638. Whether he was trying to prove himself, or his military rank compelled him to do so, he insisted on commanding the advance guard of

2 Fritz Redlich, *The Germany Military Enterpriser and his Work force: A Study in European Economic and Social History* (Wiesbaden: Franz Steiner, 1964), vol. 2, p.431.

the Imperialist Army himself and blundered into a narrow pass at Wittenweier, where he was defeated by Bernard of Saxe-Weimar on 30 July 1638. According to Franz Redlich he was to be court-martialled for this, but his aristocratic status prevented it and instead he returned to the diplomatic life.[3]

Another veteran of the Long War had a very different experience. Johann von Tilly was born in South Brabant in 1559 of a noble family. He served with the Spanish Army under the Duke of Alva in 1580, before entering Imperial service in 1598. After the peace with the Ottoman Empire he entered Bavarian service commanding the state's militia. So by the outbreak of the Thirty Years War he had considerable experience in warfare and Maximilian appointed him commander of his army.

Unfortunately, he is best remembered for the sack of Magdeburg and his defeat at the battle of Breitenfeld in 1631, but he was one of the best generals of the Thirty Years War, although he has been overshadowed by Gustavus Adolphus and Wallenstein. It was said that a fog had come down during the battle of the Lech which obscured the Swedish movements, which prompted Tilly to confess to the Duke of Bavaria that 'he had no good opinion of his actions, seeing daily heaven and earth did favour and second the King of Sweden.'[4]

Despite being 72 by this time he was wounded at Breitenfeld, and mortally wounded at the crossing of the River Lech, which opened Bavaria to invasion by the Swedish. Scottish officer Robert Monro admired Tilly, of whom he records,

> Wherein we have a notable example of an old expert General, who being seventy two years of age, was ready to die in defence of his Religion and Country, and in defence of those whom he served … [which] should encourage all brave Cavaliers … to follow his example in life and death.[5]

After Tilly's death Maximilian appointed Lord Grants to succeed him, but he was described as not being 'beloved nor respected' by his men and so seems to have been sidelined, and the rank Tilly held appears to have remained vacant. Whether appointed by patronage or merit it was important that an officer had the respect of his fellow officers, and as Robert Monro points out, 'When officers and soldiers conceive an evil opinion of their leaders, no eloquence is able to make them think well of them thereafter … [and they] are despised by their followers.'[6]

Monro also admired General Gottfried von Pappenheim whom he describes as 'a worthy brave fellow, though he was our enemy his valour and resolution I esteemed so much.' He added that if an enemy army was near him they could 'never [be] suffered

3 Sommeregger, 'Savelli, Herzog Friedrich von' in *General German Biography 53* (1907), pp.720–721, online, <http://www.deutsche-biographie.de/pnd115775617.html?anchor=adb> (accessed November 2015); Redlich, vol. 2, p.385.

4 The National Archives (TNA): SP 101/30, Newsletters, foreign, Germany, 1632–1634, f.172.

5 Robert Monro, *His Expedition with the Worthy Scots Regiment (Called Mac-Keyes Regiment) levied in August 1626* (London: William Jones, 1637), part II, p.118.

6 *Ibid.*, part II p.174.

to sleep sound' for fear they would be attacked by him.[7]

Pappenheim was born on 29 May 1594 in Treuchtlingen, Bavaria. His father died when he was only six years old and his mother married Adam von Herbersdorf. In 1616 he converted to Catholicism, and when the war broke out his status and the patronage of his stepfather guaranteed him a high position within the army, even though he had no military experience. At first he was a captain in Herbersdorf's Regiment of Cuirassiers, becoming the regiment's lieutenant colonel by October 1621. In April 1622 Pappenheim had become a full colonel; two years later he entered Spanish service, but was recalled in 1626 to help Maximilian put down the rebellion in Upper Austria. In November 1630 he rose to the rank of field marshal of the Catholic League; he seems to have fallen out with Tilly during the siege of Magdeburg and so transferred to Imperialist service without too much difficulty, although no doubt much to the sorrow of Maximilian and Tilly at the loss of a good general. However, Pappenheim was killed at the battle of Lützen on 16 November 1632.

2. Gottfried von Pappenheim, the cavalry general whose reputation was tarnished by his actions at Breitenfeld.

Gottfried von Pappenheim left only one son, Wolfgang Adam von Pappenheim, who was born in 1618. Despite his age the status of his family was such that he succeeded his father as the colonel of his regiment of foot in 1632. However, the regiment would be commanded by its lieutenant colonel, Hans Ulrich Gold, until Wolfgang was old enough to command it in person. He was eager to take command of his regiment, which brought about several demands to Maximilian over the years. At the siege of Hohenasperg his regiment lost 400 men in two weeks while under his command, trying to storm the town. He was killed fighting a duel with Colonel Colloredo in Prague on 30 June 1647. Another Pappenheim to serve in the army was Phillip von Pappenheim who was Gottfried's cousin, although he only rose to the rank of captain.[8]

The highest rank in the Bavarian Army was field marshal, which would be held by six men during the war, including Johan Jakob Count von Anholt. In 1620 Anholt was appointed colonel, then major general of foot and then major general. Two years

7 *Ibid.*, part II, pp.136, 142.
8 Biography of Wolfgang Adam von Pappenheim, online, <http://www.30jaehrigerkrieg.de> (accessed October 2015).

3. Johann von Werth, an able cavalry commander who was able to raid deep into France.

later he was appointed field marshal and second only to Maximilian and Tilly in command of the Bavarian Army. Other field marshals included Joachim von Wahl who had been a captain in 1620 and by 1626 had become the lieutenant colonel of Tilly's own regiment of foot. He became field marshal on 29 May 1640, however in 1644 due to ill health he was appointed the governor of Ingoldstadt so that he could still enjoy his status as an officer. He was succeeded by Franz Freiherr von Mercy, who was killed at the battle of Allerheim on 3 August 1645.[9]

Of course, not all officers reached the heights of field marshal. There would be 11 generals of cavalry or general of the ordnance, five lieutenant field marshals and 21 major generals. True, the higher up the social ladder a person was the higher command he was initially appointed to. However, this is not to say that all the officers came from the nobility. Between 1635 and 1649 the army consisted of 13 regiments of foot, 16 of horse and two of dragoons commanded by 51 colonels; of these only 16 came from the nobility, the rest from gentry or peasant families, although of the army's generals 18 out of 22 were from the nobility. Whereas in the Imperialist Army in 1633 only 13 out of 107 colonels were commoners, although this number was slowly rising as the war progressed.[10]

Among those officers who came from a peasant family was Johann von Werth who was born in 1594 and enlisted as a trooper in the Spanish service in the Netherlands. In 1631 he transferred to the Catholic League as the major of Colonel Eynatten's Regiment of Horse, and in December 1632 took over the regiment. In 1636 he led an invasion of France, but was captured two years later at the battle of Rheinfelden. It was not until 1642 that he was finally exchanged. However, despite being a renowned light cavalry commander, after his release he was bypassed for promotion twice and so in 1647 joined the Imperialist Army.

Johann von Sporck was also born a peasant and he enlisted in the Bavarian Army in 1619 aged about 18. However, by 1631 he had risen to the rank of cornet in Bonnighausen's Regiment and two years later was a captain. In 1636 he was recorded as the Obristwachtmeister or major of De Maestro's Regiment of Horse. He later

9 Redlich, p.198; Johann Heilmann, Kriegsgeschichte von Bayern, Franken, Pfalz und Schwaben von 1506 bis 1651 (Munich, 1868), vol. 2, part 2, pp.1110–1111.

10 Andreas Kraus, *Maximilian I: Bayerns Grosser Kurfürst* (Graz: Styria, 1990), p.152; Redlich, vol. 2, p.418.

reentered Bavarian service and rose to the rank of colonel. In 1647 both Sporck and Werth once more swore allegiance to the Emperor, after Bavaria had made peace. Unfortunately they tried, and failed, to take a large part of the Bavarian Army with them, and so were branded traitors: a reward of 10,000 *talers* was placed on Werth's head, with lesser sums being offered for Colonels Holtz and Creutz, who were also incriminated in the plot. Although they lost their Bavarian estates, they were rewarded by Ferdinand III and Sporck became a baron and received compensation for his losses. After the Peace of Westphalia he continued to serve with the Imperialist Army against the Poles and then the Turks, finally retiring from army life in 1675. By the time of his death in 1679 this lowly peasant had become a count and a general, and was one of the richest landowners in Bohemia with a fortune of three million florins. Werth married three times and on the last two occasions to countesses, which was a far cry from his humble roots.[11]

Another officer said to be a bricklayer before joining the army was Gil De Haes. It is said that he came from the Netherlands and was a Jewish convert to Catholicism. By 1632 he was a colonel in the Imperialist Army and had become a major general in the Bavarian Army in 1642, although in July 1646 his regiment passed to Colonel Johann Elter. Gil De Haes later served with the Venetian Army and died in 1657 in Croatia.[12]

When he was about 19 years old Augustin von Fritsch enlisted in Colonel Schmidt's Regiment of Foot as a musketeer in time to fight at the Battle of White Mountain. After 11 years' service, having risen through the lesser officer ranks, he became an officer and on average every three years he advanced in rank until he became a colonel. In 1649 he was discharged from the army when his regiment was disbanded.

As with the rank and file, the officer corps was a mixed bag of nationalities. In September 1645 a troop in Gil de Haes' Regiment of Horse was commanded by a captain from Lucerne, whilst its lieutenant was from Livonia and cornet from Naples, the sergeant was from Strasbourg and the leader was from Zürich, and the farrier was from Basel. Its corporals were from Lübeck, Württemberg, Candia, Überlingen, Holland and Mantua. It also had two reformado lieutenants from Franconia and Silesia and two cornets from Poland and Styria.[13]

Having 'foreign' officers within a regiment was not unique to the Bavarian Army: the Dutch and Swedish Armies had many Scottish, English and German officers, while in the Danish Army a list drawn up in June 1627 of 19 cavalry and 30 infantry companies showed about a third were commanded by Bohemians, Moravians and Silesians. The Dutch even divided their army into brigades of French, English, and Scottish regiments.[14]

However, with the origins of most of the officers being unknown it would be a mistake to suggest that the officer corps of the Bavarian Army, or in fact any other

11 Redlich, vol. 2, pp.191–192; biography of Johann von Sporck, online, <http://www.30jaehrigerkrieg.de> (accessed October 2015).

12 TNA: SP 101/3, Newsletters, foreign, Flanders, 1638–1667, unfolio.

13 Online, <http://www.30jaehrigerkrieg.de> (accessed October 2015).

14 J. V. Polisensky, *War and Society in Europe, 1618–1648* (London: Cambridge University Press, 1978), p.117.

army, was made up of foreign officers or peasantry who had risen through the ranks, although no doubt this was helped by the longevity of the war. Moreover despite being the same rank those from the nobility would enjoy a higher social status than the gentry or those who had risen from the ranks.

Of course many soldiers were not promoted, and if they were they just reached the rank of sergeant. Peter Hagendorf enlisted in Pappenheim's Regiment of Foot in 1627 as a lance corporal, since he had seen previous service. He was promoted to corporal, and in 1633 he was acting sergeant, when he was captured by the Swedish Army at Straubing on the River Danube. His captors respected his rank and appointed him a sergeant in the Red Regiment. In his memoirs he appears to have willingly been part of the Swedish Army whilst his old captain seems to have been quickly exchanged and returned to the Bavarian Army. However, Hagendorf was captured again at the battle of Nördlingen in 1634, and he and all the other former Bavarian and Imperialist soldiers were allowed to return to their old regiments. Unfortunately, for Hagendorf this meant becoming a corporal once more.[15]

Military careers did not necessarily end with the Peace of Westphalia. Being born on 10 August 1612 Franz Graf von Fugger was about 15 years old when he became the major of Schmidt's Regiment in 1627, although it would not be until 1643 when he became the lieutenant colonel of Holtz's Regiment and then colonel. However, when his regiment was disbanded in 1649 this did not end his military career: in 1663 he was promoted to major general of infantry and artillery and commanded a regiment of foot in the Hungarian campaign. He was killed on 1 August 1664 at the battle of St Gotthard against the Turks and was buried in Ingoldstadt aged 51.

However, he was not the last officer who had served in the Bavarian Army during the Thirty Years War, and who had continued to serve after the war had ended. This honour appears to go to Ferdinand von Puech, who in 1631 was an ensign in Johann von Tilly's Regiment. Ten years later he was the lieutenant colonel of Haslang's Regiment of Foot and on 16 September 1644 became its colonel. In 1657 he was again commissioned as a colonel of a regiment of foot in the Bavarian Army and in 1678 became a lieutenant field marshal, but it was not until 1685 that he resigned his commissions.

Pappenheim, Johann von Werth and Johann von Sporck were converts to Catholicism, but despite Maximilian being an advocate of the Counter-Reformation, not all his officers were Catholic. True, on 4 November 1629 he did order Tilly to expel all Protestant officers, but at one least continued to serve. He was Jurgen Ackermann, who had served under Count Ernst von Mansfeld and then in the Danish service. In 1627, having received no pay and being forced to surrender to General Pappenheim at Wolfenbüttel, where his company was reduced to just 15 men, his captain recommended Ackermann to his cousin Johann Reinhard von Stein Callenfels, who was a captain in Pappenheim's Regiment of Foot. 'I was promoted

15 Hagendorf's account printed in *The Thirty Years War, A Documentary History*, edited and translated by Tryntje Helfferich (Cambridge Mass.: Hackett Publishing Company, 2009), p.289. Helfferich states that Hagendorf was a captain, but the original account edited by Jan Peters says corporal (p.62).

so that I had command of a beautiful company of 300 men,' he recalls. He was also appointed to be the regiment's quartermaster and continued to serve in the regiment at Magdeburg and the battle of Breitenfeld in 1631. Jurgen Ackermann appears to have retired from the army shortly afterwards using the money he had plundered during the war to buy some land. However, his former profession did not stop him being plundered by soldiers later in the war.[16]

It was an age when commanders were still expected to lead by example, and so there was always the danger of being killed in battle or dying on campaign. Tilly, Johann von Götz, Werth, and Pappenheim were all wounded during the war. In 1632 Tilly would be mortally wounded at the battle of the Lech and Pappenheim killed at the battle of Lützen later that year. General of the Ordnance Furstenberg died on 15 November 1627 and General of the Ordnance Otto von Schonberg and Major General Dietrich von Erwitte were killed at the battle of Breitenfeld in 1631, Major General Hans Schellhammer died at Speyer in 1635. Being a company commander could also be dangerous: Peter Hagendorf, who wrote an account of his military career during the war, records that at the siege of Magdeburg his captain was shot dead by the garrison. On 22 March 1631 John Galgart 'was brought in as our captain', but he was also shot dead on 28 April. He was succeeded by Tilge Neuberg on 6 May, but 10 days later he resigned his commission. On 26 May he was replaced by Johan Phillip Schultz. How long Captain Schultz lasted is not recorded but it is clear that in the space of two months Hagendorf's company had four different captains. Unfortunately, Hagendorf does not record the number of casualties his whole company suffered during the time; they must have been heavy, but death in battle or from disease opened the door for promotion.[17]

An easier way for promotion was to join a newly raised army, so that with the expansion of the Imperialist Army in 1625 many of the officers in the Catholic League resigned their commissions in order to seek employment in Wallenstein's army, knowing that they might obtain advancement in rank. However, the exchange went both ways. When Franz von Mercy entered Maximilian's service he received 3,000 *fl* as a reward for leaving the service of Duke Charles of Lorraine.[18]

In 1628, dissatisfied with not being promoted to the rank of general after serving as a colonel for just four years, Johann Philipp Cratz, Count of Scharffenstein, transferred to the service of Lorraine. Rather than appointing a new colonel to Cratz's old regiment Wallenstein decided to disbanded it. Still not satisfied with this service either, two years later Cratz petitioned Wallenstein for another commission, but before this was granted he found better terms in Maximilian's service, who finally promoted Cratz to the rank of general. By now this was not enough for Cratz either, and in 1633 his plot to betray Ingoldstadt to the Swedes was discovered and he fled to the Swedish

16 BHA File 236, f.39, Maximilian to Tilly, 4 November 1629; Robert Volkholtz, *Juergen Ackermann, Kapitaen beim Regiment Alt Pappenheim* (Halberstadt: J. Schimmellburg, 1895), p.13.

17 Hagendorf's account in *The Thirty Years War, A Documentary History*, pp.282–283.

18 Redlich, vol. 2, p.332.

service. At the battle of Nördlingen the following year he was captured and beheaded for treason.[19]

Usually when a colonel transferred from one service to another he was expected to leave behind his regiment and all the money he had invested in it. However, there are exceptions. In 1647 when Colonel Caspar Schoch entered Bavarian service he brought his regiment of dragoons with him; Schoch was another officer of lowly birth, being born on 25 November 1610 at Kleinholzleute, which belonged to the Isny Monastery. Since he was good with horses he became a groom and entered the army aged just 13, and slowly rose through the ranks. Hans Wolf von Salis appears to have swapped his regiment, which formerly belonged to Colonel Erwitte, with that of Colonel Eynatten's Regiment of Cuirassiers. In 1634 he again exchanged this regiment with Werth, for his regiment of foot.[20]

Of course being captured in battle could stifle an officer's prospects. When Bernard of Saxe-Weimar defeated an Imperial–Bavarian Army at the battle of Rheinfelden in 1638 he is reported to have captured four generals, including Savelli, Johann von Werth, Enkerfort and Sepreuter, four colonels, Neumeher, Götz, Henersheim and Wolf, plus three lieutenant colonels and four majors, including Anthony de Werth, 31 captains, 22 lieutenants and 32 cornets.[21]

Both Major General Alexander von Haslang and Hans Wolf von Salis died as prisoners of war. In 1620 Haslang fell ill, and while he was being transported to Bavaria his small escort was ambushed by some enemy cavalry. Haslang was taken to Rakoniz where he died on 3 November. Salis died before he could be transported to Sweden, whether this was due to his harsh treatment by the Swedish is not known. However, Salis' treatment is completely different to that received by the Bavarian Colonel von Gayling who was allowed freedom of movement and actually persuaded Colonel Seckendorf of the Swedish Army to desert, but Seckendorf was captured and beheaded.

Officers would remain prisoners until they were swapped for an officer of similar rank or they paid a ransom, the price of a major general being 4,000 *fl* and a general 8,000 *fl*, while a colonel was worth about 1,000 *talers*. However, in 1634 this was reduced to 600 florins for a cavalry colonel and 500 *talers* for a colonel of a regiment of foot. Despite this reduction, when Colonels Gayling and Hagenbach were captured in 1641 General Wahl petitioned Maximilian to act on their behalf since they lacked the means to pay their ransoms. Maximilian also paid the ransoms of several Bavarian colonels in the 1640s but he deducted the amount from Gronsfeld's pay because he blamed him for them being captured in the first place. Some officers were too valuable to release and Werth would remain a prisoner for four years, while the Swedish General Gustavus Horn was imprisoned for a staggering eight years.[22]

19 *Ibid.*, p.193.
20 Biography of Caspar Schoch, online, <http://www.30jaehrigerkrieg.de> (accessed October 2015); Redlich, vol. 2, p.174.
21 TNA: SP 78/105.
22 Redlich, pp.396–397.

2

The Rank and File

A warrant would be issued to an officer, known as the *werbepatent* (levy patent) or *werbekontrakt* (levy contract), stating where he was to recruit his company or troop and the number of men that he was expected to raise. This patent was to be shown to the authorities within the area as proof he had been granted authority to raise the men.

In February 1623 it was reported that 20,000 men were being raised around Strasbourg and 10,000 in Lotharingia for Ferdinand, while Count von Furstenberg was levying 18,000 men for the Duke of Bavaria. Some of these levies were destined to join Montenegro's Army, since Bethlen Gabor had once again declared war on Ferdinand and it was feared that he would join forces with the Marquis de Jagendorf and Count Thurn. However, obtaining recruits was a constant problem and at the end of November 1623 Ferdinand was again recruiting in Austria and Germany to reinforce his army; the following January it was said that the recruits came in 'slowly for want of money.'[1]

On 30 April 1625 The Duke of Bavaria also complained of the 'long delay' in providing men 'for the security of the Empire which is threatened by so many foreign princes, particularly the king of Denmark and Sweden.' The problem was that too many armies from various nations were being raised, so that a man wanting to join the army would choose whoever was offering the best terms. When Count von Fugger was raising his regiments he could afford to pay each recruit three dollars plus a shilling a day as soon as they accepted his service. On the other hand in Nuremberg the soldiers being recruited for the Emperor are said to have quickly deserted because they were not paid. These were probably members of the regiment of Colonel Hirchperger, who is known to have been recruiting in Nuremberg at this time but without any assistance from the city's officials, and so was unable to raise his regiment.[2]

1 *Weekly News* (London, 14 March 1623), no. 23, p.13; *News from Foreign Parts* (London, 28 February 1623); TNA: SP 101/46, Newsletters foreign, Holland (U. Provinces), 1623–1626, f.26; *News from the Hague*, 29 Nov to 6 Dec 1623.

2 TNA: SP 101/42, Newsletters foreign, Germany, Austria, Bohemia and Hungary, 1620–1665, ff.169, 431; SP 101/28, Newsletters foreign, Germany, 1620–1625, ff.9, 28; SP 101/46, Newsletters foreign, Holland (United Provinces) 1623–1626, f.104; SP 101/30, Newsletters foreign, Germany, 1632–1634, ff.15, 22.

4. Sydnam Poyntz. Originally a London apprentice, he ran away to the European wars and rose to become a major general.

Therefore when Wallenstein received his commission to increase the size of the Imperialist Army in November 1624 it was said that a 'great provision of money and cloth is made for the paying of the soldiers', and in April 1625 Wallenstein had issued over 100 commissions to raise his army.[3]

At the beginning of Wallenstein's second generalship he again boasted that he would field an army of 80,000, but as a pamphlet recalled, 'it is well known there is want of both men and money'. However, on 29 February 1632 Anstruther wrote to Vane,

> The Duke of Friedland's [Wallenstein] Army consists already of 24 regiments. It is meant perhaps so many colonels (which yet is much) but the question is whether or not every one of them (if he have so many) hath a regiment complete. They give out here that there are already within the Emperor's domains at Moravia and Upper and Lower Austria above 100,000 veterans and new levied soldiers.[4]

Unfortunately when the strengths of the regiments were printed in newsletters etc., they always quoted the number of men the colonel had been commissioned to raise, i.e. 3,000 men, rather than the accurate figures, so it is difficult to know how successful the recruiting of new levies was and also to calculate the exact number present when it came to a battle. Certainly, despite Wallenstein boasting that he would have an army of 70,000 men, on 8 July 1625 it was said that the levies raised by him 'are not so great as it was reported' and in April 1627 another newsletter recalled that Wallenstein's army was only 20,000 strong rather than the 80,000 men previously reported.[5]

On 21 May 1628 Maximilian granted more commissions to raise 12,000 foot and 3,000 horse, and on 22 April 1631 he issued further commissions to bring the field army of the Catholic League up to 40–50,000 men.[6]

Despite offering good enlistment money Count von Fugger was forced to send commissioners as far as Hungary and Poland to recruit. This was not unique: as long as they had the ruler's permission, they could recruit anywhere. England and Scotland supplied many regiments to the Dutch, Swedish and German armies during the war and

3 *The Continuation of our Weekly Newes* (London, 30 May 1625), no. 24, p.8; TNA: SP 101/28 f.145.
4 TNA: SP 101/29, Newsletters foreign, Germany, 1626–1631; SP 80/8, Anstruther to Sir Henry Vane f.167.
5 *Ibid.*, f.141, 431.
6 *Ibid.*,f.115, 207.

King James I even allowed Spain to recruit in England. However, recruiting parties did not always get a warm welcome. In October 1622 one news-sheet reported that in Frankfurt,

> Here arrived a Bavarian commissioner in the name of his Imperial Majesty and his Highness of Bavaria, his request is that the Burgomaster of the city would permit him to levy certain soldiers in our town and there about, for the Emperor's Service and that they might likewise be maintained at the charge of the citizens and be billeted in their houses until the general muster. But the Burgomaster hath excused himself from granting either request.[7]

In August 1628 some captains who had been commissioned by the Duke of Bavaria to make some levies of men about Ulm and Augsburg, but 'the commissary of those parts hath refused, saying it would be prejudicial to the Emperor's [service].' Nuremberg also refused appeals from officers of the kings of Denmark, France and others who wanted to raise recruits in the city. However, on 10 March 1629 Nuremberg gave Captain Christopher Fontana of Wallenstein's army permission to recruit in the suburbs without the beat of the drum, the traditional sign that a company or regiment was to be raised, and he was not allowed to recruit any citizens of the town, only 'foreigners' and travellers. Fontana's company was to leave Nuremberg as soon as it had been recruited and to not be a burden to the city.[8]

Some officers resorted to tricks in raising their men: such as one Swedish officer in 1643 who, failing to find enough recruits, is reported to have thrown money into the streets of Erfurt and anyone who picked it up was instantly recruited into his company. If they refused, he imprisoned them until they finally agreed to enlist.

Men joined the army for many different reasons. In 1624 at the age of 16 the future Parliamentarian General Sydnam Poyntz recorded that he enlisted having been 'bound an apprentice that life I deemed little better than a dog's life and base. At last I resolved with my self thus, to live and die a soldier would be as noble in death as life, which resolution took strong root in me, that not long after ... [I enlisted as] a private soldier.'[9] For Sir James Turner it was a choice between his studies and fighting for the Protestant cause under Gustavus Adolphus. Unfortunately Augustin Fritsch, who wrote an account of his life in the Bavarian Army, does not record why he enlisted in 1618 as a musketeer in Colonel Schmidt's Regiment of Foot, aged 19. However, Peter Hagendorf records in his memoirs that on 3 April 1627 'I have took it upon myself to enlist in Pappenheim Regiment [of Foot] at Ulm as a lance corporal, because I was completely down and out.' Social deprivation was a major cause for many enlisting in the army. A survey of 1,069 recruits in the Bavarian Army between 1638 to 1648 shows the following trades.[10]

7 *Courante relating to divers particulars concerning news out of Italy, Germany and Turkey*, 1 November 1622.
8 TNA: SP 81/13, State papers foreign, Germany, f.174, *Advise from Swabland*, 13/23 August 1628.
9 Sydnam Poyntz, *The Relation of Sydnam Poyntz, 1624–1636* (London: Royal Historical Society, 1908), p.45.
10 Jan Peters, *Ein Soldnerleben im Dreissigjährigen Krieg* (Berlin: Akadamie Verlag, 1993), p.42; Cordula Kasper, *Die Bayerische Kriegsorganisation in der zweiten Hälfte des Dreissigjährigen Krieges* (Aschendorff: Munich, 1997), pp.271–273.

Trades	Number	Percentage
Shopkeepers	17	1.6
Food and guest trades, inc. butchers, millers, brewers	173	16.2
Clothing & textile trades	299	28
Building, wood & metal processing trades	178	16.7
Transport trades, e.g. carters	12	1.1
Paper trades, inc. papermakers & binders	12	1.1
Educated, e.g. students & teachers	16	1.5
Agriculture, e.g. labourers, cattle breeders	203	19
Soldiers' sons	23	2.7
Other trades, e.g. servants, cooks, basketmakers	70	6
Unskilled	51	4.7

This can be compared with the French Army where 52 percent of recruits came from towns, although between 1635 and 1643 the percentage from the country was higher than the townsmen.[11]

Sir James Turner states that:

> Most captains conceive sixteen to be too young, and if so I swear sixty is too old; they need not be twenty ... [but] they may pass muster of eighteen; and if they be not infirm wounded or mutilated, they may well enough continue [being] soldiers till they be fifty and upwards, though some think they should not serve after the forty six years of their age.[12]

A survey of 900 soldiers serving in the Bavarian Army between 1638 and 1648 shows the following ages:

Age	15–19	20–25	26–29	30-35	36–39	40–45	46–49	50–55	56–59	60
No.	159	405	108	80	33	49	8	8	3	0

This should be compared with 377 soldiers who left England between 30 December 1628 and 31 July 1629, whose ages are known:[13]

Age	21–25	26–29	30-35	36–39	40–45	46–49	50–55	56–59	60
No.	187	56	66	22	21	10	11	3	1

11 Robert Chaboche, 'Les Militaires et la societe', *Revue D'Historie moderne et contemporaraine*, no. 20 (1973, pp.10–24), p.16. Before 1635 107 were townsmen, 86 from the country; from 1635–1643, 187 from towns and 208 from villages, and from 1643–1648, 177 from towns and 160 from villages.

12 Sir James Turner, *Pallas Armata* (London, 1683), p.166.

13 Kasper, p.269; TNA: E157/14, Register of soldiers taking the oath of allegiance, and register of licences to persons to pass beyond the seas, 1628–1629.

Presumably in the case of the English recruits there were younger soldiers going to enlist in the various armies at this time, but anyone under 21 was considered a minor and therefore was not listed in the port books.

Like most armies at this time the Bavarian Army was not just composed of Bavarians, as the following chart shows:[1]

	Gil de Haas' Regiment of Foot, 11 February 1645		Bartel's Regiment of Dragoons, 20 December 1648	
Nationality	**No.**	**Percentage**	**No.**	**Percentage**
Bohemian	14	1.35	12	1.72
Brabantian	-	-	2	0.28
Burgundian	43	4.15	2	0.28
Croatian	2	0.19	-	-
Dalmatian	18	1.74	-	-
English	-	-	1	0.14
Flemish	-	-	4	0.57
French	15	1.48	9	1.29
German	534	51.64	632	90.67
Greek	26	2.51	-	-
Hungarian	5	0.48	2	0.28
Irish	1	0.09	1	0.14
Italian	218	21.08	6	0.86
Lorrainese	24	2.32	10	1.43
Dutch	-	-	2	0.28
Polish	54	5.22	4	0.57
Scottish	2	0.19	0	0
Sicilian	1	0.09	0	0
Slovenian	51	4.93	0	0
Spanish	11	1.06	1	0.14
Swedish	0	0	1	0.14
Swiss	0	0	2	0.28
Turkish	15	1.48	0	0
Walloons	0	0	4	0.57
Total	**1,034**	**100**	**695**	**100**

1 Kasper, quoting Kurbayern Ausseres Archiv 2809 f.115, and 2608 ff.279–291.

On 8 October 1646, of the 55 soldiers in Colonel Fritsch's Regiment who received clothing 12 had Italian names and one came from the Tyrol. This is not to say that no Bavarians served in the army: of a sample of 1,417 soldiers who enlisted between 1638 and 1648 from 34 German states and towns, 649 were born in Bavaria, 45.75 percent of the total figure.[2]

An examination of the origins of foreign invalids who served with the French Army shows a similar mixture of soldiers:[3]

Nationality	No.
English	1
Irish	27
Scottish	5
Dutch	1
Danish	1
German	109
Barrois	15
Savoyard	3
Monacan	2
Avignese	3
Spanish	16
Swiss	75
Polish	9
Italian	13
Ottoman	3
Total	**283**

There were exceptions to these mixed nationality regiments. Johan von Tilly's Regiment of Foot were said to have been composed of 2,000–3,000 Walloons, whereas 2,000 Frenchmen formed Florenville's Regiment. The Dutch Army segregated each nationality into regiments, with the Dutch, English, Scottish and French forming their own regiments and brigades. Therefore there was no language barrier in these units and it also encouraged rivalry between each nationality. On the other hand this meant they could not easily recruit each regiment and so many were under-strength until a new draft from their respective country arrived.[4]

Although Maximilian usually relied on volunteers to fill the ranks of his army, and with Bavaria about to be invaded he resorted to conscription. On 30 January

2 Kurbayern Ausseres Archiv MS 2883; Kasper, p.253.
3 Chaboche, p.17.
4 Walter Goetz, *Die Politik Maximilians I von Baiern und seiner Verbündeten, 1618–1651*, vol. 2 part IV (Leipzig: B. G. Teubner, 1907), p.5.

Vera Effigies
Jacobi Turner Equitis Aurati.

5. Sir James Turner travelled from his native Scotland to fight in the German Wars. He was to publish the famous military treatise 'Pallas Armata'.

1632 he held a general muster of all his subjects between the ages of 18 and 40, but only 24,000 men appear to have been present. He also wrote to Tilly that he was putting the militia into a posture of defence and that 'a number of single peasants' sons can be impressed … taken from our lands of Bavaria so that the infantry regiments that have lost heavily can be nearly brought back up to strength.' On 14 February 1632 Amberg reported to Maximilian that 2,000 single men had arrived, although at Sickenhausen only about 300 of the 3,380 men conscripted arrived, many having run away. It was the same story in Haimburg where the single men who had been chosen to serve refused to turn up at their rendezvous.[5]

Maximilian was not the only head of state to rely on conscription. In May 1623 when the Duke of Brandenburg decided to raise an army of 3,000 foot and 500 horse he conscripted one man in every five in the towns and cities and one in every 10 in the countryside. Moreover, despite his use of foreign mercenaries Gustavus Adolphus had to rely on conscripts from Sweden, who were in theory were meant to be between the ages of 18 and 40, but as the war dragged on it became more and more necessary to call up boys as young as 15 and men as old as 65. Usually those who were a burden on a parish or town were conscripted first, but from 1627 in Sweden it was forbidden to employ a substitute to take their place. This resulted in some conscripts mutilating themselves to avoid military service.[6] Whatever their age or background the recruits assembled at the *laufplatz* within their various towns and villages, from where they would be sent to the rendezvous or *sammelplatz* (assembly place) in the district, before finally being marched to the *musterplatz* (muster place). Sometimes the recruits appear to have made their own way to the muster place, which had been common practice in the sixteenth century.[7]

5 TNA: SP 101/30, Newsletters foreign, Germany, 1632–1634 unfolio; Eugene von Frauenholz, *Das Heerwesen in der Zeit des Dreissigjährigen Krieges* (Munich, 1938–39), vol. 2, pp.247–248.
6 Michael Roberts, *Gustavus Adolphus, a History of Sweden 1611–1632* (London: Longmans, Green and Co., 1958), vol. 2, p.208.
7 Redlich, vol. 1, pp.272–273.

On enlistment a recruit's name would be written on a muster roll, which usually also included a brief description of the man, their age and profession. The recruit would receive a sum of money, or *werbgeld*, which was also known as *handgeld*, which depend on how much demand there was for recruits at the time, but it marked his process from a civilian to a soldier. He would also receive an allowance, or *laufgeld*, which would cover his travelling expenses to the muster place, which was between eight and 13 *talers* a day. Between 1619 and 1631 accounts show that Bavaria spent 158,942 *fl* 32 *kr* on *werbgeld* and *laufgeld*. An account for the Catholic League's army dated 5 February 1621 records that about 22,500 *fl* was spent on *laufgeld* due to raising three regiments and a further 157,800 *fl* was needed to train these recruits.[8] Raising recruits was one thing but getting them to the rendezvous was another, however, as Prince Charles Louis, Frederick V's eldest son, found: 'When I write to you by Colonel Steinacher I had a list of above 800 new levied men … [but] there is arrived here not about 300, the rest run away, after they had been brought with a great deal of pains and charges and wanted nothing. Of these there were 70 English who ran all away, except very few.'[9]

When Salis raised his regiment of horse he first chose the town of Mühldorf for his muster place and then in March he also gathered soldiers at Eichstadt. Originally his commission ordered him to raise just five troops, but in 1634 he was ordered to raise an additional three. Among his troop commanders was Major Johann von Werth.[10]

A regiment might have more than one muster place: in October 1644 when Gil de Haes raised his regiment of foot he chose Wasserburg, Rosenhelm, Wellheim, Schongau, Tolz, Landesberg and Friedburg, presumably one town for each company.

Unfortunately Hagendorf does not mention much about his time as a new recruit in Pappenheim's Regiment, saying only that 'from there [Ulm] we moved out to our muster place in the Upper Margraviate of Baden. There we lay in our quarters, gorged and boozed, and it was good.' He also found time to marry the 'highly virtuous Anna Stadlerin', from Bavaria.[11]

In 1611 Maximilian had instructed these muster places to be kept open for six days. Once all the company had arrived they were issued with weapons and clothing and on the ninth day they were to be inspected by their officers. Finally the recruit would take an oath of allegiance to his officers and ruler. It has also been suggested that the soldiers may have hammered a nail into the staff of their ensign or cornet, so sealing their oath. Finally the provost would read out the laws of war, which laid down the strict discipline the soldier was to follow.[12]

Not all towns wanted to be muster places. In 1627 Nuremberg bribed Hans George Margrave of Brandenburg 16,500 *fl*, and Julius Heinrich Duke of Saxe-Lauenburg and his lieutenant colonel received 900 *fl* and 183 *fl* respectively, not to use the city as

8 Heilmann, 1868, vol. 2, p.885; Redlich, vol. 1, pp.272–273, 483–484; Duch, pp.75–76.
9 TNA: SP 81/45, State Papers Foreign, Germany, Prince Charles Louis to Secretary Roe, 30 October 1638, ff.204–205.
10 Salis, pp.71–74.
11 Helfferich, p.280.
12 Herbert Langer, *The Thirty Years' War* (Poole: Blandford Press, 1978), pp.92–93.

a muster place. Nuremberg also made other payments to officers to make their troops move on quickly, or if they were forced to quarter the troops within the city then the officers were to guarantee their good behaviour.[13]

One way of obtaining a large number of well-trained soldiers was offering prisoners of war the option to change sides. After the battle of Nördlingen in 1634, 1,494 men from the Swedish Army reenlisted in the Bavarian Army and a further 2,487 Frenchmen after Herbsthausen. However they were not always reliable, as Robert Monro recalled of the 1,000 strong garrison of Donavert in 1632 who were 'forced to take service' with the Swedish Army, but 'being Papists of Bavaria, as soon as they smelt the smell of their fathers' houses, in less than ten days they were all gone.' In 1648 Maximilian ordered that only German deserters could enlist in regiments of foot of the Bavarian Army.[14]

On 2 January 1632 it was reported from Nuremberg that, 'Hither do daily come running from their colours 10 or 12 of Tilly's soldiers at once who reenlist in the Swedish service.'[15] At the same time Tilly was said to have 'brave cavalry but very poor

Date	Gayling's Cuirassiers	Mercy's Foot
Mar 1639	924	-
Nov 1640	930	1,327
1642	967	1,500
Dec 1642	840	660
1643	888	842
Jan 1644	934	1,087
Dec 1644	940	1,031
Nov 1645	872	822
Feb 1647	891	688
Jul 1647	868	707
Feb 1648	985	603
Nov 1648	941	703

and impotent foot forces. In their march from Ansbach to Guntsbach they left behind them in the streets and ways above 1,500 sick and dead soldiers.' However, soldiers did not necessarily have to change sides. When Wallenstein was raising his army, many of Tilly's soldiers deserted to enlist under Wallenstein, knowing that newly raised regiments would have better resources available to them.[16]

13 TNA: SP 101/46 f.104; Redlich, pp.339–341.
14 Wilson, p.829; Monro, pp.114–115; Redlich, p.456.
15 British Library Burney MS, LR 263/C/7, *The Continuation of our Foreign News since 24 to 30 January 1632.*
16 British Library Burney MS, LR 263/C6/5, *The Continuation of our Foreign News since 2 to 12 January 1632.*

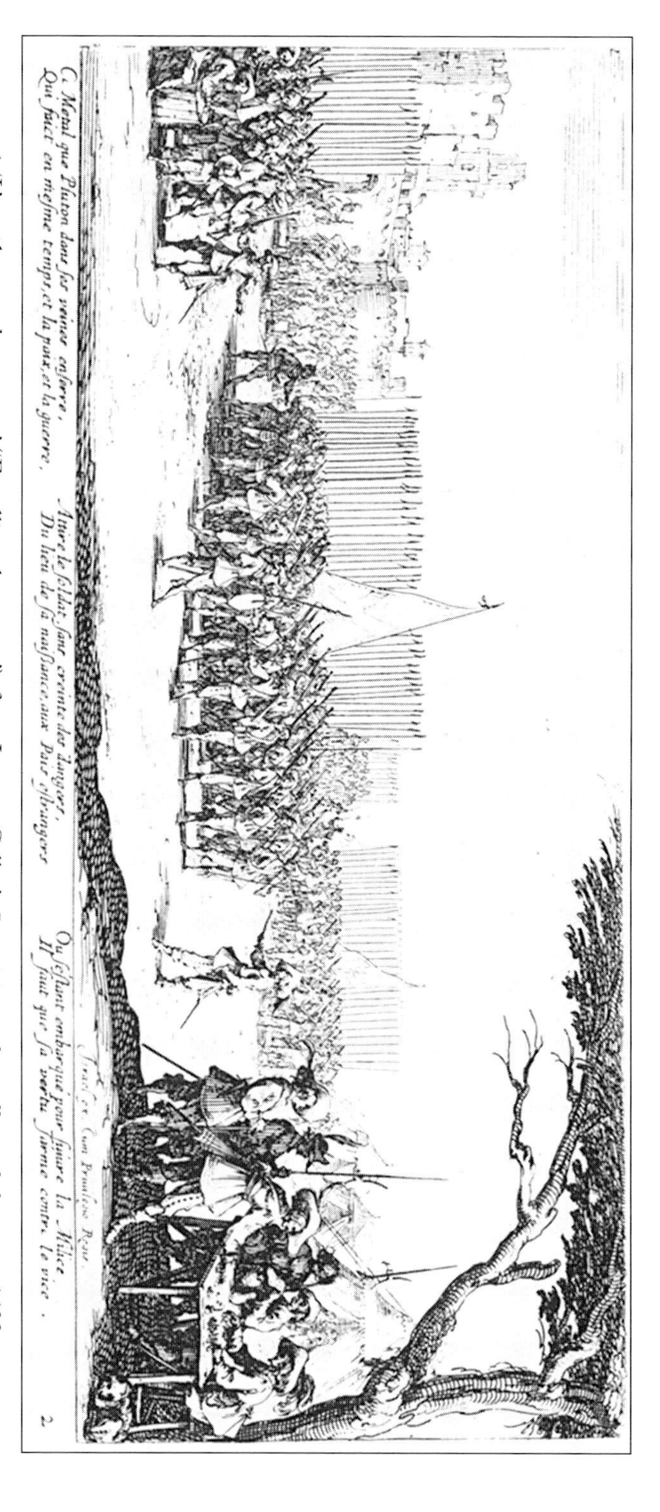

6. 'L'enrôlement des troupes' ('Enrolling the troops'), from Jacques Callot's *Les misères et les malheurs de la guerre*, 1633.

Once a regiment or company had been raised, recruits were always needed to keep it up to strength, although this was practically impossible, especially after a battle as the following chart shows:[17]

Gayling's regiment had been raised in 1620 and Mercy's in 1619, although they were not the original commanders. Between 1639 and 1648 Gayling's Regiment saw action at the battles of Wolfenbüttel, 1641; Tuttlingen, 5 May 1643; Herbsthausen and Allerheim, 1645; Zusmarshausen, 1646; and Mercy's at Freiberg, 1644; Jankow, 23 February 1645; 2nd Nördlingen and Zusmarshausen. How many of the soldiers with these regiments in 1620 were still with the colours in November 1648 is not known.

For many, life as a soldier was a family affair. In 1627 the Duke of Holstein's Regiment of Foot mustered 1688 men and 897 women, and in 1646 a Bavarian regiment of foot which mustered 480 men also had 314 women, 74 servants and three sutlers. A regiment of horse had 481 troopers, with 236 servants, 102 women and children and nine sutlers. They also had 1,072 horses across the regiment. Of these soldiers 961 or 66 percent were veterans. Peter Hagendorf records that he had two wives during his military service: his first wife and their four children all died, and from his second marriage of the six children only two survived.[18]

Sir James Turner wrote that:

> Women are great helpers to armies, to their husbands, especially those of the lower condition ... They provide, buy and dress their husband's meat, when their husbands are on duty or newly come from it; they bring in fuel for fire, a soldier's wife may be helpful to others, and gain money to her husband and herself; especially they are useful in camp and leaguers, being permitted (which should not be refused them) to go some miles from the camp to buy victuals and other necessaries.[19]

There were three types of women who followed the army: soldiers' wives, whores, who were unmarried but performed the same duties as a soldier's wife, and prostitutes. 'Whores' might attach themselves to a soldier for a campaign or two, although a late sixteenth century German engraving called *The Mercenary's Whore* warned:

> If you're not into gluttony and boozing
> I don't want to follow you for long
> If I stay near you for any length of time
> I'll certainly let you have the French disease.[20]

In the late 1490s, shortly after the discovery of America, syphilis, or 'the French disease' appeared in Europe. Often it is said that it came from the New World,

17 Kasper, pp.221–249.
18 <http://www.Kriegsbuch.blogspot.co.uk> (accessed December 2015); Redlich, *Military Intelligencer*, pp.521–522.
19 Turner, *Pallas Armata* (London, 1683), p.277.
20 Quoted in Keith Moxey, *Peasants, Warriors and Wives: popular imagery in the Reformation* (Chicago: University of Chicago Press, 2004), p.81.

although there is no evidence for this. The Articles of War stated that prostitutes were to be whipped from the camp, but despite these women helping spread syphilis throughout the army, the article seems to have been largely ignored. The regimental staff included a *hurenwebel* or whoremaster, whose job it was to control the women.[21] There was a hierarchy: a sergeant's wife was higher than a musketeer's, who was higher than the musketeer's whore, who was higher than a prostitute. A woman's status in the camp depended also on whether she walked, or sat in a baggage wagon. An attempt to rise above her place could cause disorder among the soldiers concerned, who often became embroiled in the quarrel. If a soldier's wife became a widow she would have to quickly find herself another husband to survive the campaign and not slide down the pecking order of camp society. No doubt widows were in great demand amongst the unmarried soldiers.[22]

Sometimes the presence of women could be a detriment to military discipline. In August 1633 part of the garrison of Erfurt was ordered to dig some fortifications, but 'their women began to wonder where their men had gone and they went looking for them. They brought food and drink with them. Once they had begun to settle in, little work was done afterwards. More pints of beer and wine were drunk than carts of earth moved.'[23]

On 5 June 1629 among the 47 prisoners 'condemned of felonies' from Newgate and Bridewell gaols, there was an Elizabeth Leech who were ordered to be delivered to the Swedish Ambassador for service in Gustavus Adolphus' army. What Elizabeth's role was intended to be is not specified, but in 1634 a doctor of Hildesheim discovered a woman who was had been wounded in a skirmish dressed as a musketeer. She may have belonged to Colonel Sorbus Ordre's Regiment, which belonged to the Swedish Army and was quartered in the town from 10 April 1634. Other than camp followers, this is one of very few examples of women serving in the ranks.[24]

21 Langer, p.97; Hubsch, *Das Hochstiff Bamburg* (Bamberg: 1895), p.120.

22 John Lynn, *Women, Armies and Warfare in Early Modern Europe* (Cambridge: Cambridge University Press, 2008), p.67.

23 Quoted in Holger Berg, *Military Occupation under the Eyes of the Lord* (Gottingen: Vandenboeck & Ruprecht, 2010), p.58.

24 John Bruce (ed.), *Calendar of State Papers, Domestic Series. Charles I, 1628–1629*, p.568; Casper von Schoch, <http://www.30jaehrigerkreig.de> (accessed December 2015), note 5; Reinhard Jordan, *Chronik der Stadt Mülhausen im Thüringen* (Mülhausen; Danner, 1906), vol. 3, p.78.

3

Organisation

During the war the Bavarian Army consisted of 21 regiments of foot and 30 regiments of horse, 18 of which were raised between 1619 and 1620. The remaining regiments were raised throughout the war, although 11 would be disbanded during this time. However, this was the exception rather than the rule: regiments within the army had a surprisingly long regimental history compared with other armies, although all regiments changed colonels several times during the war. One regiment of cuirassiers commanded by Colonel Herman von der Lippe from 1619 passed to Adolphus von Eynatten in July 1620; in 1624 a Colonel de Grana took command of the regiment, but despite this poor start it was finally disbanded in 1649, albeit with three further colonels having commanded it.

As well as commissioning new regiments Maximilian also increased, and decreased, the strength of those already existing, by commissioning new captains to raise men. This not only had the benefit of making strong regiments, but also it did not drain Bavaria's war chest by paying for additional colonels, majors and other regimental staff. Although commissioning a regiment or company to be raised was one thing, paying for its existence was another. Pappenheim's 'new' Regiment of Foot cost 548,738 *fl* 57 *kr* between 1626 and 1644, whereas his regiment of horse cost 436,462 *fl* 46 *kr* between 1620 and 1624. It is usually stated that in 1627 Pappenheim took command of the regiment which had originally been commanded by Colonel Hans Ernest Sprinzenstein, but these accounts suggest they were two different regiments, with Sprinzenstein's costing 817,635 *fr* 52 *kr* between 1622 and 1631. The six companies of the regiment had passed to its Lieutenant Colonel Hubner in 1624 and three were massacred in the Upper Austria in 1626 along with their colonel, while the other three remained in the Upper Palatinate.[1]

In 1621 the cavalry varied in size and strength from two to six troops, with Colonel Franz von Herzelles' Regiment of Cuirassiers being the strongest at 669 men

1 Walter Goetz, 'Die Kriegskosten Bayerns und der Ligastände im Dreissigjährigen Kriege' in *Forschungen zur Geschichte Bayerns* vol. 12 (Munich and Berlin: R Oldenbourg, 1904), pp.121, 123; Franz Weber 'Gliederung und Einsatz des bayerischen Heeres im Dreissigjahrigen Krieg' in Hubert Glaser, *Um Glauben und Reich, Kurfürst Maximilian I* (Munich: R Piper & Co., 1980), p.470.

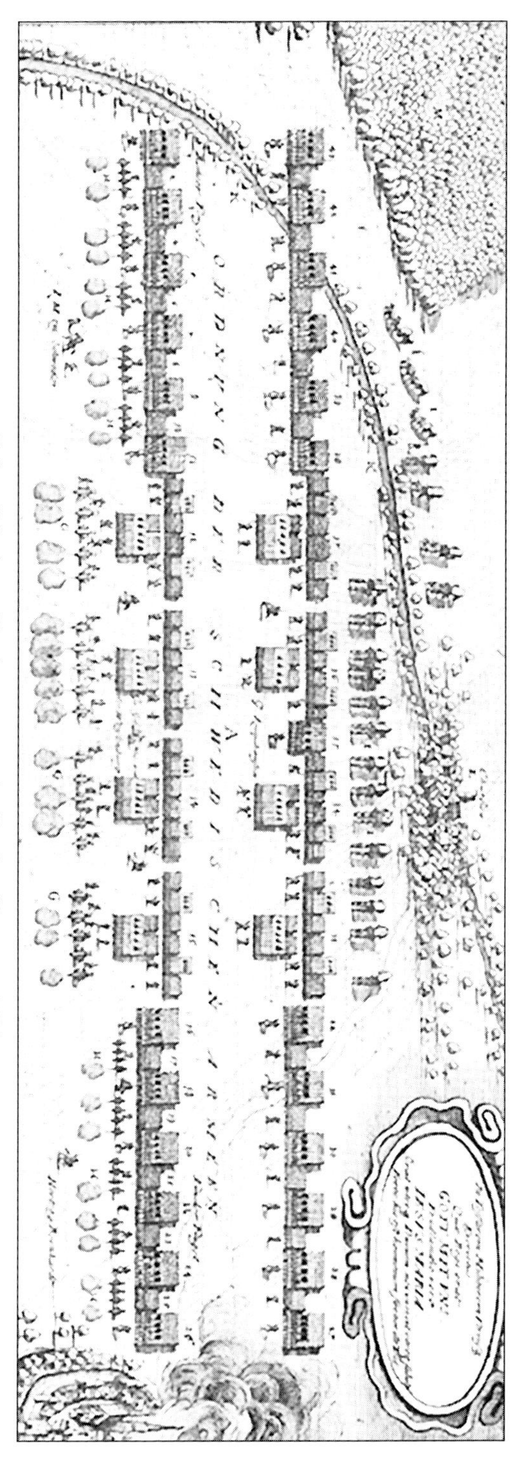

7. Swedish Army Deployment at the Battle of Lützen, 1632.

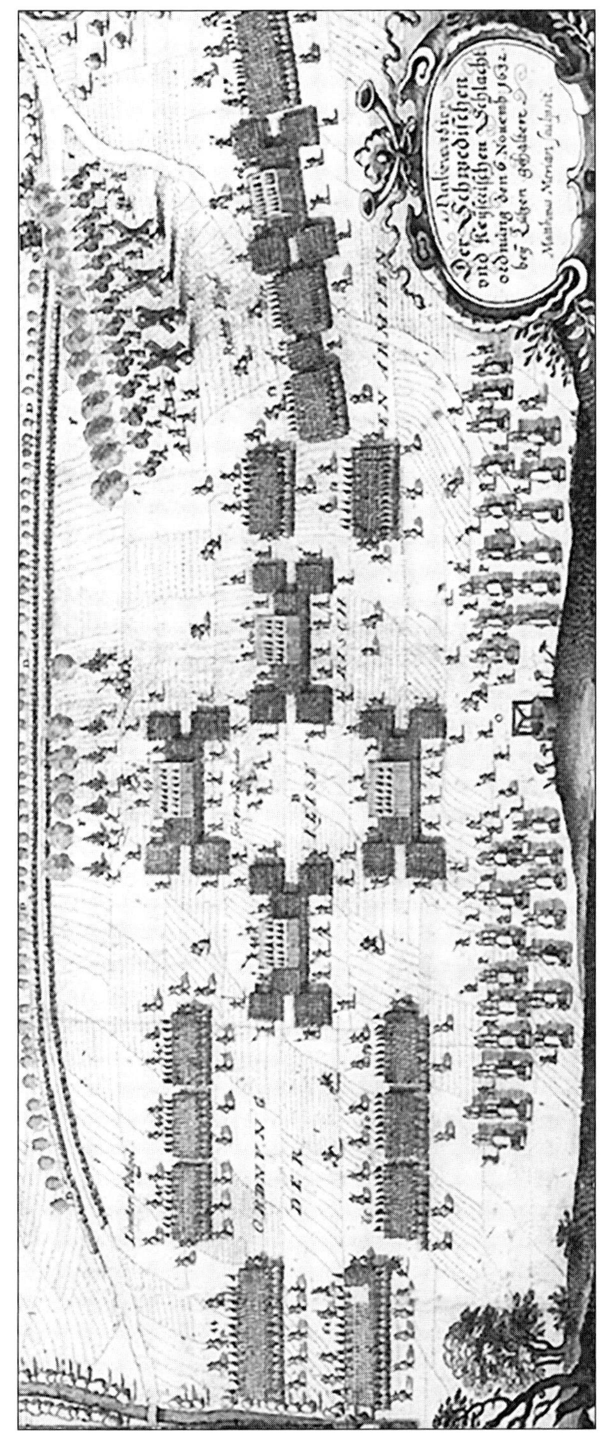

8. Imperial Army Deployment at the Battle of Lützen, 1632.

and Cronberg's being the weakest with just 179. On 10 April 1623 due to losses on campaign, Maximilian ordered that 31 troops of horse and six companies of foot be disbanded and the men dispersed into the remaining units. This meant that the army's cavalry regiments now consisted of four or five troops per regiment and the infantry eight companies, although Anholt's Regiment of Foot continued to have 14 companies.[2]

However, by 13 February 1626 there had been an increase in the strength of cavalry with Cronberg's Regiment mustering 823 troopers in eight troops and in 1633 the regiment had 1,078 men in 13 troops. On the other hand Billehe's Regiment mustered 621 men in nine troops in the same year. Not all troops were with their colonel: Johann von Werth's Regiment, which was commissioned to be raised in 1631, mustered 2,020 men in 18 troops in 1634, although only 12 were serving with the main field army, the other six had been detached for other duties. Likewise three of Cronberg's Regiment were at Munich, while the other 10 were with the army.[3]

Unfortunately these numbers could not be kept up indefinitely, and in 1635 only Werth's, Billehe's and Furstenberg had 10 or more troops, the other 11 regiments of horse having five or six troops. A newssheet dated 15 March 1632 reported that Tilly's cavalry 'are old beaten soldiers, being some of those that were at the battle of Leipzig and these are good men generally one with the other. As for his foot they be raw and new levied fellows for the most part made here to serve against their will and such have no heart to grapple with the king of Sweden.' Like many newssheets it was published for propaganda purposes so must be used with some care; although many probably did wish 'they had much rather be at home at their ploughs and spades' as the newssheet claimed, this was due to them not wanting to be soldiers rather than any fear of the Gustavus Adolphus.[4]

Moreover, finding recruits to fill their ranks was one thing, finding horses for the cavalry was another matter. At a muster held on 21 January 1639 the regiments were divided into mounted and dismounted troopers as follows:[5]

Regiment	No. of Troops	Mounted	Dismounted	Total
Götz	10	800	200	1,000
Wahl	10	400	160	560
Behlen	10	400	140	540
Wartenberg	10	350	150	500
Harthausen	6	300	150	450
Truckmuller	6	300	166	466
Kolb	9	400	200	600
Redetti	6	150	80	230

2 Maximilian to P. Valeriano, 10 April 1623, printed in Goetz, *Die Politik Maximilians I von Baiern und seiner Verbündeten*, p.121.
3 Heilmann, 1868, pp.919–923.
4 British Library Burney MS, LR 263/C6/10, *The Continuation of our Foreign News*, 15 March 1632.
5 Heilmann, 1868, p.924.

Regiment	No. of Troops	Mounted	Dismounted	Total
Meissinger	5	218	72	290
Lohn	2	150	50	200
Ruischenberg	6	-	-	-
Croats	1	90	40	130
Total	**81**	**3,558**	**1,408**	**4,966**

Most of these figures appear to have been rounded up, but the same cannot be said of the figures for the 19 November 1640 when the Bavarian cavalry mustered as follows:[6]

Regiment	No. of Troops	Mounted	Dismounted	Prisoners	Total
Werth Cr	8	396	180	30	606
Gayling Cr	9	770	111	49	930
Kolb Cr	8	483	234	43	760
Lowenstein Cr	9	725	274	55	1,054
Werth Ha	9	593	210	23	816
Reuneck Ha	8	277	164	-	441
Truckmuller Ha	9	495	210	141	846
Sport Ha	8	555	209	-	764
Wolf Dr	6	294	287	-	581
Ossena Dr	5	-	-	-	443
Total	**78**	**4,588**	**1,879**	**341**	**7,049**

Cr = Cuirassiers; Ha = Harquebusiers; Dr = Dragoons

In other words about a fifth of the cavalry could not perform their duty since they did not have enough horses. It was not just the lack of horses that hindered a regiment, as the following chart of a muster taken in October 1643 shows:

Regiment	Total Strength	On foot	Hurt horses	Captured	Sick & Wounded	Missing
Werth	935	58	111	15	16	-
Mercy	682	26	74	6	8	1
Reihling	888	80	42	10	17	5
Druckmuller	845	70	103	12	12	16
Kolb	752	35	93	11	2	-

6 *Ibid.*

Regiment	Total Strength	On foot	Hurt horses	Captured	Sick & Wounded	Missing
Sporck	1,060	32	111	26	22	-
Lapierre	753	87	100	16	6	-
Kongisbeck	371	90	49	1	-	-
Total	**6,286**	**478**	**683**	**97**	**83**	**22**

To put it another way, of the total of 6,286 men, only 4,965 were mounted leaving about a third of the cavalry on foot or mounted on wounded horses.[7]

Despite this shortage of horses, on 14 February 1647 the staff of Sporck's Regiment was allowed 166, including 17 for the colonel and 10 for his lieutenant colonel; Sporck himself as a major general was allowed 35. In addition the regiment was allowed 1,632 to pull its baggage train.[8]

The staff of a regiment of horse included not only the senior commanders, i.e. a colonel, lieutenant colonel and major (who also all held the rank of a captain), but also a chaplain, quartermaster, wagon master and a provost and his deputy who were responsible for imposing discipline in the regiment.[9]

Each troop consisted of the following officers, and no matter how strong the troop was, it always had its full complement of officers:[10]

German Ranks	English Ranks
1 Rittmeister	Captain
1 Leutnant	Lieutenant
1 Wachtmeister	Cornet
Fourier	Quartermaster
2 Corporal	Corporal
Musterschreiber	Clerk
Feldscherer	Surgeon
3 Trompeter	Trumpeter
Sattler	Sadler

The cavalry were divided into four types at this time. Cuirassiers were heavy cavalry armoured from head to knee, with their lower legs protected by leather riding boots. They were usually armed with two pistols and a sword. However, the armour was heavy and according to Sir Edmund Verney, who wrote about his experience during

7 Johann Heilmann, *Der Feldzüge der Bayern in den Jahren 1643, 1644 & 1645* (Leipzig: Goedsche, 1851), p.18.
8 Heilmann, 1868, pp.926–927.
9 Ronald Sennawald, *Das Kursächsische Heer im Dreissigjährigen Krieg* (Berlin: Zeughaus, 2013), p.593.
10 *Ibid.*

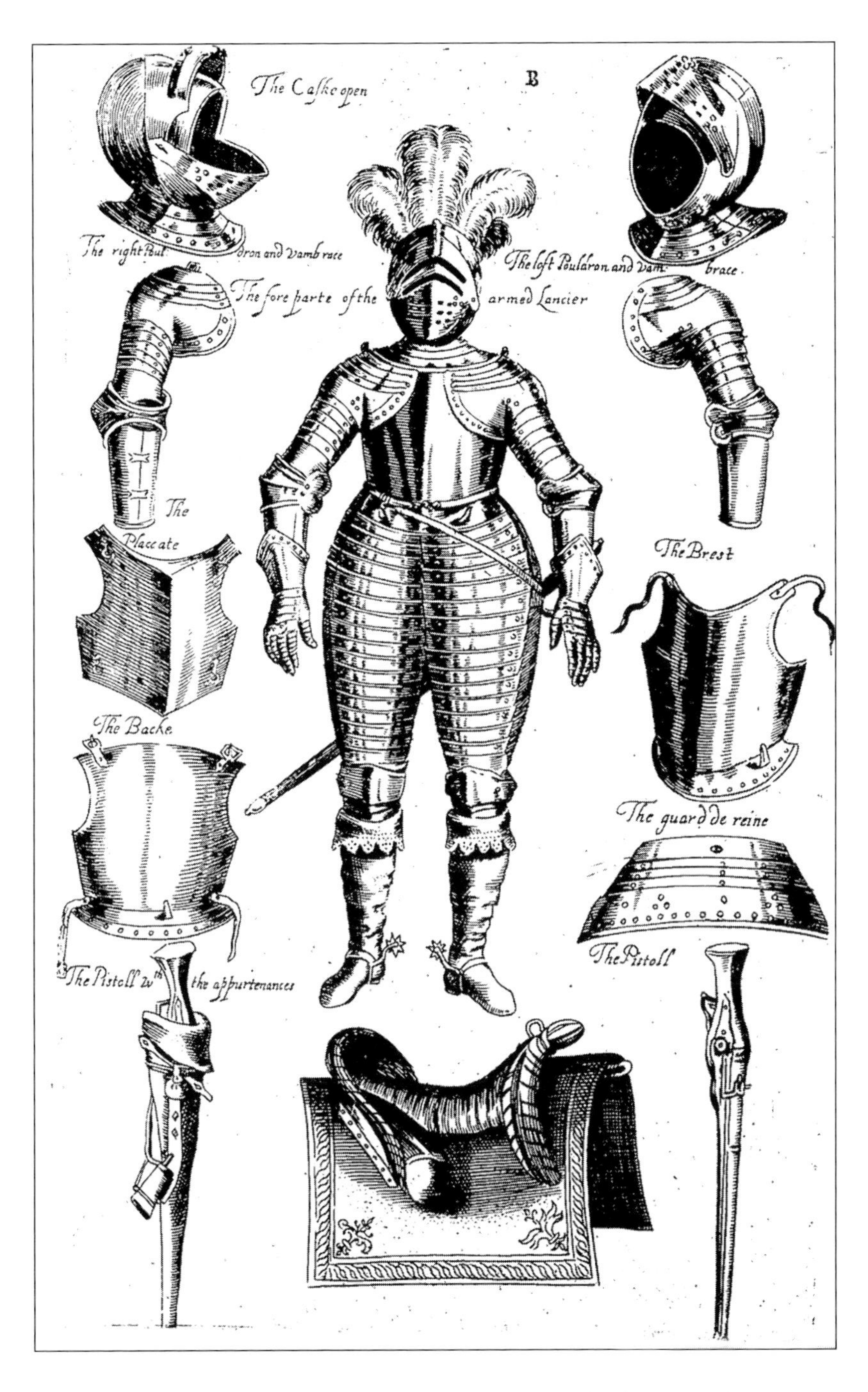

9. The arms and armour of a cuirassier, from the first part of Henry Hexham's *Principles of the Art Military*, 1642 edition.

the English Civil War, 'It would kill a man to serve in a whole cuirass. I am resolved to use nothing but back, breast and gauntlet.' The Parliamentarian Edmund Ludlow agreed; being dismounted, he records, 'I could not without difficulty recover on horseback being loaded with cuirassiers arms.' It was because of these difficulties and their expense that many discarded their cuirassier armour, even though they were seen as the senior form of cavalry. When the Imperial General Montecuccoli wrote to the Duke of Modena he suggested that the cuirassier 'should be equipped with breast and back harness, storm hat [helmet] together with two pistols and a sword. This is the way the Swedish cuirassiers are armed.' Lancers were armoured similarly to the cuirassiers but also had lances.[11]

When General George Monck wrote his *Military and Political Affairs* he stated, 'I have omitted here to speak anything of the armour of the cuirassier, because there are not many countries that do afford horses fit for the service of cuirassiers.' John Cruso does not say how many hands a cuirassier horse should be, but that it should 'not [be] inferior in stature and strength, though not so swift.' Cruso does record that a lancer's horse should be '15 hand high at the least, strong swift and well managed', which was the same phrase he used for a harquebusier's horse.[12] In theory harquebusiers wore a buff coat underneath their back and breastplates and a helmet, although in practice they might wear either a buff coat or a back and breast plates. Their offensive arms were two pistols, a carbine and a sword.

Although regiments were often referred to as a cuirassier or a harquebusier regiment they often had a mixture of troops. In 1621 Colonel Adam von Herbersdorf's Regiment of Horse consisted of four cuirassier troops and three of harquebusiers, even though it was referred to as a cuirassier regiment. In 1622 Herbersdorf recruited additional troops which once mustered were divided into three regiments, two commanded by Herbersdorf himself and the other by Gottfried von Pappenheim, who had been the regiment's lieutenant colonel the previous year. In fact Herbersdorf appears to have been one of only a few commanders in the Bavarian Army to have commanded more than one regiment. Pappenheim's Regiment consisted of five troops, four of which were harquebusiers and his own troop were cuirassiers. While in 1647 Colonel Casper Schoch's Regiment consisted of six troops of harquebusiers and two companies of dragoons, which were mounted infantry.[13]

Originally dragoons were armed with pikes and flintlock muskets. According to Cruso a dragoon's horse was to be the 'least price, the use thereof being but to expedite his march, alighting to do his service.' Whether there were any dragoons armed with pikes in the Bavarian Army is not known, but in 1634 there were 16 companies of dragoons in the Bavarian Army, a total of 1,080 men, although five companies were

11 Quoted in David Blackmore's *Arms and Armour of the English Civil Wars* (London: The Trustees of the Royal Armouries, 1990); Thomas Barker, *The Military Intellectual and Battle; Raimondo Montecuccoli and the Thirty Years War* (Albany: State University of New York Press, 1975), p.110.

12 John Heath, *Observations upon military and Political Affairs written by the Most Honourable George, Duke of Albemarle* (London: Henry Mortlocke, 1671), p.25; John Cruso, *Militarie Instructions for the Cavalrie*, ed. Brigadier Peter Young (Kineton: The Roundwood Press, 1972), pp.28–29, 31.

13 Barbara Stadler, *Pappenheim und die Zeit des Dreissigjährigen Krieges* (Winterthur: Gemsberg-Verl., 1991), p.112.

attached to cavalry regiment, leaving just two regiments of dragoons: Werth's, which mustered 350 men in six companies, and 250 men in Metternich's Regiment of five companies. However, in 1639 there was just one regiment, Wolf's, which mustered 423 men. The following year in addition to Wolf's Regiment there was also Ossena's Regiment mustering a total of 1,024 men. The Bavarian Army would continue to have just two regiments of dragoons until 1648, when one appears to have been disbanded.[14]

The lightest cavalry were the known as Croats, or Crabats, although this was a term given to all light horseman no matter where they came from, which was usually Poland or one of the Cossack tribes. It was these 'Croats' who were often blamed for the worst atrocities committed during the war, and were even said to have eaten children. They were armed with a harquebus, sword – which was rumoured to be poisoned – a dagger ,and pistols. As well as having complete regiments of Croats, there were also troops attached to regiments of horse, such as Colonel Otto Fugger's Regiment of Horse.

Those recruits who enlisted into a cavalry regiment who could not ride, would be taught how to mount a dummy horse, at first without arms and then holding a sword and a pistol. They would then progress to the horse itself and weres taught how to ride and manoeuvre in formation with a dummy sword, or as Lord Herbert of Cherbury records, 'reasonable stiff riding rod,' and then finally with a real sword. Troopers would also have to learn how to discharge their firearms on horseback, before they were ready to take the field.[15]

In theory a German regiment of foot was composed of 10 companies each of 300 men, plus officers. However, when Maximilian was issuing commissions between 1619 and 1620 to raise his regiments of foot six were to be 3,000 men strong, one was to be 2,000 strong and one, Colonel Theodor von Haimhausen's Regiment of Foot, was to be just 1,000 men. Why Maximilian chose different sized regiments is not known, but when a muster was held on 5 July 1621 only one regiment, Gaisberg's, was at its full complement of 3,000 men. Mortaigne's Regiment, which was also meant to be 3,000 strong, mustered just 1,417 men, whereas Herliberg's, which was meant to be 2,000 men strong, mustered 2,598. The situation had not changed by 26 June 1622, but now Mortaigne's Regiment was 1,400 strong, although on paper it still mustered 3,000 men. During 1624 he had brought his regiment up to 1,900, but it was still short of the number of soldiers he had been commissioned to raise.

The regimental staff was similar to that of a cavalry regiment; like the cavalry new companies were raised to keep up the regiment's strength, so that during the early 1620s only a few regiments had 10 companies, but in 1627 most had more, with Anholt's Regiment, which still had 3,000 men, mustering between 13 and 16. By 1635, however, with the decline in the strength of the army most regiments had under 10, with only six out of the 11 regiments mustering over 1,000 men. The strongest was Wahl's Regiment with 2,000 men in 11 companies. Three years later 13 regiments

14 Kasper, pp.222–247.
15 Edward, Baron Herbert of Cherbury, *The Expedition to the Isle of Rhe* (London: Whittingham and Wilkins, 1860), pp.84–85; Jacob von Wallhausen, *Art militaire a Cheval. Instruction des principes et fondements de la cavalerie* (Frankfurt: Paul Jacques, 1616); TNA: SP 101/42, State Papers, Foreign Newsletters, f.243.

of foot mustered just 9,975 men in 93 companies and on 6 December 1642 the situation was even worse with just 8,700 men in 102 companies. In 1648 the 10 companies of Kolb's Regiment had just 805 men, giving an average of about 80 men per company.

10. A Croat light horseman. Soldiers such as these were recruited from the military border with the Turkish Empire.

Fortunately for Maximilian he did not need to commission large numbers of regiments, and of the 21 regiments of foot raised during the war 14 were raised between 1619 and 1625 and a further four between 1631 and 1632. Only five regiments were disbanded during the war, whereas the Imperialist Army raised and disbanded many regiments during this time.

Each company contained a captain, a lieutenant, ensign, two sergeants, three corporals, three drummers, 25 lance corporals, a surgeon and possibly a fifer, and each company was divided into three types of soldier: musketeers, halberdiers and pikemen. In some companies the harquebus, a lighter and less powerful musket, was still being carried, although by the end of the war halberdiers and harquebusiers had disappeared.

The pikemen took their name from their main weapon, the pike, which was between 16 and 18 feet long and made of ash about 1¾ inches thick. It had a steel head with two metal strips about two feet long, running down the shaft of the pike, 'well riveted' to its side to prevent the head being cut off. It has been suggested that pikemen would cut down their pikes to a more manageable size, but in the Dutch Army at least, this was forbidden since it would put him at a disadvantage when it came to battle and make a weakness in the formation. The pikeman also had a sword and to protect himself and had, in theory, a back and breast plate; tassets, which protected the thighs; a gorget, which protected the neck; and a helmet. The halberdiers were armed similarly to the pikemen but carried a halberd which was also a pole weapon but with an axe-shaped head.

The musketeers were usually armed with a matchlock musket, although flintlocks were also issued and came in handy when guarding the gunpowder, and for night assaults when the lighted match of the matchlock, would give away a soldier's position. It was estimated that a musketeer could used two fathoms of match every 24 hours, so even on the march, or on sentry duty, musketeers would be burning match even before they came within sight of the enemy. To save match musketeers could extinguish it leaving just the file leader's match still alight, but this could lead to a desperate scramble for the other musketeers to light their match if the enemy was spotted. During the

11. A typical depiction of a mounted harquebusier from the early part of the Thirty Years War.

English Civil War a detachment of Sir Miles Hobart's Regiment of Foot at the siege of Newark in 1644, being relieved from guard duty, extinguished their match only to be cut to pieces by Royalist cavalry. Those who were not killed were taken prisoner.

Since matchlock muskets were heavy they needed a rest to steady the musketeer's aim, but as muskets became lighter rests were discarded. To carry their gunpowder the musketeers were issued with a powder flask and a set of bandoliers, which consisted of small wooden bottles attached to a leather belt with cord. Since there were usually 12 of these bottles they have erroneously been referred to as the 'Twelve Apostles', but there is no contemporary evidence for this nickname.

Wallhausen, who wrote about his experiences during the sixteenth century, suggested that each regiment should have 1,600 musketeers, 1,200 pikemen and 200 halberdiers or targetiers, but experiences during the 'Long War' with the Ottomans had shown the need for firepower. As early as 1622 Colonel Sprinzenstein's Regiment contained 874 musketeers and 400 pikemen, being a ratio of about one pikemen to 2.2 musketeers and Florainville's Regiment also had 1,400 musketeers and 600 pikemen, which was also a ration of about 2.2 musketeers to one pikeman.[16]

On 17 July 1621 Maximilian ordered the delivery to Herbersdorf for his regiment one partizan, five commanders' halberds, one drum, 100 soldiers' armour, 80 long pikes, 200 muskets with bandoliers and powder flasks, 50 musket ball flasks, 20 common halberds and 202 coats. When Pappenheim raised his regiment in 1627, 1,500

16 Wallhausen, *L'Art Miliatire pour l'Infantrie* (Uldrick Balck, 1615), p.101; Bavarian Archives KAA no. 2329 p.147.

12. The somewhat idealised depiction of a musketeer going through his postures of drill.

muskets, 300 pike and 350 halberds were supplied to him by the Bishop of Würzburg, a further 1,000 muskets came from the city of Strasbourg and 200 muskets and 700 pike came from other sources; a total of 2,700 musket, 1,000 pike and 350 halberds or ratio of two musketeers to every pikeman/halberdier. Not all regiments had this ratio: in 1627 the Duke of Holstein's Regiment had 1,361 musketeers and 327 pikemen.[17]

In the summer of 1631 Otto Fugger obtained for his regiment 700 muskets with rests from Augsburg weapons dealers Jakob Banz and Hans Roth, as well as 1,000 bandoliers, for 3,200 *gulden*. Roth also supplied 80 sets of pikemen's armour for 164 *gulden*, while the city's armoury supplied 950 muskets with bandoliers, 700 long pikes 180 halberds and some partisans, 600 sets of armour and 17 drums for 7,200 *gulden*.[18]

Dragoons were organised along similar lines as the infantry regiments having the following contingent of officers in each company:[19]

German Ranks	English Ranks
1 Hauptmann	Captain
1 Leutnant	Lieutenant
1 Fahnrich	Ensign
1 Feldwebel	Sergeant Major
1 Musterschreiber	
Fourier	
Wachtmeister	Sergeant Major
Fahnenjunker	
Feldscherer	Surgeon
3 Korporale	Corporal

17 Dr Hans Wertheim, *Der Tolle Halberstädter, Herzog Christian von Braunschweig im Pfälzischen Kriege* (Berlin: Internationale Bibliothek, 1929), vol. 1, p.112; Stadler, pp.210, 249–250; <http://www.Kriegsbuch.blogspot.co.uk> (accessed December 2015).

18 Stephanie Haberer, *Otto Heinrich Fugger (1592–1644): biographische Analyse typologischer Handlungsfelder in der Epoche des Dreissigjährigen Krieges* (Augsburg: Wissner, 2004), pp.339–340.

19 Sennawald, p.595.

However, an army would not be complete without its train of artillery, which not only included its pieces of ordnance and gun crews, but also support wagons which carried the gunpowder and shot not only for the artillery but for the rest of the army as well. In 1622 the Bavarian Army's train of artillery contained 129 wagons and 568 horses, including 28 wagons to carry 512,500 musket shot, 16 wagons for 160 cwt of gunpowder and 33 wagons for 330 cwt of match. There was also a wagon for petards, another to carry 555 shot for the two falconets, and two to carry the 72 mortar balls for the army's three mortars. In addition there was an army of artisans, carpenters, blacksmiths, wheelwrights etc., all of whom were needed to repair the artillery pieces and the wagons if necessary.[20]

According to Sieur Du Praissac there were six calibres of artillery: the cannon, the culverin, the bastard culverin, the minion, the falcon, and the falconet. One of the largest guns, the great culverin, fired a shot weighing 15 and a quarter pounds, which needed 10 pounds of gunpowder per shot and was served by two cannoniers, two extraordinary cannoniers and 24 pioneers who could fire it about 10 times an hour. Although for this rate of fire it needed three wagons pulled by 12 horses per day, which does not include the number of horses needed to pull the piece itself. The smallest piece, the falconet, could be fired 20 times per hour and fired a three-quarter pound shot. It was served by one cannonier and four pioneers and a wagon, which was pulled by a horse. The wagon could carry enough ammunition and powder to last for three days if it was in constant use.[21]

When the Swedish Army occupied Munich, according to Monro:

> Before his Majesty [Gustavus Adolphus] coming, by the Duke's Command the great cannon were buried side by side in the magazine house, whereof his Majesty being much acquainted there were digged [sic] up out of the ground and carried away to Augsburg, above one hundred and forty pieces of cannon, great and small, whereof there were twelve Apostles and other cannon which formerly were taken from the elector Palatine and the Duke of Brunswick, with their names and arms on them.[22]

An inventory was taken dated 12 August 1634 of the guns in Bavarian armouries and mentions seven of these '12 Apostles', so Gustavus must have only taken five of them. Those remaining guns were engraved with the names of 'St Andreas, Mathias, Simon, Jakob minor, Thomas, Jakob major and Paulas.' Underneath these names was engraved the arms of Maximilian of Bavaria.

Others guns were called after animals: the 'Steinbock' (wild goat); 'die Lowen' (the Lion); and the 'Storchen' (the Stork); or other names such as 'Die wilde Mann' (the Wild man) and 'die wilde Frau' (the wild woman), both of which had been captured from the Brandenburg Army. On 27 September 1622 it was reported that Maximilian

20 Heilmann, 1868, vol. 2, p.953.

21 Sieur Du Praissac, *The Arte of Warre, or military discourses*, translated from the French by John Cruso (Cambridge: Roger Daniel, 1639), pp.118, 121.

22 Monro, p.125.

had ordered these two guns to be transported from Amberge in the Upper Palatinate to Munich, while six full cannon and some demi-cannons were also sent from Mannheim to Munich.[23]

Other pieces mentioned in the inventory bore the head of state's monograph, their coat of arms, or an inscription engraved on them with the date they were cast. It is usually believed that it was Gustavus Adolphus who introduced regimental guns, but this inventory also includes an entry for 'short Danish regimental pieces, 14 of seven and 12 pounds', which were possibly captured at the battle of Lutter in 1626, certainly no later than 1629 when Christian IV of Denmark made peace with Ferdinand.[24]

23 *The Continuation of the Weekly News* (London, 27 September 1622), p.5; *Weekly News* (London, 28 January 1623), No. 15, p.2.

24 Heilmann, 1868, pp.964, 966.

4

Clothing the Soldiers

Writing during the 1880s, Anton Gindely in his *History of the Thirty Years War* states that 'there was no symmetrical uniform at the time of the Thirty Years War, neither in colour nor in cut of the garments… [since], with the solitary exception of France and Holland, no provisions were made for the army's needs.'[1] This view has been repeated by many historians, who believe that a soldier had to equip himself with clothing and weapons at their own expense and so there was no uniformity. Another myth which has also been often repeated, is that Tilly said that he preferred a ragged soldier as long as they had a clean musket. However, both views are incorrect, since there is no contemporary evidence to suggest that Tilly ever said these words and far from the soldiers supplying their own clothes it was one of the reasons why they enlisted.

In 1620 an English volunteer wrote, at Delft, 'we mustered for the King of Bohemia and was billeted there for three weeks, where we had our apparel, our hats and Colours with our arms given to us'. Some recruits would desert once they had received their clothing which prompted Sir Dudley Carleton to recommend that the English soldiers being sent to the King of Denmark, that their 'clothes [were] not to be delivered till they come to Harwich' where they were to embark. In another letter, this time dated 20 August 1628, Carleton informed Lord Conway, 'The soldiers will hardly be drawn to return to the King of Denmark's service … Their clothes are not yet provided nor will they be ready this month yet … The clothes [are] not to be delivered till they come to the place of service.'[2]

This did not mean that their clothes did not wear out. In 1637 Maximilian of Bavaria wrote to the Emperor, saying of the Bavarian Army, 'the largest part of the cavalry marches on foot. The unfortunate soldiers are destitute, ragged, naked, worn out, starving and in such shape that we must in fairness commiserate with them. A

1 Anton Gindely, *History of the Thirty Years' War* (London: Richard Bentley and Son, 1885), Translated by Andrew Ten Brook, vol. 2 pp.391–392.

2 *A Relation of the passage of our English Companies from time to time since their first departure from England to the parts of Germanie, and the united Provinces. Sent from Frankendale in Germanie, by a souldier of those colonels, to his worshipfull* (London: Henry Gosson, 1621), p.2; British Library Add MS 18981, f.45; Geoffrey Mortimer, *Eyewitness Accounts of the Thirty-Years War, 1614–48* (Basingstoke: Palgrave Macmillan, 2002), p.18; TNA: SP 101/75, f.372; SP 101/47, Sir Dudley Carleton to Lord Conway, 20 August 1628, f.86.

period of recovery is urgently needed if it is planned to use the troops again next spring.'[3]

It is sometimes claimed that Wallenstein introduced clothing to the regiments of the Imperialist Army, but this is also incorrect, as in 1619 we find that Otto Heinrich Fugger paid Wolf Seidel, an Augsburg tailor, 4,580 *gulden* for an unspecified number or colour of *schützenröcke* or cassocks, to clothe his regiment.

Other references to clothing being made for the soldiers include George Ayermann of Nuremberg supplying Count von Mansfeld with 2,400 coats for his Imperialist Regiment in 1625, and in November 1628 Johann Wangler's Regiment of Foot being issued with clothing and shoes, although the quantity is not recorded.[4]

Furthermore it was reported on 4 October 1622 that the soldiers of the Marquis de Montenegro, 'soldiers returning from Hungary, Moravia and Silesia were so tattered, torn and in a manner of countenance, when they came to civil places that he was compelled to take order for the new arming and apparelling, [of them], dispersing great sums among them for their further satisfaction.'[5]

Neither did the supply of clothing dry up after Wallenstein's assignation in February 1634. On 13 January 1637 2,021 coats of 'course cloth' and lined, 3,018 pairs of shoes and 3,000 pairs of stockings were delivered to Adjutant General Count Ernest von Konigsbeck and on 19 January 1642 Count Rudolf Colleredo wrote to Hatzfeldt asking that clothing be sent to Cologne for his men. Also in 1642 the Swedes captured, an 'abundance of soldiers' coats and other provisions' from Piccolomini.[6]

Outer clothing, such as coats and breeches, were usually made by tailors in their own workshops. However, to increase their production Gustavus Adolphus planned to set up a magazine or factory, which was to employ between 40 and 50 tailors to make army uniforms. Unfortunately, it is not known whether he did or not since the records for this period do not survive; however during the English Civil War King Charles I did set up a similar factory in the Music School and the Astronomy School at Oxford University, and another one in Reading, to produce clothing for the main Royalist Army. So these types of factories were known at this time.[7]

Once the clothing was made it would then be taken to an appointed magazine, where it would be checked to see if it had been made correctly. There is some evidence to suggest that the clothing may have been made according to a relevant pattern;, certainly the clothing issued to English troops in the 1620s was copied from a pattern in the Royal Wardrobe, and in there is a hat said to be the pattern worn by Queen Christina's infantry during the latter part of the War. Unfortunately, for Maximilian in

3 Redlich, p.475.

4 Haberer, *Otto Heinrich Fugger (1592–1644)*, p.338.

5 *A True Relation of the Affairs of Europe*, 4 October 1622.

6 LVR-Archivberatungs und Fortbildungszentrum: Schonst 121, Count Ernest von Konigsbeck to Field Marshal Hatzfeldt, 13 January 1637, and Schonst 172, Count Rudolf Collerado to Hatzfeldt, 19 January 1642; British Library 1471.aa.4.(10), *News from Foreign parts*, July 1642.

7 Erik Bellander, *Dräkt och Uniform: den Svenska arméns beklädnad från 1500- talets början fram till våra dagar* (Stockholm: Norstedt, 1973), p.588; David Hopkins, Hillary Hopkins, *The Tale of a Soldier's Coat: The Story of the Experimental Reconstruction of a 1643 Oxford Royalist Soldier's Coat* (Stuart Press, 2000), p.5.

1632 his magazines at Würzburg and Munich fell into Swedish hands and the coats were distributed amongst Gustavus Adolphus' men rather than his own army.

As one can imagine, fashion changed considerably over the thirty years and varied from country to country. In February 1607 William Calley was to supply 6,000 'suits' and Francesco Sarra, an Italian merchant, was to supply 3,000 to the Spanish infantry. The cassocks and breeches, or hose as they were often called, were to be made of 'Reading cloth made large after the Spanish fashion.' He was also to supply a doublet made of fustian cloth. The cassocks were to be lined 'with good bayes, faced broad in the collar with rich taffeta and edged in the seams with the same. The doublet in the like manner and hose and lined with very good and strong linen and very fairly trimmed with buttons of silk at least 22 dozen of like button are employed in the trimming of the cassock, hose and doublet.'[8]

When it came to the coats and breeches issued to the Guard of the Elector of Brandenburg in 1620,they were to be made of five ells of a 'good blue' cloth, plus five ells of an unspecified colour for the lining and 12 ells of white, black and red stiff ribbon. The coats and breeches were to have 6 dozen bows and 3 dozen iron buttons, plus a hat. Plus one ell of thread to trim the cassock.[9]

Whereas in 1627 Philip Burlamachi estimated that it would cost to clothe each English soldier:[10]

Large cassock and hose, 2 yards and a half at eight shillings	20s
Cotton to line the cassock, 2 yards at 2s 6d the yard	3s [*sic*]
Lining for the hose either leather or linen	2s 6d
Making with buttons	4s
10 dozen buttons to each cassock and hose at 2d the dozen	1s 8d
Silk [thread] for button holes	8d
	31s 10d

In 1626 two thirds of the coats ordered to be supplied to the Swedish Army were to be large and the other third small. In 1633 the Swedish allowed an average of five ells of cloth per soldier, the same amount as for the Elector of Brandenburg's Guard. During the 1640s the French Army supplied the clothing to its soldiers in three sizes: small, large and regular.[11]

Among the accounts for the Swedish regiments at Stralsund in 1630 were several Scottish Regiments. Alexander Leslie's Regiments were issued with cloth which cost 9,464.34 *rikstaler* and Jacob Dubattles' Regiment of Horse was issued with cloth, furs and shoes. Colonel Hall's Regiment of Foot was issued with 4,270 ells of cloth

8 TNA: SP 77/8, Clothing for Archduke forces, 1606, f.202.

9 A. C. von der Oelsnitz, *Geschichte des Königlich Preussische Ersten Infanterie-Regiments* (Berlin: E. S. Mittler and Son, 1855), pp.18, 20.

10 J. V. Lyle, *Acts of the Privy Council of England*, 1627, Estimate of the charge of clothing the soldiers, 31 March 1627, p.194.

11 John Lynn, *Giant of the Grand Siècle: The French Army, 1610–1715* (Cambridge: Cambridge University Press, 1977), p.177.

at 5,207.24 *rikstaler* and Robert Leslie's Scottish Regiment received 1,000 ells of cloth costing 1,000 *rikstaler* and in 1631 they received breeches, shoes and stockings. Kembnitz squadron was issued with 543 *rikstaler* of cloth and shoes, Hastfehr's Regiment also received furs and shoes and in 1631 furs, shirts, shoes and stockings, while Reinhold Metstacke's Regiment was issued with furs and shoes and in 1631 furs, shirts, shoes and stockings. In 1631 Weissmeijer's squadron shoes and stockings, those of Noding's cloth, shoes and stockings, and Krigbaum's Regiment stockings and shoes. In a different order dated 1 November 1631 Robert Bremer of Brandenburg was asked to supply 500 suits of clothes, 500 pairs of stockings, 500 pair of shoes and 260 Monmouth caps to the Scottish Regiments in Swedish service, although only 360 pairs of stockings seem to have been delivered.[12]

In 1632 Metsake's and Hastfer's Finnish Regiments were issued with shoes, stockings, furs and shirts, Nodingke's Squadron received rough cloth, furs, shirts, shoes and stockings, while Monier's Regiment of Dragoons received just cloth for 1,600 *rikstaler*.[13]

On 4 October 1627 Sir James Spence wrote about the cloth being supplied by Swedish clothiers for Gustavus' Army:

> For clothing his [Gustavus Adolphus] army he hath course cloth made in his country and though it be course yet it is warm for winter, it is at 2 shillings sterling … with this he clothes his common soldiers causing to dye it a red, yellow, green and blue which makes a great show in the field and this never was done before this king's time.[14]

In 1631 the merchant Hans Barkhusen was contracted to buy 20,000 ells of cloth for the Swedish Army, preferably blue, although red or brown cloth was acceptable if he could not find enough of the former.

On 6 July 1624 a warrant to pay Philip Burlamachi £17,280 was issued for clothing and arming 6,000 foot for service in the United Provinces and in 1625 George Hooker was paid £6,666 13s 4d for 10,000 cassocks 'of good strong broad cloth' for Mansfeld's soldiers raised in England. Since the soldiers would have already received a coat from the county where they were raised, cassocks appear to have been more of an overcoat.[15]

Unfortunately, warrants for clothing do not often mention the colour of the clothing being supplied, since accountants usually care how many coats etc. were supplied and their cost rather than the colour. An exception to this is some Swedish accounts in 1620 which record that Smaland's Regiment of Foot were issued with 350 red jackets, the Vastgota Regiment of Foot 100 yellow coats with blue facings, and the Ostergotland Regiment 350 yellow coats, while the Uppland Regiment of

12 National Archives of Scotland: GD406/1/234.

13 J. Mankell, *Arkiv Till Upplysing On Svenska Krigens Och Krigsinrättningarnes Historia* (Stockholm: P. A. Norsstedt and Soner, 1860), pp.156, 205–207, 212–213, 218–220.

14 TNA: SP 95/2, Sir John Spence relations of affairs in Sweden, 4 October 1627, f. 179.

15 TNA: SP 81/33, Note of money paid to Mansfeld, 1625, f. 257.

Foot received 250 yellow coats with black facings. Each company was to be clothed the same.[16]

However, eyewitness accounts sometimes also fill this gap in our knowledge, for instance Israel Hoppe, who served with the Swedish Army's in Poland, mentions 'the German yellow coats' and 'the Swedish bluecoats under Count von Thurn Regiment.' Colonel Maximilian Teuffel is also mentioned as having 'four companies of bluecoats', and there were also 'four companies of redcoats of Colonel Hohendorf's [Regiment]'. Colonel Ehrenreiter's Regiment is also described as having red coats with Colonel Hans Nohten's as being a regiment of 'bluecoats'. Ehrenreiter's (which later became Hohendorf's) and Nohten's Regiments were known as the Red Regiment and Blue Regiment respectively. Teuffel commanded the Blue Regiment, before being appointed the commander of the Yellow Regiment and it is his former regiment that Hoppe is referring to.[17]

Several eyewitness accounts of the battle of Breitenfeld in September 1631 record that in the Swedish Army, 'the greatest part of the [foot] soldiers were clad in blue and yellow jackets'. Certainly the Blue and Yellow Regiments of the army are known to have worn these coloured coats as well as carrying the same colour ensigns, but this would suggest that not all of Gustavus Adolphus' 'Colour Regiments' were in the same coloured coats as their regimental colours, e.g. the Red and Green Regiments.[18]

It was not just the Swedish Army who had uniform coats: Wallenstein also received 1,000 ells of light blue cloth, 300 ells of carmine red and 100 red pairs of stockings, from England via Amsterdam, probably to clothe his own regiment since red and blue was his livery colours. In about 1630 a resident of Haguenau complained that he had been plundered by Colonel Collalto's blue coats, Schaffenburg's yellow coats and an unidentified militia regiment of red coats from Ortenau. This was Collalto's Life Regiment which served throughout the war, but whether it wore blue coats throughout this period is not known. Another blue coated regiment within Wallenstein's Army was Colonel Julius Hardegg's, whose coats were faced red. In 1645 Count Mathias Gallas ordered clothiers to supply pearl grey cloth for uniforms for his regiment of foot.[19]

In 1621 there were about 35 cloth mills at Reichenberg, but when Wallenstein became the town's owner he established 76 new cloth mills between 1622 and 1634. After his death these mills passed to Gallas and they continued to supply cloth to the Imperialist war effort. Under Gallas the number of clothiers appears to have increased from 20 between 1635 and 1637 and a further 28 between 1638 and 1645. In 1628 these mills were producing blue, red, black and grey cloth in two widths, 2½ and 2 ells.

16 Bellander, pp.79–80.

17 Israel Hoppe, *Burggrafen zu Elbing, Geschichte des Ersten schwedisch-polnischen Krieges in Preussen nebst Anhang* (Leipzig: Duncker and Humblot, 1887), pp.112, 138, 141, 230, 247, 270, 417, 469. Ed. Dr M. Toeppen.

18 Count Galeazzo Gualdo Priorato, *An history of the late warres and other state affaires of the best Part of Christendom beginning with the King of Swethlands entrance into Germany, and continuing in the yeare 1640* (London: W. Wilson, 1648), p.42. Translated by Henry Carey, Earl of Monmouth.

19 Anton Ernstberger, *Hans de Witte, Finanzmann Wallensteins* (Wiesbaden: Steiner Verlag, 1954), p.287; *Auguste Hanauer, La Guerre de Trente Guerre Ans à Haguenau* (Colmar: H. Hufel, 1907), pp.138, 138, 175; Geoffrey Parker, *The Thirty Years' War* (London: Routledge and Kegan Paul, 1987), p.192.

Cologne and Aachen are also known to have supplied clothing to the Imperialist and other armies.[20]

In 1620 the musketeers in at least one regiment in the Danish Army, the King's Own Regiment, were to have light blue coats with white edging, while the Red Regiment in Christian IV's service had red ensigns along with red coats with red, blue and yellow breeches.[21]

In April 1623 the King of Denmark requested 1,000 pieces of English cloth to clothe his soldiers. In March 1629 Burlamachi was ordered to be paid £7,000 to buy coarse cloth for the Danish Army, while the government of England also paid 45 shillings per suit for each soldier who enlisted in the Dutch Army in July 1624. The clothes and arms were to be issued to the men after they had landed in Holland.[22]

In 1620 the Schlieben and Goldstein Regiments of the Army of Saxony had red and yellow coats respectively. Colonel Loser's Regiment of Foot wore blue and white coats and the Life Regiment of Foot in the Army of Saxony also wore blue coats. In 1631 the Army of Saxony were issued with the following uniforms:

Loser	Red and white coats
Klitzing	Blue and red
Scherschadel	Black and yellow
Schwalbach	Red and yellow
Frei Company	Blue and yellow

Presumably the second colour mentioned is the facing colour. In 1633 one eyewitness referred '200 blue coats' of the Elector of Saxony Life Regiment, which was still in blue coats in March 1643. In 1635 another eyewitness referred to Schleinitz's Regiment, which had been Loser's Regiment, as being in red and white coats. Therefore since the regiments were meant to receive clothing each year they appear to have kept the same coloured coats, even when a new colonel was appointed.

During the 1640s Le Tellier purchased clothing for the French troops from 10 livres 6 sols to 13 livres 13 sols. During the siege of La Rochelle in 1627–1628, Paris was ordered to provide 2,500 outfits for King Louis XIII's Guard and in 1647 the city supplied a further 1,600 suits of clothing. Each town and city was to provide the French regiments with clothing. This practice continued in Germany when the city of Ulm was ordered to supply 1,000 grey coats and 1,000 pairs of shoes to the French Army under Turenne, although he had demanded 4,000 of each.[23]

20 Joseph Grunzel 'Die Reichenberger Tuchindustrie in ihrer Entwickelung vom zünftigen Handwerk zur modernen Grossindustrie' in *Verein für Geschichte der Deutschen in Bohemia. Beiträge zur Geschichte der deutschen Industrie in Böhmen,* no. 5 (Prague, 1893), pp.54, 56, 59.

21 Bellander, pp.79–80.

22 Allen B. Hinds, (ed.) *Calendar of State Papers Venetian*, vol. 21, April 1623 and July 1624; TNA: E403/2747, ff.205, 211, 224, E403/2606.

23 Lynn, *Giant of the Grand Siècle*, p.177; Hans Heberle, *Der Dreissigjährige Krieg in zeitgenössischer Darstellung: Hans Heberles "Zeytregister" (1618–1672)* (Stuttgart: Kommissionsverlag Kohlhammer, 1975), pp.209–210.

Smaller states also appear to have adopted uniform colours. As already stated in 1620 the Guard of the Elector of Brandenburg were issued a coat, breeches and stockings of 'a good blue colour'; but in 1632 blue was also adopted by the 4,000 man Brandenburg Army and by 1646 the regiments were distinguished by the following facing colours:

Colonel Conrad von Burgsdorf's regiment, blue coats faced silver lining
Colonel George Friedrich von Trott blue with yellow lining
Colonel Hans George von Ribbeck's (formerly Rochow's) regiment blue with green lining[24]

However, in June 1626 the 1,100 horse and 2,000 foot of the Brandenburg militia had red, yellow and blue and light grey clothing.[25]

When Odoardo Duke of Parma raised a small army in 1635, his regiment of foot wore green cassocks, while another regiment of horse and foot in his army wore yellow cassocks.[26]

In 1636 the Lifeguard of the Duke of Brunswick consisted of 100 horse, 50 dragoons and a company of 160 foot all of whom wore blue coats, apart from the drummers who wore grey coats, and in 1642 the Duke of Brunswick had two regiments of foot, one with blue uniforms and the other yellow.[27]

But what of Bavaria? Between 1618 and 1648 Bavaria spent 2,499,473 florins and 11 krona purchasing weapons and clothing. On 8 April 1643 it re-equipped its army, including buying 4,000 clothes, shirts, shoes and stockings for its infantry and coats for the cavalry at a cost of 55,000 florins.[28]

As early as 1526 one eyewitness is Nuremberg saw soldiers in grey and green coats, and during the 1590s the Bavarian nobleman, Albrecht Sprinzenstein, clothed 110 musketeers in red coats faced white, with blue breeches and yellow stockings. In 1610 the city raised soldiers clothed with red coats faced white and in 1614 and 1621 blue coats faced yellow. Also in 1621 Friedrich Koler supplied yellow coats faced blue and to Colonel Johan von Leubelding red coats faced white and Captain Backus' company received blue coats faced yellow.[29]

In 1619 the Bishop of Würzburg's militia had a blue hat and a blue and white coat and those of the garrison of Nuremberg mustered 1,053 musketeers and 479 pikemen in four companies, the first company having blue coats with brown facings; the second,

24 Curt Jany, *Geschichte der Königlich Preussischen Armee bis zum 1807* (Berlin: K. Siegismund, vol. 4, 1928), p.100.
25 Oelsnitz, pp.18, 20.
26 Gregory Hanlon, *The Hero of Italy, Odoardo Farnese, Duke of Parma, his soldiers, and his subjects in the Thirty Years' War* (Oxford: Oxford University Press, 2014), p.83, quoting a document in the Biblioteca Comunale Passerini-Landi di Piacensa, MS Pallastrelli 126, Cronicle Boselli, 109.
27 Dr Carl von Venturini, *Amriss einer pragmatischen geschichte des Kriegswesen im Herzogthume Braunschweig* (Magdeburg: Eduard Buhler, 1837), p.20.
28 Goetz, 1904, p.122; Heilmann, 1868, vol. 2, p.1022.
29 Franz Freiherr von Soden, *Gustav Adolph und sein Heer in Süddeutschland von 1631 bis 1635* (Erlangen: Deichert, 1865), p.48.

green coats faced white; the third brown coats faced yellow and the fourth, white coats faced red. In 1620 Colonel Johann von Leublfing commanded the garrison which was increased to six companies. The following year the companies received new coats: red with white facings, blue with yellow facings and yellow with blue facings.[30]

Cavalry could also be issued with coats. The five troops at Donauwörth in 1607 under the command of Colonel Engelbert von Bonninghausen were distinguished by the colour of their coats; blue, yellow, violet blue, sea green, and white. A sixth troop were cuirassiers and so were not issued with coats. On the other hand the garrison of Neuburg were clothed in black and yellow coats and yellow and black coats. The cavalry of Tilly's army at Breitenfeld were reported to be 'all mounted on stately horses armed with strong cuirassiers richly adorned in their apparel'.[31]

While some regiments do appear to have tried to keep the same colour coats throughout their existence, others probably used whatever colour cloth they could find. In 1621 the colonel's company of Colonel Haimhausen's Regiment is believed to have had blue coats, whereas his lieutenant colonel's company had red coats. However, whether this was two different issues of clothing with one colour replacing the other or each company having its own coat colour is not known.[32]

In 1621 Colonel Schmidt's Regiment of Foot, which also served in Tilly's Army, was issued with silver-grey coats with red facings and grey breeches, along with shirts, stockings, and shoes. Colonel Adam von Herbersdorf's Regiment was supplied with 202 blue coats faced white on 17 July 1621.[33]

In 1628 the clothiers appear to have supplied red, black and grey Loden cloth to the Bavarian Commissariat and when the Swedish Army occupied Munich in 1632 they found between 8,000 and 10,000 soldiers' clothes under the floor of the arsenal, which according to Theatrum Europaeum, were 'newly made soldiers' coats of yellow, blue, and green colour which were distributed to some regiments under the Swedish Army.' What regiments these coats had been originally intended for is not recorded, nor how they were distributed in the Swedish Army, but they may have gone to reclothe the regiments of their respective colour, e.g. the Yellow Regiment etc.[34]

In 1646 113 sick soldiers from the regiments of Colonels Goltz, Fugger, Kolb, Marimont and others received 61 coats, 89 pairs of breeches, 55 shirts, 81 pairs of stockings, 64 pairs of shoes. In addition, amongst 55 men of Colonel Fritsch's Regiment, 11 received coats, 10 received breeches, 13 received shirts, 15 pairs of stockings and 14 received shoes. Some received a full set of clothes whereas others received a pair of stockings and shoes. The breeches appear to have been made from

30 Heilmann, 1868, vol. 2, pp.865, 871, 911.

31 *Ibid.*, pp.839, 914–915; British Library, Add MS 39,288, f.20.

32 Karl Freiherr von Reitzenstein, *Der Feldzug des Jahres 1621 mit der Besitzergreifung der Oberpfalz* (Munich: F. Straub, 1887), p.147.

33 Dr Hans Wertheim, *Der Tolle Halberstädter, Herzog Christian von Braunschweig im Pfälzischen Kriege 1621–1622* (Berlin: International Bibliothek, 1929), vol. 1, pp.112, 394.

34 Dr Adolf Danner, 'Der Kommerzienrat in Bayern im 17. jahrundert. Buch 1, Unter Maximilian I', *Oberbayerisches Archiv für Vaterlandische Geschichte* (Munich: 1910), p.277; Bellander, p.590; Monro, part II p.125; Johan Philip Abelin, *Theatrum Europaeum* (Frankfurt, 1643), vol. 2, p.645; Franz Khevenhueller, *Annales Ferdinandi* (Leipzig, 1722), vol. 12, p.142.

two ells of cloth, whereas the coats were made from either 2, 2¾ or even 3 ells of cloth, presumably depending on the size of the soldier. Unfortunately, the colour of this clothing is not recorded.[35]

Shirts were made of lockram or Osnabruck linen. The Spanish in 1607 received two shirts 'of reasonable fine linen cloth with falling bands and cuffs of Holland, sewed to them edged with bone lace and strings.' On the other hand the clothing issues supplied to the British Army in 1627 by Philip Burlamachi and other armies raised in Germany appear to have allowed only one shirt.[36]

A soldier was meant to receive a new set of clothes each year, usually before the onset of winter. Warrants for shoes and stockings are the most common since they wore out more quickly that the other items of clothing. In February 1626 Wallenstein wrote to his administrator, Gerhard von Taxis,

> Also have 10,000 pairs of shoes made for the infantry so that later I can divide them out among the regiments. Have them made in my towns and markets and pay a fair price for them in cash. See especially that the shoes are always carefully bound pair by pair, so that one will know which belong together. At the same time have leather prepared for I shall shortly order a further few thousand boots to be made. Have cloth ready also for it may be that clothes will be required.[37]

The city of Cologne supplied Colonels Pappenheim and Comargo with 20,000 pairs of shoes and 3,000 boots along with several thousand musketeers' bandoliers and pistols. On 1 February 1634 Anton Morel of Lothringen was appointed shoemaker to the Bavarian Army. In October 1638 4,000 pairs and stockings and shoes were ordered for the Bavarian Army and in 1647 Maximilian ordered 1,327 suits of clothing from Nuremberg. The coats were made of loden, which is a rough cloth, while shirts were made of linen.[38]

The making and issuing of shoes and stockings are the most common warrants since they wore out more quickly than the other items of clothing. In April 1627 Burlamachi was ordered to immediately supply 1,000 pairs of shoes to the soldiers waiting to be embarked for Denmark, and on 27 November 1636 the Landgrave of Hesse Darmstadt purchased 3,000 pairs of shoes and stockings for his army. Maximilian I sent shoes and stockings worth 4,000 *fl* to his soldiers at Cologne.[39]

On 13 January 1637 Johan Pluckhandt of Würzburg received an order worth 3,804 *fl* and 12 *batzen*, for shoes and stockings for General Johan von Götz. Pluckhandt was required to sort the 1,866 pairs of stockings into four bundles of 300, 380, 100 and

35 Bavarian Main Archives, Kurbayern Ausseres MS 2883.

36 TNA: SP 77/8 f.204; Lyle, *Acts of the Privy Council of England 1627*, Estimate of the charge of clothing the soldiers, 31 March 1627, p.194.

37 Quoted in Francis Watson, *Wallenstein, Soldier under Saturn* (London: Chatto and Windus, 1938) pp.177–178.

38 Heilmann, 1868,, vol. 2., pp.242, 910.

39 LVR-Archivberstatungs und Fortbildungszentrum: Schonst 35, Landgrave Hesse Darmstadt, 27 November 1636; Schonst 49, Maximilian I, 29 January 1642.

286 pairs, with each bundle being numbered one to four respectively. The 1,701 pairs of shoes were to be in eight bundles of 160, 193, 91, 192, 500, 181, 139, and 131, respectively numbered from one to seven, and nine. No doubt other items of clothing were similarly bound up in bundles and numbered with each numbered bundle being allocated to a company or regiment.[40]

Since both sides wore the same clothing, field signs were worn in battle to distinguish one side from the other. According to John Cruso 'Every man must wear a scarf of the prince's colour who he serveth … by which means (besides the ornament) … being subject thereby to be distinguished and upon occasions of battle they shall by that means not to offend each other.'[41]

Each nation was identified by the following coloured sashes (or 'scarves'):

Baden	Yellow red?
Bavaria	White (1620), light blue or blue and white; red from 1635?
Bohemia	Blue (1620), red and white
Brandenburg	Black and white
Brunswick	Yellow and red
Catholic League	Black, white, white golden, red, yellow; red (after 1635)
Denmark	White
Dutch	Orange
England	Dark blue or pink
France	White
Hanseatic States	Black
Hesse	Blue or sky blue
Imperialists	White (1620), then red
Mansfeld (1620–1622)	Red and white, or black and white
Protestant States	Green
Saxony	Red (1620–1624, and after 1635) Yellow, yellow and black, or green (other years)
Spain	Pink
Sweden	Green or blue
Weimar	Green, green and yellow; white (in French service)

Of course, to confuse the enemy soldiers are known to have changed their sashes so that they would be taken for the opposite side. Moreover, paintings of officers in these armies show different coloured sashes from that they were meant to be wearing, such as paintings of the Dutch militia showing officers in orange and white sashes and also light blue sashes. In these paintings some sashes are worn over the shoulder, while others are worn around the waist. Some even wore them around both!

40 *Ibid.*, Schonst 36, Johan Götz to Johann Pluckhandt of Würzburg.
41 Cruso, *Arte of Warre* (Cambridge, 1639), p.17.

Not all soldiers wore a sash. Often they had to make do with a field sign chosen on the day and a field word such as 'Jesus Maria'; a white ribbon tied about the arm was chosen for the storming of Magdeburg in May 1631. At the battle of Wittstock the Swedish used the word 'God with us', while the Saxons and Imperialists said 'God willing'. The Swedes wore green ribbons about their arms and the Saxons white ribbons, some with a handkerchief upon their hats.

Portraits of the senior officers often depict them in three-quarter armour, but Marshal Grammont saw Tilly at the head of his army 'mounted on a small white Croatian pad [horse] in a green satin doublet with slashed sleeves and trousers of the same stuff, a little cocked hat with a red ostrich plume in it … a belt round his waist of two inches breadth, to which hung his fighting sword with a single pistol only in one of his holsters.' Officers appear to have had to supply their own clothing and there are newssheets criticising German officers wearing the 'foppish' French style of dress with laced collars and cuffs on their shirts and feathers in their hats, with the boots turned down, which was seen as positively un-German. Other newssheets criticised gentlemen who served as volunteers within the ranks for wearing elaborate styles of clothing other than their regimental clothing.[42]

42 Quoted in Walter Harte, *The History of the Life of Gustavus Adolphus* (London: G. Hawkins, 1759), vol.1, p.lvi.

5

Arming the Soldiers

As well as an army of tailors who clothed the soldiers, there was also an army of people who made weapons and armour. Among the arms manufacturing towns were Essen, Nuremberg, Liège and Suhl, who were willing to supply weapons to both sides during the war. Pieces of artillery could be bought from Nuremberg, Frankfurt, Augsburg, Strasbourg and Ulm. Essen's gun foundries dated back to the fifteenth century, while Nuremberg, situated near the Elbe and Rhine, could easily transport arms throughout Europe, including to Denmark, Sweden and Russia. As well as the armourer's mark, the city's examiners would stamp the city coat of arms on the weapons and armour as proof of its quality.[1]

Liège would become one of the greatest firearm producing towns in Europe, its trade dating back to the sixteenth century. Since it was situated in Northern Europe it usually supplied arms to the Dutch and French armies, but in 1621 the merchants received 50,000 florins to arm Mansfeld's and Brunswick's Armies.[2]

The arms trade in Suhl dated back to 1535 and specialised in good quality weapons for common soldiers. The city's muskets were stamped with the gunsmith's mark and 'SVL' to identify them as coming from Suhl. Between 1619 and 1632 it supplied at least 61,000 muskets at a cost of between 2 and 3 *reichtalers* per musket; among the many orders placed during the war was one in 1619 to equip 1,000 musketeers for the government of Bamberg for 3 *fl* each, divided as follows:[3]

Musket	2 *fl* 1 *batzen*
Powder flask	5
Bandoliers	5
Musket rest	6
Bullet mould	6
Cleaning equipment and worm	4

1 Peter Krenn and Walter J Karcheski, *Imperial Austria, treasures of Art, Arms and Armour from the State of Styria* (Australia: Art Exhibitions Australia Ltd, 1998), p.43; Monro, part II, p.212.
2 Jaroslav Lugs, *Firearms Past and Present* (London: Greville, 1973), vol. 1, pp.450–453.
3 Heilmann, 1868, vol. 2, p.910.

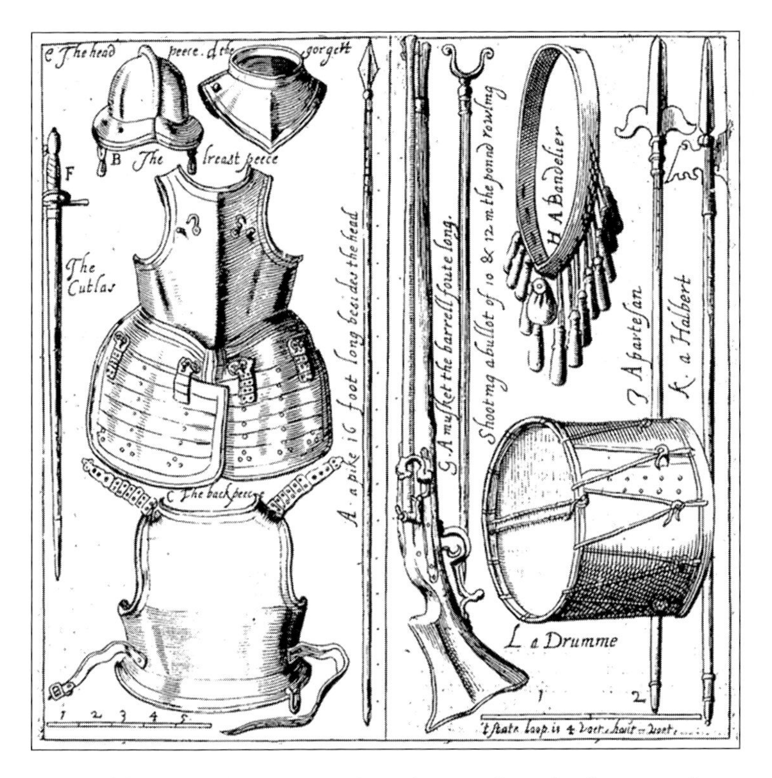

13. The arms of pikemen and musketeers, from the first part of Henry Hexham's *Principles of the Art Military*, 1642 edition.

In 1622 just one Suhler gunsmith, Simon Stohr, received an order for 4,000 muskets for the Imperialist Army, and Wallenstein placed orders with six Suhler gunsmiths to equip his army; 28,950 muskets were ordered in 1631 alone. Unfortunately, the archives of the Suhler gun makers have not survived so the exact number is probably considerably more. Suhler muskets weighed 4.5–4.7 kg (around 10 lb), and were 140 cm (55 inches) long, the barrel being 102 cm (40 inches), which was shorter than the muskets being produced by Sweden at this time. Swedish muskets were 156 cm (61 inches) long, with a barrel 115–118 cm (45–46 inches) long. The lightness of these muskets meant that the musketeers were able to discard their musket rests, although the older heavier muskets continued to be used.

Like most towns when it came to business Suhl was neutral, supplying weapons and armour to both Wallenstein and the Protestant general Bernard of Saxe-Weimar. Unfortunately this may have been one of the reasons why Isolani's Croats burnt down the town in 1634, thus robbing both causes of a valuable supplier.[4]

4 Anton Ernstberger, *Wallenstein als Volkswirt im Herzogtum Friedland* (Reichenberg i.B.: F. Kraus, 1929) pp.137–140.

However by 1639 the gunsmiths of Suhl were producing arms once more, and during the summer of 1639 the Jung family were ordered to deliver 4,000 muskets to Vienna. In 1643 another order was placed, this time for 20,000 muskets, 4,500 pistols, 400 carbines and 1,000 pistol holsters, and in 1645 Nicholas Jung received another order from Vienna for 8,000 muskets, 1,000 carbines and 4,000 pistols. The Jung family were not the only arms manufacturers to receive such orders: Valentine Schneider also received an order in 1639 for 4,000 muskets and 2,000 pistols, so the Suhler gunsmiths had clearly recovered from Isolani's raid.[5]

Meanwhile in Hamburg the English government placed an order with Albert Balzer Bearne and Leonard Mercellus on 16 April 1639 to supply 3,000 muskets, 700 cuirassier arms, 700 pairs of holsters and 1,500 pikemen's armour, all 'according to the patterns already delivered', which were to be supplied in just eight to 10 days. This contract was one of several placed in April 1639. Probably like shipments from other cities these muskets etc., would be packed in cases, while the accoutrements, such as the bandoliers, spanners and flints would be packed in 'dry fats' which were numbered, so that they could be easily distributed to a regiment. The English government seems to have been lucky and the arms were delivered on time, but such was the demand for firearms that orders outstripped production, so there was sometimes a long delay in completing orders.[6]

The largest producer of arms was Nuremberg. In 1625 an order was placed by Hans de Witte for furnishing seven complete regiments of Wallenstein's army. These were sent to Eger five weeks ahead of schedule, and among its merchants was Ulrich Loser who supplied hundreds of back and breast plates, pikes and muskets in 1631; while in March 1638 the city supplied 3,000 muskets, 2,000 pairs of pistols and 2,000 pikes to the Imperialist Army. The city also supplied Bavaria with cuirassier armour.[7]

However, the Dutch arms trade was one, if not, the largest in Europe: not only did it supply its own armed forces, but in 1621 the merchants in Amsterdam supplied 300 harquebusiers, 400 carbines, 1,000 muskets with rests and bandoliers, 1,000 suits of armour, 1,000 pikes, 30 halberds, 16 drums, and 1,000 pounds of lead, match and gunpowder to the Protestant Union. The following year, as well as supplying arms to the Danish and Swedish armies, the Dutch also supplied 3,000 muskets, 3,000 suits of pikemen's armour, 3,000 pikes, 1,000 back and breast plates, 1,000 harquebusiers with bandoliers, to Christian of Brunswick's army, in addition to 10,000 lb of gunpowder, 20,000 lb of match and 10,000 lb of lead shot.

During the 'Danish period' of the war Christian IV purchased 33,000 muskets, 15,000 pikes and 20,000 sets of armour, in addition to 400,000 lb of gunpowder and 1.7 million pounds of match.[8]

5 H. Ebner, *Festschrift Othmar Pickl zum 60. Geburtstag* (Graz: Leykam Verlag, 1987), p.685.
6 TNA: SP 81/46, ff,214, 220, 243, Arms from Hamburg, 13, 16 and 28 April 1639.
7 Ernstberger, pp.137–140.
8 Hans Vogel, 'Arms Production and exports in the Dutch Republic, 1600–1650', in M. Van Der Hoeven, *Exercise of Arms: Warfare in the Netherlands 1568–1648* (Leiden: Brill, 1997), pp.201, 207.

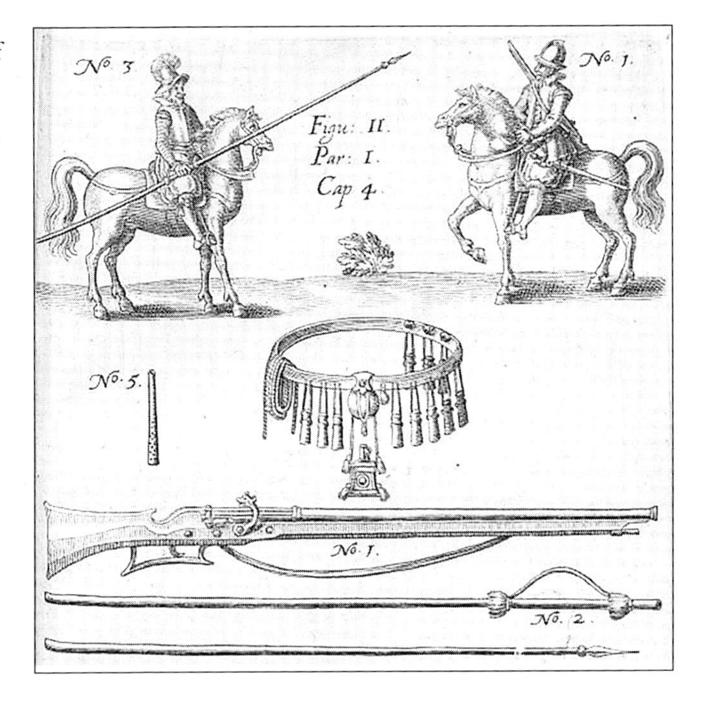

14. The depiction of dragoons and their equipment from a military manual of the time. Dragoon pikemen were used in the early stages of the war.

As well as these old industrial towns,during the war new centres for manufacturing of arms and armour were established, such as Munich, Graz, Dresden and Vienna and the bell founders of Nuremberg and Regensburg converted their foundries to make cannon.

Prices varied: a musket supplied by Nuremberg in 1638 cost 2½ *reichtaler*, whereas those from Cologne and Hamburg cost 2¼ *reichtalers*. On 29 July 1634 Cologne supplied the following arms to the Bavarian Army:

1,000 cuirasses @ 8 *reichtaler*
2,000 other armour @ 3½ *reichtaler*
1,000 pistols @ 7½ *reichtaler*
3,000 carbines @ 3½ *reichtaler*
2,000 muskets @ 2¼ *reichtaler*
1,500 long and 500 short pikes @ ½ *reichtaler*

For a total of 38,500 *reichtaler*[9]

When Louis de Geer was equipping the Swedish Army during the war he purchased arms not only from the German arms manufacturers at Liège, Cologne, Namur, Aachen, Solingen and Suhl, but also from Holland, before he set up his own

9 Christian Bartz, *Köln in der Dreissigjährigen Krieg: die Politik des Rates der Stadt (1618–1635); vorwiegend anhand der im Historischen Archiv der Stadt Köln* (Frankfurt am Main: P. Lang, 2005).

factories in Sweden.[10] Unfortunately, receiving arms from different cities and even armourers had its drawbacks, in that the calibres for the various firearms differed, with musket calibres ranging from 17.5 to 19.7 mm, or in the case for those in Holland, 21.6 mm, and in England between 19.0 and 22.6 mm. The calibres for pistols also varied between 10.0 and 14.9 mm. This made it difficult to supply the appropriate musket shot with the number of musket balls varying from eight to 15 balls to the pound. There are accounts of the shot having to be melted down and recast or even the musketeers having to gnaw the musket balls down to make them fit in the barrel. Calibres also changed during the war. Nuremberg supplied muskets with 18.3 mm calibre or 14 balls to the pound in 1631, but in 1634 the city was supplying muskets with a 17.5 mm calibre or 16 balls to the pound. Even when the same gunsmith was supplying muskets or pistols they could vary in weight due to the design of the stock.[11]

Harquebusiers wore buff coats which could be sleeveless, or have cloth or leather sleeves. An account dated October 1632 records that hides from 2 elks were bought to make Gustavus Adolphus' buff coat, while another buff coat weighted around 7½ lb (3.35 kg), although it was embroidered. Troopers' buff coats varied, the 33 belonging to the Littlecote Collection in Wiltshire, England, which are now stored at the Royal Armouries in Leeds, vary in weight between 4 and 7 lb (1.9 to 3.1 kg). They are made of four pieces of leather for the body panels and four panels for the sleeves stitched together with linen thread. The sleeves are lined with linen, while the main body of the coat was lined with coarse canvas. The Littlecote buff coats are bright yellow, but underneath the linings they are natural leather suggesting they were stained after they were made, possibly before they were displayed at Littlecote House. These coats were fastened by a cord or leather thong down the front, although several buff coats preserved at the Army Museum in Paris are fastened by hooks and eyes down the left side.[12]

Since all the armour was handmade there was also a variant in weight; the collection of harquebusier armour preserved in the Royal Armouries, made between 1625 and 1630 weighed 6,245 g (almost 14 lb) for a breastplate and 4,905 g (just under 11 lb) for a backplate. However by 1651 the weight had been reduced to between 2,865 and 4,600 g (6½ and 10 lb) for a breastplate and 1,190 to 1,530 g (around 2½ to 3½ lb) for a backplate. Straps were attached to the shoulders of the backplate which were attached to the breastplate with two small pommels on the chest and sometimes locked into place by a catch. Two small belts were also attached to the waist to fasten it at the front by a buckle. These plates could either be lined with leather, which made it more expensive, or left without any lining. Although despite what the various military manuals say many harquebusiers appear to have either had a buff coat or armour to protect them. In addition a harquebusier might also have a helmet, and this could weigh between 1.4 and

10 E. W. Dahlgren, *Louis de Geer, 1587–1652: hans lif och verk* (Uppsala: Almquist och Wiksell, 1923) vol. 1, p.106.

11 Peter Engerisser, 'Matchlock Musket, Suhl approx, 1630' <http://www.engerisser.de/Bewaffnung/weapons/Matchlockmusket.html> (accessed 8 May 2015).

12 *17th Century War, Weaponry and Politics: 10th congress Stockholm 1984* (International Association of Museums of Arms and Military History), p.191; Thom Richardson and Graeme Rimer, *Littlecote, The English Civil War Armoury* (Leeds: Royal Armouries, 2012) pp.132–161.

1.8 kg (3–4 lb). True, these relate to English harquebusier armour, but there is no reason to suggest those produced on the Continent varied greatly in weight;[13] the European cuirassier armour preserved in the Wallace Collection in London weighs as follows:

Pieces of Armour	Savoy, *c*.1620–1635	Augsburg, *c*.1620	French, *c*.1640
Helmet	2.11 lb	2.11 lb	5.7 lb
Gorget	0.652 lb	0.974 lb	1.45 lb
Breastplate	3.51 lb	5.2 lb	3.85 lb
Backplate	4.05 lb	2.488 lb	3.115 lb
Tassets			
Left	1.88 lb	3.135 lb	Not mentioned
Right	1.585 lb	1.74 lb	Not mentioned
Garde rein	1.92 lb	0.510 lb	Not mentioned
Pauldrons & Arms			
Left	2.54 lb	5.975 lb	8.0 lb
Right	2.46 lb	4.105 lb	8.45 lb
Gauntlets (pair)	6.12 lb	2.15 lb	2.55 lb

Pikemen wore a back and breast plate and tassets to protect the thighs, although during the late 1620s tassets seem to have gone out of fashion because there are examples of armour having a metal 'skirt' at the front. However, by the early 1630s tassets were back in fashion. As with the cavalry armour they could be lined with leather for comfort. In 1622 Francis Markham recommended that pikemen should wear:

> Spanish morions well lined within which a quilted cap of strong housewives linen; for Buckram which is the usual lining is too course and galleth the soldier's head, as also is too stiff and unplyable by which means it will not guilt like the other. The ear plates shall be lined also.

There are several surviving examples of helmets having cotton lining, including two at the Wallace Collection in London. One is a red woollen and linen cap filled with raw cotton wadding, although this was designed for a burgonet helmet. The other is made of canvas and linen padded with bast.[14]

However, armourers were not always honest about their orders, sometimes sending obsolete armour, which was found to be unserviceable. Also the sign of a good breastplate, whether it was for a trooper or a pikeman, was a small dent, which was a proof mark that showed it had been tested by firing a pistol bullet at close range,

13 Richardson and Rimer, pp.2–69.

14 Francis Markham, *Five Decades of Epistles of Warre* (London, 1622). p.39; Sir James Mann, *Wallace Collection Catalogue, European Arms and Armour* (London: William Clowes and Son Ltd, 1962), vol. 1, pp.83–90.

indicating that it was 'pistol proof'; however unscrupulous armourers would often make the dent with a hammer instead.

If this was not bad enough, at least one manufacturer of gunpowder in the Lower Saxony circle in 1634, John Kip, was guilty of mixing his gunpowder with large quantities of salt rather than saltpetre, making the power useless. This deceit was only discovered when the barrels it was stored in were opened.[15]

Gunpowder was essential in battle for the musketeers and troopers to shoot their firearms and the gunners needed large quantities to fire their artillery pieces. Nuremberg, along with Cologne, Salzburg, Ulm, Hamburg, Aachen and Southern German states including Bavaria itself also supplied gunpowder. Gunpowder was also imported from Italy and Poland. When it was issued to the musketeers they carried it in bandoliers, which according to Francis Markham were:

> About their bodies baldrickwise from the left shoulder under the right arm, he shall carry bandoliers of broad leather ... and to this bandolier shall be fastened by long double stings (at least a quarter of a yard in length a piece, that they may with more ease be brought to the mouth of the musket) one large priming charge ... and at least twelve other charges of wood, all made of some tough light wood or else of horn, and covered with leather.[16]

Gervase Markham suggested 12 or 13 charges which 'must contain powder according to the bore and bigness of the piece by due measure.' This powder was poured down the musket barrel, and 'a charge greater than the rest ... for pan powder.' Sometimes a musketeer would be equipped with a separate triangular-shaped flask.[17]

An order for bandoliers to be used by the New Model Army stated that they were to be 'of wood with whole bottoms, to be turned within and not bored, the heads to be of wood, and to be laid in oil (viz), three times over, and to be coloured blue with blue and white strings with thread twist and with good belts'.[18]

However, the badge of the soldier was the sword, and Solingen was famous for its swordmakers inasmuch they were greatly sought after to set up sword factories in other towns and countries. Most illustrations of soldiers, whether in a print from a manual on tactics or in paintings by such artists as Peter Snayer or Philip Wouvermans, show them wearing rapiers which had long blades. However, there are many surviving swords of this period with short blades, either curved or straight, which must have been more practical during a melee and must have been produced in their 10,000s. In April 1627, of the 3,000 recruits who were to be sent to the King of Denmark's army with Sir John Burlacy, 2,200 were issued with swords, 300 with rapiers and 500 with 'Turkey swords', which presumably had a curved blade. These usually had a simple hilt with a bar to protect the soldier's hand.

15 Ernstberger, Wallenstein, pp.141–145; TNA: SP 81/42, f.83.
16 Francis Markham, *Five Decades of Epistles of Warre* (London, 1622) p.34.
17 Gervase Markham, *The Souldiers Accidence* (London: John Bellamie, 1625), p.3.
18 Gerald Mungeam, 'Contracts for the Supply of equipment to the New Model Army', in *The Journal of the Arms and Armour Society*, 1968, vol. 6, no.3, pp.88, 90.

When the armour etc., had been delivered it would be stored in a magazine or 'zeughaus' until it could be distributed to the regiments. In 1627 an inventory of the Munich armoury included:[19]

1,383 Suhler muskets large bore
441 Suhler muskets small bore
90 firelock muskets
51 muskets engraved with the Bavarian coat of arms for the Lifeguard of Foot
628 half musket barrels (17 with match and firelocks)
745 harquebusiers with large bore
949 harquebusiers with small bore
40 carbine barrels
628 pistols and holsters

Unfortunately for Maximilian, in April 1632 when Augsburg fell to the Swedish the city's magazine was said to have been 'so well furnished' with arms that Gustavus was able to arm 30,000 men 'all after the newest fashion.'[20]

Gustavus probably needed these arms because no matter how well, or badly, the arms and armour were made they would quickly be broken, whether during battle or just wear and tear. Swords might be broken due to soldiers cutting firewood and the mechanisms in firearms would seize up, particularly wheellock pistols if they were 'spanned', i.e. wound up, too long so that the spring would not drive the wheel against the flint to cause the spark which ignited the gunpowder.

19 Swedish Army Staff, *Sveriges Krieg Supplementary*, 1611–1632, Bilagsband vol. 1 (Stockholm: V. Pettersons Bokindustriaktiebolag, 1936), p.141.
20 TNA: SP 101/42, f.36, News from Vienna, 18 May 1624; SP 101/30 f.196.

6

Regimental Colours

Each troop of horse was issued with its own cornet or standard and each company of foot an ensign. Dragoons on the other hand were issued with small guidons which usually had a swallow tail, which sometimes also had a fringe. There does not appear to have been a standard size for these regimental colours, but the ensigns at least were certainly smaller than the huge standards carried during the sixteenth century. The trumpets carried by each troop also had a banner either bearing the captain's coat of arms in the centre of the banner or, if he did not have a coat of arms, the same device which appeared on the troop's cornet or similar to the troop's cornet. The drums of a company also appear to have borne the same system. There is evidence to suggest that when a soldier joined a company or troop they would hammer a nail into the colour's staff. However, if a troop or company or even a regiment dishonoured itself by breaking its oath of allegiance, not only would the soldiers be punished but the head of state's monogram would be removed from its colours and the colours ripped from their staffs and publicly burnt by the public executioner. This happened to the Imperialist regiments of Colonels Sparr and Niklas von Hagen for their poor conduct at the battle of Lützen in 1632.

During the eighteenth century Walter Harte boasted that he had seen an illuminated manuscript showing all different types of colours: 'what surprised me was, that those belonging to the Croatians were the best imagined of any.'[1] Unfortunately he did not have a pen to take any notes, nor did he say where he had seen the manuscript, although since he was researching Gustavus Adolphus it could have been the one now held in the Army Museum in Stockholm which was compiled by Olaf Hoffman at the end of the seventeenth century.

In 1685 a survey was held of all the colours captured by Sweden, and it found that there were 1,821, of which 261 were standards, 48 were dragoon guidons and 621 were ensigns that had been captured during the Thirty Years War. During the eighteenth and nineteenth centuries the colours were held in various places, including the Riddarholm Church, where on 28 July 1835 they were nearly destroyed when lightening struck the

1 Harte, vol. 1, p.28.

building and set it on fire. During the 1840s some of the staves which the colours were attached to were shortened to give them a more uniform appearance while on display; some of the cannons which had been captured were melted down or sold to bring in income. Tourists were able to take souvenirs, including a fragment of a green cornet which is now in the Shakespeare Birthplace Trust Library.[2]

In 1907 another survey was held of all the colours, which by now had been supplemented by colours captured during other wars, and it found that the collection consisted of 1291 infantry colours; 385 staves with fragments of infantry colours; 382 cavalry and dragoon standards; 202 staves with remnants of cavalry and dragoon standards and there were 280 staves without any colours on them at all. Fortunately, since Hoffman was able to drawn the colours in the seventeenth century many of his illustrations include details that have been lost over the centuries where the original colour has deteriorated or no longer exists.[3]

Another manuscript held by the Saxon State Archives in Dresden was composed by Balthasar Böhme between 1632 and 1633 and comprises two volumes, the first with 92 illustrations and the second with 160. Then there is Reginbaldus Mohner's manuscript mainly of Swedish colours, which he saw in Augsburg between 1632 and 1635 and is now preserved in the Augsburg Cathedral Library. There also appears to a manuscript of several colours belonging to Mansfeld's Army in 1620, which is held at the Museum of the Thirty Years War at Wittstock.[4]

Another manuscript of late sixteenth and early seventeenth century colours is held by Royal Library in Copenhagen and there are several manuscripts at the National Library in Paris. Although these cover the latter part of the reign of King Louis XIV, one does record the number of colours captured by the French Army, beginning with 250 ensigns and cornets captured at the battle of Rocroi on 19 May 1643 and 400 ensigns and cornets captured at the battle of Lens on 20 August 1648. Unfortunately, there are no descriptions to these colours and the numbers appear to have been exaggerated.[5]

Such was the value of regimental colours that victories were judged in the number of them captured, inasmuch the number was often exaggerated; at the battle of Breitenfeld one source states that 66 ensigns and 22 standards were captured, whereas another source gives 70 standards and ensigns. A third source says 120 cornets and 60 ensigns, plus 25 pieces of ordinance and Tilly's baggage. Unfortunately, the provenance of the majority of captured colours preserved at the Army Museum in Stockholm is unknown, so we do not known the correct number. Judging from the number taken

2 T. J. Petrelli and E. S. Liljedahl, 'Standar och dragonfanor', in *Antiqvarisk Tidskrift for Sverige*, vol. 14. no. 3, p.4; Fred Sandstedt and Lena Sandstedt, 'Proud Symbols of Victory and mute witnesses of bygone Glories', in *Hoc Signo Vinces, A Presentation of The Swedish State Trophy Collection* (The National Swedish Museums of Military History, 2006) (Stockholm: National Swedish Museums of Military History, 2006), pp.78–87; Shakespeare Birthplace Trust Library Reference no. DR762/332.

3 Sandstedt and Sandstedt, p.88.

4 Hans-Christian Huf, *Mit Gottes Segen in die Hölle, Der Dreissigjährige Krieg* (List Taschenbuch, nd) pp.239, 383.

5 Bibliothèque Nationale, *Drapeaux et Étendant pris depuis le commencement du regne de Louis 14 jusqu'en 1688*, FR14166 unnumbered page.

the second battle of Leipzig on 23 October 1642, that battle seems to be an even greater victory for the Swedish Army than the first one, with 120 ensigns and '70 odd' cornets captured although as usual no descriptions are given.[6]

According to the Annales Ferdinandi 100 cornets and ensigns were captured at the battle of White Mountain on 8 November 1620. These were sent to the Pope and paraded through the streets of Rome before being lodged in the Carmelite church of Santa Maria della Victoria. Unfortunately, they were destroyed by a fire in 1833.[7] However, in a biography of Father Dominico – who helped rally the Catholic Army during the battle – there are a number of colours mentioned, but the text does not say whether they belonged to a cavalry or an infantry regiment; these included an image of a Christ and several with an orb, the trappings of monarchy. One had two crowns, presumably those of Bohemia and the Palatinate.[8]

Also in 1622 Mansfeld lost eight colours on 30 August which were presented to the Infanta Maria in Brussels, including an orange colour with three white roses joined together and a second which was red with the motto, 'Pro Libertate'. When the Imperialist Army under Montenegro surrendered to Bethlen Gabor in December 1623 he sent all the ensigns and artillery to his ally the Marquis of Jagendorf, and in 1626 Maximilian, who was then seriously ill, sent the colours captured at the battle of Lutter to the Pope to help his recovery. It was reported that 115 ensigns and cornets were captured, and after the Spanish-Imperialist Army's victory at Nördlingen in 1634, the King of Hungary offered to pay 80 *talers* for every captured banner or standard delivered to him. What happened to these colours is not known.[9]

However, those colours captured by the French forces and Bernard of Saxe-Weimar's Army were sent to Paris and displayed in Notre Dame Cathedral, from where, in 1793, they were transferred to Les Invalides. Unfortunately, in March 1814 with the allies at the gates of Paris, the city's governor ordered them burnt in the courtyard so that they would not fall into enemy hands. Despite various enquiries to the military archives and libraries in France I have been unable to trace any descriptions of these colours for the Thirty Years War period, although there is a colour at the Chateau of Chantilly in France which was captured at the battle of Rocroi in May 1643. This colour is white bordered by blue 'flames' and has the Imperial Eagle in the centre.

These colours varied in design from simple to elaborate images. Some were comical such as that of Colonel Dietrich von Taube's Saxon Regiment of Dragoons which had a wolf dressed in a priest's surplice and hat preaching to some chickens. Another company had a bear trying to get honey out of a beehive. Other devices used

6 BL Add MS 39,288 f.20; TNA: SP 101/30, f.294; Thomason Tract E127/30, *A True and perfect Relation of a great and bloudy Battell fought the 23 October [1642]*, p.8.

7 Annales Ferdinandi, vol. 9, p.1104; Guglielmo Matthiae, *Santa Maria Della Vittoria* (Rome: Ats Italia Editrice, 1999), pp.3, 13.

8 Juan Caramuel de Lobkowitz, *Caramuelis Dominicus hoc est, Venerabilis P Dominici a Jesu-Maria* (Vienna, 1655), pp.400–424. See Appendix 2 for details.

9 TNA: SP 81/41, f.129, *Geschichte des Bayerischen Heeres* (Munich, 1901), vol. 1 p.92; Barker, p.165; TNA: SP 101/46, f.249; *News from the Hague 28 December 1623*; BL Harl 390, Collection of letters of Joseph Mead, Jan 1626–Apr 1631, f.121–122.

mythological beasts or people such as Fortuna, the Greek goddess of fortune, who is depicted as a naked woman waving a veil above her head.

Sometimes colours had borders which makes sorting them into regiments easier, albeit an unknown one; while the many Spanish and Imperialist Regiments bore the Burgundian cross on their colours. The Virgin Mary was also a popular device for Catholic Regiments, while others bore the monogram of their sovereign, i.e. 'F II', for Emperor Ferdinand II, or that of the Virgin Mary, which varied between 'sDMVBs', 'MAR' or 'MRA', or Mediatrix Reparatrix Auxiliatrix (or Adjutrix), or in the case of 'MR', Maria Regina.

Regiments might also receive new colours when they entered the service of another prince, since it was reported in October 1625 that, 'The horse of the Duke of Holstein which were lately dismissed are now again taken in the service of the Emperor and get new colours seeing they rent the others from their lances as soon as they were dismissed.'[10]

In 1619 the garrison of Nuremberg had at least two troops of horse during the war, one troop had a red damask cornet with an armoured arm holding a sword with the inscription, *Pro aris et focis*, while the second troop in March 1622 had a white damask cornet with the Virgin Mary and an eagle with the inscription, *In Deo et Fortuna*. Whereas the garrison of Neuburg had colours of white, blue, red, yellow and black with the inscription, *Iustitia liberabit a morte*.[11]

Some countries such as Sweden, Hesse, Denmark and Brunswick had 'coloured regiments', which were known as the Blue, Yellow and Red Regiments and Mansfeld's Army of 1622 also had a Red and a Blue Regiment.[12] What the difference was between these and other regiments is not known. Wertheim suggests that it was referring to the coat colours, but the Swedish coloured regiments also had the same coloured ensigns, although it is uncertain whether the Green and the White Regiment also had coats in these colours. On the other hand Schlieben's and Goldstein's Regiments of the Army of Saxony are known to have had the same coloured ensigns as their coats, but they were not known as a 'coloured' regiment.[13]

In one action the Imperialist General Holk lost two standards of his regiment of horse, one having 'Fortuna and the motto "Audacter" inscribed beneath and [on the other] a serpent writhed in spires rolled itself around a drawn sword, alluding to the wisdom of the animal and the bravery the weapon implied and the motto, "His Ducibus sitis Imperterriti".'[14]

Unfortunately, the provenance of many of these Thirty Years War colours is not known. For years it was suggested that several large white colours in Stockholm belonged to Wallenstein's Regiment, but it is now suggested that they belong to Karl

10 *A continuation of all the principall occurrances...* London, 1 December 1625.
11 Heilmann, 1868, vol.2, pp.871, 841.
12 Sweden and Hesse also had a Green, a White and a Black Regiment.
13 Wertheim vol. 1, p.425; BL Add MS 39,288 f.20.
14 Harte, p.367.

von Lichtenstein's Regiment.[15] However some colours, at least, can be identified as belonging to Bavarian regiments since they have the monogram 'M' for Maximilian painted on them. Among them is a blue ensign, 290 by 260 cm (114 by 102 inches), with a white St Andrew's cross with a white 'M' in the centre of a white circle. Other colours of this unidentified regiment had a red 'M' in the centre of a red circle, a red St Andrew's cross with a green 'M' in the centre and a red cross and 'M'.

An ensign preserved in the Bavarian Army Museum, 219 by 238 cm (86 by 93 inches), has light blue and white horizontal stripes, with a light blue and white border in diagonal stripes, and in the centre is the symbol of the Jesuits, 'IHS' and the letters 'MRA' surrounded by a laurel wreath.

A further ensign, 294 by 261 cm (115 by 102 inches), has light blue and white diamond pattern with orange and light green chevrons around the border. In the centre is a white disc with which is the image of the Virgin Mary surrounded by the inscription *Clypevs Omnibvs in Te Seperantibvs*. On the other side of the ensign is the image of St Patrick with the inscription, *1626 St. Patrick Erzbischof.* The colour pole for this ensign is 275 cm (108 inches). Since this ensign has St Patrick on one side with an orange and green border it has been suggested that it belonged to a company of Irish soldiers, but this is mere speculation.[16]

Other ensigns were more elaborate, like the ones believed to have been issued to Alt Tilly's Regiment of Foot. These were 300 by 240 cm (118 by 94 inches) and had the image of the Virgin Mary above the church at Altötting, with grass surrounded by a fence and some lime trees. The ensign itself was divided into four with two white segments and two yellow. Another ensign from the regiment was identical except that it had blue rather than yellow segments. Usually the Virgin Mary is depicted in a red dress with a blue cloak, but she appears in different colours, presumably to identify each company.

The regiment of Werner von Tilly, or Jung Tilly as he is sometimes known, had a blue field, 259 by 283 cm (101 by 111 inches), with a light blue and white 'tooth-shaped' outer border and a black and white 'toothed' inner border. In the centre is the Madonna and child with John the Baptist kneeling at their feet with a lamb, and the motto *Ecce Angnvs Dei Qvi Tollis Precata Mvndi, Zabvlo Terribilis Acies Casrorum Protvs et Refvgivm sis Christianorvm,* in a wreath. On the reverse is the motto, *Domina Sancta Maria Salvm Fac Imperatorem Nostrvm et Exavdi Nos in Die Qva Invocaverimvs Te.* This colour is believed to have been captured in 1633 at Rinteln and belonged to the colonel, because there is another colour with an identical border, but without a device in the centre.[17]

However, not all Bavarian colours were the light blue and white colours of the Wittelsbach family: a Bavarian regiment of foot with 12 companies was seen at

15 Eva Turek, *Under False Colours: A case of miskaten identity – are the colours those of Wallenstein or Liechtenstein?* (Stockholm: Armémuseum, 1996), pp.1–46.

16 Swedish Army Museum accession no. ST 14:1; Sandstedt, *In Hoc Signo Vinces*, p.212. At this time the colours of Ireland were green and red, not as the authors suggest, orange.

17 Swedish Army Museum accession nos. ST 14:3, ST 14:8.

15. Although showing a scene from the Dutch Revolt, this contemporary image by Pieter Snayers clearly shows the location of the colours in a foot regiment on the battlefield. Many contemporary military manuals advocated the ensign to swap his colour for the pike of an experienced soldier in the middle of the formation and fight in the front rank.

16. Bavarian Cavalry Cornets.
(All drawings by Dr Lesley Prince)

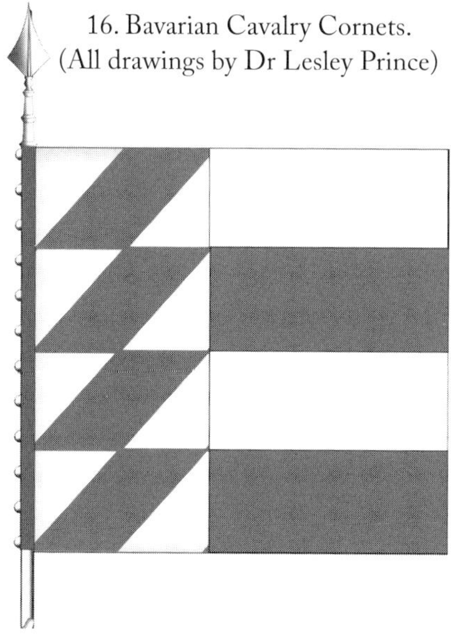

White and light blue

White and light blue lozenges; wreath green; hand proper; sleeve violet with white cuff; fringe light blue; cravat and tassels light blue

Red field; fringe red and gold; arm, snake and script gold; cloud and sword silver

Light blue field; fringe light blue and white; arm and sword silver.

17. Bavarian infantry colours. (All drawings by Dr Lesley Prince)

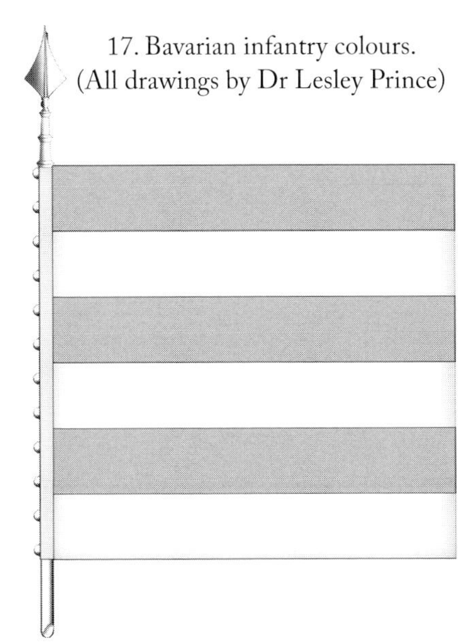

This pattern occurs frequently. The above alternates light blue & white stripes; another alternates white & light blue. Others have varying numbers of stripes, all variants on the white & light blue theme.

Edge red and white; blue-green field; golden flames; black cross

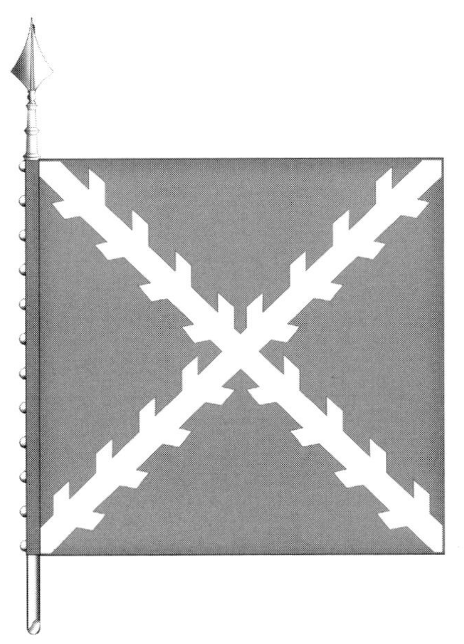

Light blue field; white Burgundian saltire

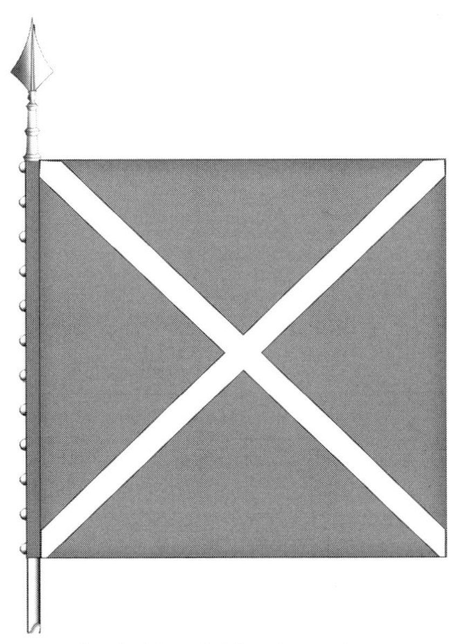

Light blue field, white saltire

Augsburg, where the colonel's ensign was white with a purple and green cross in the form of diamonds with yellow rays of light emerging from the monogram of 'MAR' in the centre of a green circle. The remaining ensigns all had a light blue and white diagonal cross, one had a yellow, green, red and white segments, another white, red, white and yellow segments, while another had a green field and another a yellow field. Then there were seven colours with the same cross, with various patterns of yellow, blue, green, red and white.

Among the colours preserved at the Swedish Army Museum at Stockholm, and believed to be of Bavarian origin, is a light blue damask dragoon guidon, 111.5 by 227 cm (43 by 89 inches), with a swallow tail and white flames, which is believed to have belonged to a Bavarian regiment. It has the image of a crucified Christ with the motto *Jesvs Nasarenvs Rex Ivdeorum* written above the image, and below, *titulus triumphalis ab omnibus me defendit malis*. On the other side is the image of the Virgin Mary with the inscription, *Maria Mayer Dei Ora pro me*. It has a thin blue and white fringe.[18]

Also preserved in Stockholm is a blue cavalry cornet 55 cm wide by 64 cm high (21 by 25 inches) with the letter 'M' over the arms of the Wittelsbach family surrounded by a laurel wreath, and on the other side is the image of a crucified Christ. This image is also surrounded by a laurel wreath and the cornet has a blue and yellow fringe.[19]

Some cavalry cornets are so elaborately painted that they would not be out of place in an art gallery. Among them is a blue cavalry cornet, 52 by 45 cm, with a white fringe with a painting of a penitent Mary Magdalene sitting under a tree on one side and the Virgin Mary being blessed by an angel on the other. In the four corners is the monogram 'sDMVBs'.[20]

An English newssheet concerning the battle of Wiesloch, near Prague, records several standards of Tilly's army that were captured in May 1622:

> Two great standards or banners, one of white damask, wherein were these words 'In Domino Sperantes, co non confundantur' The other standard was of red damask, having on the one side a black eagle and on the other side the Arms of Bavaria, with the golden fleece round above it and under it was written "Adiutorium Domini sit inimicis terror."
>
> In a third great cornet much spoiled there stood fortune, but it was so torn and tattered that the motto could not be read.
>
> There were also six ensigns of footmen found, but so spoiled with rain and mire, that they could not be known.[21]

Among a list of colours captured at the battle of Wittenweier in 1638 include,

> The cornet of the Guard company of Goetz, made of blue damask with a cross of Burgundy, silver embroidery with this symbol. 'Pro Imperatore et Fide'.

18 Swedish Army Museum accession no. ST 14:1; Sandstedt, *In Hoc Signo Vinces*, p.211.
19 Swedish Army Museum accession no. ST 14:11.
20 Swedish Army Museum accession no. ST G.7.
21 *A True relation of all such battles as have been fought in the Palatinate ...* (London: 1622).

> A red standard of the Goetz's Guard regiment with a cross of Burgundy with this symbol. 'Pro Imperatore et Fide'.

> A white standard with the Jesuits' mark and embroidered in gold on one side and on the other these letters 'MR'.[22]

However, the list describes just 25 of the 66 colours said to have been captured during the battle. Another source describes a cornet of General Goetz's Regiment of Cuirassiers which was captured at Wittenweier as being, 'very fair and embroidered with silver and gold'. In 1633 Colonel Peter Goetz raised a regiment with red colours and a Colonel John Goetz's regiment of horse had white colours. The original colours were taken to Paris and destroyed in 1814.[23]

As well as manuscripts and newssheets, sometime descriptions of colours can also be found in memoirs, such as those of Count Gualdo Priorato who describes one wing of Tilly's cavalry at the battle of Breitenfeld as having '70 Standards of several colours, with several impresses; among the which one was a great Imperial Eagle, which held in her right talon a Pontifical Crown and in her left the Imperial Sceptre; the word was "Pro Ecclesia, et pro Imperios".' The vanguard consisted of '48 ensigns of diverse colours and with several inscriptions'.[24]

However, he also records the Swedish infantry had, '72 ensigns of various lovely colours, upon which was set the king's arms and upon that a great crown, the motto was Gustavus Adolphus Rex Fidei Evangelica defensor.' However, Reginbaldus Mohner, who drew these colours in Augsburg in April 1632, disagrees with Count Gualdo Priorato, and only a few regiments carried this monogram. It may be that Priorato was not present at the battle since he does say that he has used other sources to fill in any gaps in his account.[25]

22 TNA: SP 81/45, ff.125–126, see Appendix 2 for further descriptions.
23 *A supplement to the sixth part of the German History* (London, 1634), pp.51–52.
24 Priorato, p.45.
25 *Ibid.*, p.42.

7

Rations and Pay

Rations

Raising an army was comparatively simple, since once raised the soldiers could go without pay and wear rags that were once clothes etc., but keeping them fed was another matter. A typical soldier's ration was 2 lb of bread, 1 lb of meat and 8 pints of beer, or to put it another way a regiment of 1,000 soldiers needed about 2,000 lb of bread, 1,000 lb of meat and 8,000 pints of beer per day, while a corporal and sergeant received 2 lb of meat and bread. On the other hand a corporal of horse and a trooper serving in the Bavarian Army in 1634 could expect 10 pints of beer, 2½ lb of bread and 1½ lb of meat. Captains received almost 15½ lb of bread and about 10 lb of meat plus two measures of wine and 15 measures of beer, and a colonel 24 measures of beer, 15 measures of wine, and 40 lb of bread and meat per day.

The meat was probably salted to stop it going bad. During the Napoleonic Wars it was estimated that 2 lb of salt was enough to preserve 8 lb of meat and so often had to be soaked in water to make it edible, whereas the officers probably had fresh meat. However, on one occasion Peter Hagendorf was sent out with a foraging party and managed to bring back a whole flock of sheep to the army, which he estimated to be 2,000 strong, so they had fresh meat for several days. Hagendorf recalls he kept two sheep for himself which he slaughtered.[1]

The recipe for the bread seems to have been a mixture of rye, oats and flour. The alcohol content of the beer would have been low, which in England was known as 'small beer'. The provisions would be weighed on a pair of scales, but no consideration was taken of any bone or fat within the meat, so if they were unlucky then their meat ration for that day would be mostly bone or gristle.

When an army could not rely on the local bakers then brick ovens were built. G. Perjes estimates that it would take about 500 bricks to build an oven, which was big enough to bake between 599.85 and 1,125 kg (1,322–2,480 lb) of bread per day. Therefore an army of 10,000 men would need between eight to 15 ovens or 4,000 to

1 Helfferich, pp.292–293.

7,500 bricks, which would have to be transported along with the firewood to heat the ovens, as well as the ingredients to make the bread, and the bread itself once baked. Where possible these ovens would continue to bake the bread for a number of days while the army was stationary.[2]

However, for many soldiers it was a case of feast or famine. At the beginning of November 1620 Father Henry Fitzsimon recorded in his diary:

> At Raconitz we had no bread, and no drink, except the turbid waters of Bohemia. Our food was meat killed on the spot, and spoiled by the smoke of fir trees. Our enemies, to sport with our want, sent us the present of a little bread, and we in turn sent them a sheep, as they were suffering from scarcity of meat. Our soldiers, notwithstanding their privations, were kept in good spirits by the self denial and good humour of their general.[3]

Therefore an army which was short of rations could still be an effective force if its morale held up; however that cannot be said of Montenegro's Imperialist Army when it was defeated in December 1623, when it was said his army had 'endured so great a want as they had no bread during the space of three or four weeks and were constrained to eat dead horses and dogs.' It was said that this defeat resulted in Bethlen Gabor massacring all the Italians, Spanish and Walloons and only sparing the Germans.[4]

Therefore a commander needed to accumulate large quantities of supplies. In June 1626 it was reported that Tilly was gathering all the corn and other provisions he could, and that in his camp a dollar could buy an oxen or six sheep. On 17 November 1631 he demanded 100,000 three pound loaves of bread from Nuremberg to feed his army.[5]

Peter Hagendorf recalled that 'on Good Friday we had bread and meat enough, but on Holy Sunday, we could not get even a mouthful of bread'. However, the diet was monotonous as Hagendorf further recorded, 'we got tired of eating beef and had to have geese, ducks or chicken instead.'[6]

Accounts speak of towns being laid waste, but in Ratisbon at the end of December 1633 the price for provisions fell because there was such an abundance of bread, wine, beer and meat. In fact there was so much food that some had to be sent to Nuremberg and other places.[7]

Campaigns were conducted not only for strategic purposes, but also to find fertile land where an army commander could feed his army. The newssheet *More Newes from the Palatinate*, published on 5 June 1622, records:

2 G. Perjes 'Army provisioning, logistics and strategy in the Second Half of the 17th Century', in *Acta Historia Academiae Scientiaruim Hungaricae*, vol. 16 (1970), pp.8–9.

3 Father Henry Fitzsimon, 'Diary of the Bohemian War of 1620', in *Words of Comfort to persecuted Catholics* (Dublin: Gill & Son, 1881), p.94.

4 TNA: SP 101/46, State Papers, Foreign Newsletters, f.249; *News from the Hague*, 28 December 1623.

5 TNA: SP 81/34, f.71; Heilmann, 1868, vol. 2, p.314.

6 Helfferich, pp.280–281.

7 TNA: SP 101/31, State Papers, Foreign Newsletters, f.28.

> Count Mansfeldt had the advantage of them [Tilly's Army] for when the soldiers had eat up their victuals which they brought with them in their knapsacks and drunk out all their water out of their water bottles (those that had it) their wine out of their Borachoes there was no stay for them ... their hunger which breaks through stone walls and fears no worst enemy then it selfe.[8]

Another newsletter, this time for July 1623, records that in Tilly's army:

> The thirst all this while said to be very sore in his Army; for want of water, was said to be one of the main reasons of his [Tilly's] so sudden retreating; (there being no river near to his former camp, nor other water but such as was brought on horseback in buckets, water-budgets, Borachoes and the like, which made it to be sold extreme[ly] dear.[9]

Nothing had changed by August 1631, when another newssheet reported that Gustavus Adolphus:

> Hath his provisions and victuals coming to him without any let, whereas Tilly hath none but what is brought very far down from Germany to his army, where there is already such a dearth, that a loaf of bread costs a florin of gold ... whereby it is thought that Tilly must either go back again or tarrying but a while longer [and] suffer extremely.[10]

Once the army had eaten the provisions of an area the local merchants would increase their prices due the scarcity of the food. On 20 January 1623 Tilly's Army was quartered at Hanau, Solms and Isenburg and that 'everything grows very dear seeing the soldiers have devoured and consumed almost all the provisions hereabouts'. A week later it was reported that 'they are likely to ruin the Boars and other people living in open and unwalled places'.[11]

However, it was not just Tilly's Army that was suffering. In Prague at the beginning of 1623 the Hungarians had invaded Moravia and the Marquis of Montenegro had to send for reinforcements even though provisions 'grow daily all things dearer, the bread is made very small and the beer taxed higher and we are likely to sustain want of flesh and other victuals seeing the soldiers which lie upon the country consume all and stay in conveying of the provisions hitherwards, taking it from the country people upon the highways.'[12]

Unfortunately, the weather did not help matters for the local population: in the Palatinate in February 1623 there was 'such famine that many die for want of victuals

8 *More newes from the Palatinate* (London, 5 June 1622).
9 *The Continuation of Our Weekely News* (London, 29 July 1623), no. 24.
10 *The Continuation of Our Forraine Avisoes* (London, 9 August 1631).
11 *Weekly News* (London, 20 January 1623), no. 14, p.14; *Weekly News* (London, 28 January 1623), no. 15, pp.1–2.
12 *Weekly News* (London, 11 February 1623), no. 18, p.23.

Rank	Measure of Wine	Measure of Beer	Pound of Bread	Pound of Meat
Colonel	15	24	40	40
Lieutenant Colonel	7	10	12	8
Oberstwachmeister	4	6	8	6
Quartermaster		7	8	6
Schltheiss		7	8	6
Chaplain		7	8	10
Provost with staff		12	14	3
Wagon master		5	5	3
Scharsrichter mit 2 stickenknechte		5	6	3
Troop of Horse				
Captain	2	15	15	10
Lieutenant		9	8	6
Cornet		8	7	5
Wachtmeister	5			3½
Farrier	5			3½
Musterschreiber		5		3½
Corporal		5		3½
Trumpeter		2½	2½	1½
Blacksmith		2½	2½	1½
Plattner		2½	2½	1½
Trooper		2½	2½	1½
Company of Foot				
Captain	2	15	15	10
Lieutenant		9	8	6
Ensign		9	7	5
Fuhrer		3	2	2
Furier		3	2	2
Clerk		3	2	2
Feldscherer		3	2	2
Corporal		3	2	2
Spielleute		3	2	2
Lance Corporal			2	1
Soldier		2	2	1

Bavarian government's regulation for soldiers' daily rations, 24 January 1634 (Heilmann, *Kriegsgeschichte von Bayern*, vol. 3)

and especially in the villages many starve of late when the earth was frozen so that they could not dig roots out of the ground which many feed as if they were hogs.'[13]

Of course in enemy territory the army did not have to worry about paying for their food. On 28 June 1623 Heinrich Rodingus, the rentmaster in Sontra, wrote to the Landgrave of Hesse-Kassel:

> The Bavarian cavalry and several servants of the Lieutenant Colonel Herbersdorff forced me with violence and great threats to open the grain supply to them and they took the available wheat, spelt and oats from me to feed the animals, but they did not stop there, but also broke open the lock on the stalls and took away your entire supply of hay and used all the coal.

However Rodingus does not mention any other valuables being stolen, so Tilly's army must have been looking for provisions rather than plunder. Nevertheless this would leave the population short of food, particularly if it was stolen during the middle of winter.[14]

To carry their provisions a soldier would be issued with a knapsack. Usually it was a leather bag, although sometimes it was made of canvas, and was a cylindrical bag fastened at both ends with a cord and a strap to enable the soldier to carry it over his shoulder. Contemporary illustrations show that it was only large enough to hold about a day's rations along with any personal items the soldiers might have.

The soldiers' provisions were usually issued to them daily, probably in the evening, after they had set up camp. Each regiment had its own wagons to carry its provisions, ammunition, etc., for its soldiers, which was controlled by the regimental wagon master. During the 1622 campaign some of Tilly's regiments of foot possessed the following:

Regiment	Army Wagons	Horses	Calash	Horses	Sutler Wagons	Horses
Anholt	27	148	8	16	-	-
Herliberg	17	68	17	34	10	40
Schmidt	20	80	9	8	9	32
Mortaigne	20	80	-	-	-	-
Würzburg	24	96	-	-	-	-

Given their popularity it would be highly unlikely that Anholt's, Mortaigne's and Würzburg's Regiments did not have any sutlers attached to them.

The number of wagons in Tilly's army at this time was not unique: in 1622, Duke Ernest of Saxe-Weimar's army of 3,000 foot and 1,000 horse had 500 wagons or a

13 *Weekly News* (London, 14 March 1623), no. 23, p.13.

14 Quoted in J. C. Theibault, *German Villages in Crisis: rural life in Hesse-Kassel and the Thirty Years' War, 1580–1720* (Atlantic Highlands, New Jersey: Humanities Press, 1995), p.142.

ratio of eight soldiers to one wagon. On the other hand, in 1626 Mansfeld had 800 wagons for his 18,000 men and 36 pieces of ordnance or a ratio of four wagons to nine soldiers. The regimental wagons may have been distinguished by flags identical to those carried by the regiment, but there are no surviving examples or references in archives to confirm this.

In 1625 Spanish general Ambrogio di Filippo Spinola ordered the Estates of Brabant to supply 500 wagons to carry 'provisions of meal and oats' for his army, which was estimated as just 10,000 strong. When the town of Breda fell to the Spanish in 1625 Spinola demanded a further 4,000 wagons to carry away the corn which the Spanish had found in the town. How many wagons he already had is not recorded.[15]

In 1644, to help feed the soldiers, the Bavarian Army had two commissary generals, eight war commissaries and under them four provision administrators, eight provision officers and 1 provision-master baker, one provision leader and one provision henchman.[16]

However, it was not just the soldiers and their families who needed feeding: the horses for the cavalry, the baggage train and those owned by the officers also needed feeding.

A horse doing a moderate day's work needs 25,000 calories per day and so needs to eat about one to three percent of its body weight to stay healthy or 6.8–9 kg (15–20 lb) per day. Therefore a regiment of horse around 500 strong needed 3,400–4,500 kg (around 7,500–10,000 lb) of fodder per day. On the other hand a horse employed in heavy work burns 33,000 calories so would need more fodder, plus about 10 gallons of water, so the regiment would also need 5,000 gallons of water per day. Since a horse has a small stomach it needs to be fed several times per day, but unfortunately for the horse a campaign would take a heavy toll on a cavalry regiment.[17]

Any cattle kept for fresh meat would also have to be fed; on average one head of cattle consumes about 11 kg (24¼ lb) of hay per day, plus water.

Pay

As well as being issued with daily rations, a soldier could buy extra from the many sutlers that accompanied the army. Unfortunately for the soldier they were rarely paid on time: Maximilian, like most heads of state, preferred to spend the money in his war chest on weapons, supplies and raising new levies rather than on the soldiers themselves, so their pay soon fell into months, if not years, of arrears. It was only when the soldiers were required to take the offensive that Maximilian reluctantly paid part of their arrears.

15 TNA: SP 77/18, List of Spanish forces in the Netherlands, 1625, f.12–13; Substance of Spinola's letter to the State of Brabant and their answer, 16 June 1625, f.169; SP 101/28, State Papers, Foreign Newsletters, 1620–1625, f.152; SP 101/29, State Papers, Foreign Newsletters; BL Harl MS 7,364, *A book of tactics in Charles I's time*.

16 Friedrich Munich, *Geschichte der Entwickelung der bayerischen Armee seit zwei Jahrhunderten* (Munich: Lindauer, 1864), p.5.

17 Robin Higham, 'Some Thoughts on the 30 Years War' in Jan Vilím, *Bellum Tricennale* (Prague: Historical Institute of the Army of Czech Republic, 1997), p.340, and on horse feeding at <http://ecoquine.wordpress.com> (accessed December 2015).

At least at the beginning of the war a Bavarian soldier was lucky, in that he received higher pay than in other armies: 18 *fl* per month if he was a cuirassier, 16½ *fl* if a harquebusier, and 8 *fl* if a pikeman or musketeer. Whereas, a harquebusier in the Imperial service received 12 *fl* and a cuirassier 15 *fl* a month.

On the other hand, during the early 1620s Tilly was paid 2,000, later 3,000, florins per month, as the lieutenant general of the Catholic League, and his subordinate Lieutenant Field Marshal Anholt received 1,500 florins per month in 1622 and 3,000 florins in 1628. However, as the war dragged on there appears to have been a decline in the wages of the senior officers: General of Cavalry Johann von Werth only received 1,200 *fl* per month in 1636 and General of Artillery Franz Royer was paid 2,000 *fl* in 1648, plus free lodging. In contrast, when Wallenstein was commander of the Imperialist Army in 1625 he received 6,000 *fl* per month, and the pay of his subordinates was also higher in the Imperial Army than in the League's Army, although there was later parity between them.[18]

To help finance their war effort, an army could impose taxes on the local population, especially if they were in hostile territory, in which case a soldier would be more likely to get paid. However, as with other armies this 'contribution' system only worked when it controlled large areas of land. When it lost control of these territories, as in 1645, the system broke down and Maximilian had to rely on his own finances to keep the army in the field. As early as May 1624 it was reported that the Catholic League was in debt to Bavaria for six million florins.

The terms of pay differed between nations. The Dutch Army received three shillings a week, but 12 pence was deducted for the captain to buy the soldier's clothing which was issued once a year. If the soldier was maimed while in service he would continue to receive his pay even after he was discharged from active service. A soldier in the Spanish service received the equivalent of 16 shillings a month, although a financial 'month' could be between six and eight weeks long. On the other hand soldiers in the Swedish and the Imperial service received six shillings a week, but 'theirs is a hard service to lye out wet and dry' in the fields, i.e. on campaign. The Polish Army also paid its soldiers six shillings a week but cashiered most of its soldiers just before winter.[19]

The soldiers were going so far unpaid that as early as the beginning of June 1622 'The Bavarian soldiers fall daily to Mansfeld, I have seen it and have heard it of his officers that they go twelve or sixteen in a day out of a company. And two days ago there was money going to pay for four months, but Mansfeld soldiers took it.'[20] On 8 March 1623 it was reported that Tilly could only pay his army four months pay and that it was 16 months in arrears. To save money in June 1623 it was reported that 'The Duke of Bavaria hath paid the army for four months and hath reformed 15 troops of horse, having cashiered the officers.'[21]

18 Redlich, pp.311–314.
19 Frederick Boas (ed.), *Diary of Thomas Crosfield* (London: Oxford University Press, 1935), p.67.
20 TNA: SP 101/28, State Papers, Foreign Newsletters, ff.23.
21 *Copies of Letters*, 30 May to 11 June 1622; *More news*, 30 May to 10 June 1623.

This was still not enough, and in January 1624 it was reported that Tilly's men were 14 to 15 months in arrears and that some troops had had enough and torn up their colours and sought employment elsewhere, including with Mansfeld or the Duke of Brunswick, although the former had the reputation of rarely paying his soldiers. In May 1624 it was reported that, 'a great sum of money hath been sent to Frankfort towards the payment of Tilly's Army, but [it is] not sufficient to content them'. At the beginning of the following year the situation had not improved, '[Tilly's] troops were commanded to march all, but they do not stir yet ... The troops of the emperor and those of Bavaria cry out for money'. Without their arrears the soldiers refused to march.[22]

The situation had not improved by 3 January 1627, when it was reported that:

> Some colonels and captains of Tilly's army are at Vienna for the pay of their troops that are now in Bohemia ... The regiments of Tilly's Army winter here and there in the circles of Bohemia. The other horse which Tilly sent since began to mutiny in Franconia and would go not further till the arrears of their pay were paid them, which because they would not serve against Bethlen Gabor they pretended to be due up to then for 14 or 15 months. Some companies tore [up] their cornets and seek new masters. Many of them are gone to Mansfeldt and Brunswick.[23]

In September 1631, when Tilly invaded Saxony, he wrote 'In all the days of my life, I have never seen an army so suddenly and totally deprived of all that it needs, from the greatest to the smallest requisite ... And I am utterly astonished that the poor soldiers remain so long in such necessity'. While Colonel Snetter who commanded the Bavarian forces in Ingoldstadt appealed, for 'Heavens' sake' send more provisions. When Tilly died early in 1632 he bequeathed 60,000 *talers* to his army.[24]

Not getting paid was one thing, but during the early 1620s there was hyperinflation, known as 'Wipper and Kipper', when the value of the currency fell dramatically so what little money a soldier did have was practically worthless. Sir Horace Vere probably echoed many commanders when he wrote on 6 May 1622:

> The miserable estate of the soldiers through abuse in the valuation of money growing daily worse and worse, and finding that without reformation in that point it will be impossible to continue their or raise new troops ... and not sufficient for food, I conceive it a thing worthy [of] compassion.[25]

Fortunately by the mid 1620s there was a significant improvement in the inflation rate, with the old debased coinage being recalled and a new currency issued. But there was another problem with not paying the soldiers, in that it bred indiscipline. True,

22 TNA: SP 101/28, State Papers, Foreign Newsletters, ff.23, 242, 189.
23 TNA: SP 101/46, State Papers, Foreign Newsletters, *News from the Hague*.
24 Quoted in Geoffrey Parker, *Europe in Crisis: 1598–1648* (Glasgow: Fontana, 1984), p.223; Redlich, p.508.
25 TNA: SP 81/24, Sir Horace Vere, 6 May 1622, ff.144–145.

there were military laws preventing plundering, rape and murder: on 1 August 1641 a general order issued by the Imperial Headquarters read:

> Swearing will be punished the first time according to the discretion of the authorities; thereafter it is punishable with death. Stealing a cow or a horse secretly or by force will without judgement and investigation and without mercy be punished by hanging. If one is in possession of a stolen horse and cannot show from whom it was purchased, he will be punished as if he were their thief. Whoever mistreats or tortures a civilian or attacks anyone on the highway will pay with his life.[26]

Unfortunately for the civilian population, like the edicts before this one, the officers felt unable to impose the harsh punishments these laws prescribed while their men were in arrears, since without money they could not buy food or other essentials and the only way to obtain it was to steal it.

This did not mean that the officers always turned a blind eye to crimes committed by the men, particularly when it came to discipline within the regiment: for offences such as hitting an officer, giving the password to the enemy or being asleep on guard duty, a soldier could expect death by hanging. If there was more than one soldier involved then lots might cast by throwing a dice and the soldier with the lowest score would be executed. Alternatively they might draw a ticket from a hat and the soldier who drew the piece of paper with a gallows on it was hanged. On the other hand an officer who committed a crime might be shot or beheaded as a mark of respect for his status. For other crimes a soldier might be made to 'ride the wooden horse', whereby he had his hands tied behind his back and was sat on the edge of two wooden planks for a given amount of time. Weights might also be tied to his feet to make the punishment more severe.

A worse punishment was the strappado. A soldier would have his hands tied behind his back, and was then hoisted up by the hands or thumbs so that he could only stand on tiptoes or he might even be raised off the ground complete before being dropped at least once which would often result in his arms being dislocated. It was believed that the very sight of a strappado 'will do good in a wicked mind'. In his *Miseries of War* Jacques Callot shows a soldier undergoing this punishment having been raised high above his comrades. The caption reads, 'It is not without cause that great captains have well advisedly invented these punishments for idlers, blasphemers, traitors to duty, quarrelers and liars, whose actions, blinded by vice, make those of others slack and irregular.'[27]

Imprisonment was used if a soldier blasphemed for the first time, but it could also be used if a soldier was 'seen without his sword', or if he left his garrison or lodging without a pass, struck a fellow soldier or was insolent to an officer, did not keep his arms clean or even sold or pawned them. For a second offence, 'blasphemers' and 'common swearers' could expect to have their tongue bored with a red hot iron. How often this was carried out is not known.

26 Robert Ergang, *The Myth of the all-destructive fury of the Thirty Years' War* (Pocono Pines, Pa.: The Craftsmen, 1956), p.19.

27 Daniel Howard (ed.), *Callot's Etchings: 338 Prints* (New York: Dover Publications, 1974), sketch no. 274.

8

Billeting the Soldiers

Apart from marching a soldier would spend most of his time in quarters; these could be in the form of a well-designed military encampment, in a house within a town or village, or he may sleep under the stars. Sometimes soldiers had no option but to sleep in the fields since they had burnt the surrounding towns and villages to the ground. Therefore commanders could consult one of the many military manuals which contained descriptions and diagrams on how to set up a military encampment, including that they should be fortified in case they were attacked.

The military engineer Samuel Marolois recommends a ditch, six to eight feet broad and five to six feet deep 'and the parapet of the same breadth and height', whereas Robert Ward suggests that redoubts should be dug to defend the passages to the camp. For passages where the approach of the enemy was least expected, Ward recommended a triangular redoubt, which was to contain 30 or 40 men. However, for passages where the approach of the enemy was more likely, square redoubts were to be erected to protect between 80 to 100 men. Ward further adds that:

> These redoubts are to be relieved every night before sun set with fresh companies from the main camp; where no soldier is to pull off his armour or set down his pike or musket until they be all entered the work and the sentinels set out in their due places.[1]

As to the encampment itself it was to be divided into four areas separated by wide streets and named for example, north east, south east, etc. These areas were to be designated to each arm of the army, such as the artillery or cavalry. Each one of these areas would further divided and allocated to a regiment and a company would be allocated an area of land within the camp on which to quarter. This land would be divided into a number of strips depending how many companies the regiment had. A road would be measured in the middle of each strip and the company would set up their tents or shelters either side of the road. At the end of these roads were the senior officers' tents and a space was also allocated for the regimental baggage.

1 Robert Ward, *Animadversions of Warre; or a Military magazine of the truest rules and ablest instructions for the managing of warre...* (London: 1639), Book 2, p.31.

Johann von Wallhausen, who wrote a manual on cavalry and infantry at the beginning of the seventeenth century, suggests that these roads should be '16 paces wide' and each tent, or hut, should have a frontage of eight paces. Lieutenants were allowed 16 paces, and ensigns and captains 24 paces. However another contemporary source suggests that road should be '10 foot broad.'[2]

William Garrard records that a soldier should go to,

> [The] adjoining village (if time and safety from the enemy doth permit) for long straw both to cover their cabin and make their bed … another [soldier] with a hatchet … doth cut down forked bows and long poles to frame and rear up their cabin withal and provide timber and fire wood if it be winter or if need requires.[3]

Hexham states that the soldiers '[made] their huts of forks, lathes withes and straw or for if they were staying just one night, sticks and boughs or as such things as they can get.' Therefore a soldier's hut would depend on his foraging skills and what was available to hand, so some of these huts might be well built while other might just give the minimum of protection from the elements.

A contemporary military treatise describes one of these huts:

> In each hut or cabin you shall lodge two common soldiers and so you shall have 50 huts for each company, divided into ranks, each rank consists of 25, every hut is to be six foot broad and seven foot long, each hut shall be distant one from another rank [by] two feet.[4]

Other sources suggest that huts were to be eight feet by eight feet, and since the companies of the European countries were larger, being 200 to 300 strong at full strength, then there would be 100 to 150 huts per company. Most sources agree that there should be two soldiers to a hut, the Swedish appear to have had three, so were nine feet square. However, if a soldier was accompanied by his family then they would occupy his hut, rather than another soldier.

Writing around 1614, Sir Horace Vere, who served in the Dutch Army, said it was the quartermaster's duty to:

> Go through every captain's quarters to see if the soldiers have built their cabins high and wide enough and have made their beds above the ground. The captains ought every three weeks to get fresh straw to give their soldiers … and to air their cabins and to keep their quarters swept every day very clean to avoid sickness.[5]

2 Johann von Wallhausen, L'*Art militaire pour l'Infantrie* (Frankfurt, 1625), p.127; BL Harl 6,344, *A Short military treatise concerning all things needful in an army*, ff.160–169.
3 William Garrard, *The Art of Warre. Beeing the onely rare booke of Myllitarie profession* (London: 1591) p.13.
4 BL Harl 6,344, *A Short military treatise concerning all things needful in an army*, ff.160–169.
5 TNA: SP 9/202/1/18, Compendium of the Discipline of the Art of War under Sir Horace Vere, 1603–1625.

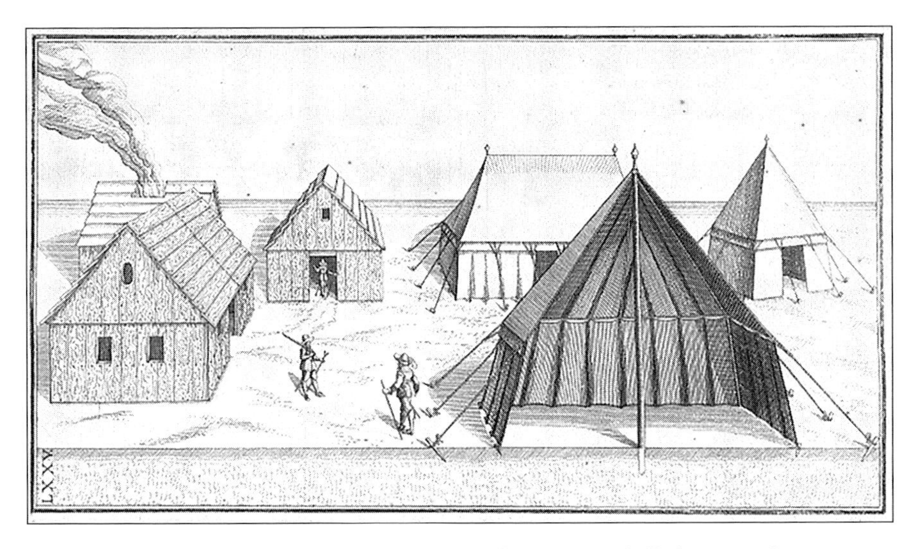

18. The ideal military encampment. 'Kriegswesen & Belagerung & Zelt & Hütte' ('A view of camp and huts'), from Wilhelm Dilich, *Peribologia, seu Muniendorum locorum ratio Wilhelmi Dilichii*, 1641.

Robert Ward, however, writing some 25 years later, said that responsibility had passed to the sergeants of the company to make sure that:

> The soldiers build their huts even and keep exactly the measurements so the streets may be even and that if it be possible that the huts be built all of one height and after one and the same fashion ... All the doors of the huts must be open to the lane that is between the ranks of the huts.[6]

The corporals and the regimental provost and his men were to make sure that the camp was kept clean, especially if they were quartered in the same place for some time.

Contemporary encampments showing tents suggest that they are composed of two upright poles and one horizontal pole with a single sheet of canvas stretched over them and staked out on the ground. They do not appear to have had a front or a back and so were open at both ends. A contract dated 3 April 1645 for 200 tents 'for the train' to be issued to the New Model Army were to be 'seven foot long, seven foot broad and six foot high of good lockram according to the pattern and with firre [?*sic* = five] staves, lines and pins and other appurtances.' These tents cost 20 shillings. On 5 May 1654 another contract for Cromwell's Army records 'the making of 1,000 tents with thread, tape and cordage; each tent to be six foot high and seven foot square to be delivered into the stores within the Tower [of London] within 10 days at 2s and 7d per tent.' The same day another contract was issued 'for tent staves, pins and mallets

6 Ward, Book 2. pp.32, 38.

for 1,000 tents; viz for each tent three poles, 17 pins and one mallet at 14d per piece to be delivered within ten days.'[7]

Officers had more elaborate tents. Johan von Wallhausen shows circular tents used by the officers, with cone tops and small flags on the top, secured to the ground by about 14 tent ropes. However, by the end of the 1620s rectangular tents for officers seem to be in fashion. Beneath a portrait of Sir Horace Vere is a scene of a soldier a outside an officer's tent, the dimensions can be estimated to be about seven feet tall and about 12 to 14 feet long with possibly six or seven small windows and a doorway with a crescent top. The roof tapers up. The tent cords are fastened to where the walls are attached to the roof and two cords are also tied to the poles holding up the roof. Presumably the walls are pegged down.

A colonel might not just have his own tent, according to Thomas Raymond, who served in Colonel Packenham's Regiment in the Dutch service:

> My colonel had a kitchen tent, a servants' tent, a lodging tent for himself and another, the largest and fairest tent of all, wherein he eat, gave audience to his officers and entertained. Which also was our church having there every Sunday morning a sermon preached by the chaplain to the regiment.[8]

Usually the tents were transported by the regimental baggage and so might not arrive in time for the soldiers to sleep in, and if they were unable to erect a hut, then they would have to sleep in the open. Thomas Raymond records during one of these times he:

> Had nothing to keep me from the cold wet ground but a little bundle of wet dried flax, which by chance I lighted on, and so with my boots full of water and wrapped up in my wet cloak, I lay as round as a hedgehog, and at the peep of day looked like a drowned rat.[9]

In an army's accounts the most common issue of tents was for the artillery, presumably to shelter the ordnance and wagons under. When it came to the horses, whether for the cavalry or artillery, they needed stabling. John Cruso, who wrote *Militarie Instructions for the Cavall'rie* in 1632, records that 'to lodge or encamp the cavalry, a special care must be had of the commodity of water, and where they may be under shelter: for one cold or rainy night might ruin the cavalry, nothing hurting a horse sooner then cold or wet.'

Cruso also suggests that the huts of each troop of cuirassiers were to be:

7 Mungeam, p.113; TNA: PRO 30/37/5, Army contracts, unfolio page.
8 Charles S. Terry, *The Life and Campaigns of Alexander Leslie, First Earl of Leven* (London: Longman, 1899), p.72.
9 G. Davis (ed.), Thomas Raymond, *Autobiography of Thomas Raymond* , (London: Royal Historical Society, 1917) pp.38–40.

> 13 foot broad and the huts of the horsemen are 10 foot broad and 8 foot long for one horseman and his boy. And betwixt two huts there is two foot of space for the drain of rain water, dropping from the thatch or covers of the huts. These huts have their chief doors or passages towards their heads of their horse and a small opening into the street where they lay their hay and straw, every one behind his own hut ... a street of five foot broad [is] between the horseman's huts and the mangers [or stables] for their horses ... Ten foot [is allowed] for the stables of their horses, which are placed with the heads towards their huts, and every horse hath four foot in breadth for his litter and eight foot for two horses; according to the length of their huts.[10]

Wearing three-quarter armour a cuirassier needed someone to help arm him, hence the boy. As to the harquebusiers, Cruso continues:

> [The] companies of harquebusiers have also 180 foot depth for the quartering of their ... huts ... but these have but 15 huts in every file doe 30 horse, having also two streets (as the cuirassiers) ... being of 12 foot broad and eight foot deep for two harquebusiers and eight foot for the litter of their two horses and 10 foot for their stable. And five foot for a street between their huts and the mangers for their horses.[11]

The officers' and trumpeters' tents or huts were at the end of each street.

Life for a soldier was usually boring while in camp. True, there were the usual guard duties but one of the activities a soldier could engage in to pass his time was gambling, either with dice or cards. On 5 September 1620 Father Pietro Drexel, who accompanied Maximilian of Bavaria during the campaign that year, records that 'the money is gambled, a musketeer lost in a round 105 guilders and won the next day 100. It is quite normal in the army.'[12] Smoking was also a common pastime, since tobacco had been brought back from America during the sixteenth century by the English and quickly spread to Europe.

They might even go to the sutlers' huts and stalls to buy beer and other goods. These were situated behind the huts of the regiment furthest away from the officers' quarters in a road about six paces wide, which was specially allocated for 'sutlers, butchers and shopkeepers.' The sutlers' tents and huts distinguished by having laurel wreaths, a tankard or a flag hanging outside.[13]

Further behind the sutlers' row was a plot of land where offal and human or animal waste was to be left to be buried, to stop the spread of disease. Alternatively the military manuals suggest that if the camp had been built near a river then not only was it good for defensive purposes, but also the waste could be thrown into it. A soldier could be fined if he left any waste in the middle of the encampment. Robert Ward also

10 Cruso, *Militarie Instructions for the Cavall'rie*, 1632, pp.66–67.
11 *Ibid.*
12 Father Drexel's diary in Sigmund Riezler, *Kriegstagebücher aus dem ligistichen Hauptquartier, 1620* (Munich: G Frans'chen, 1908), p.158.
13 Jos W. L. Hilkhuijsen et al., *Beelden van een strijd: oorlog en kunst vóór de Vrede van Munster, 1621–1648* (Zwolle:Waanders, 1998), p.251.

suggests that there was to be a gap between each regiment of 20 to 30 feet, and the commanders of the army should be in the middle of the encampment.[14]

If possible a commander of an army might try to quarter his cavalry in the surrounding villages while his infantry had to make do with building huts. However, Wallhausen wrote that 'in friendly country I will never counsel any Lord or Potentate to lodge a regiment of soldiers in villages, except that great necessity requires it, as time of frost [or] cold weather.' His reasons include that the householders cannot afford to keep them and that the soldiers might be badly behaved so cause ill feeling by their subjects.

Furthermore Wallhausen warns that being quartered in towns and villages they did not have the proper protection of a fortified military encampment, and so might have their quarters 'beaten up' by the enemy.[15] As one officer during the English Civil War put it, 'there is nothing worst than having your quarters beaten up.' Usually these hit and run raids by enemy cavalry took place at night when most of the soldiers were asleep. which added to their disorientation. While trying to put up a resistance to this raid the soldiers would try to fall back to a designated rendezvous such as a town square, or even a church's graveyard so that they had enough space to reform their ranks.

However the soldiers probably preferred being quartered on the inhabitants of a town, especially during the winter. The regimental quartermasters would chalk on the door of a house the regiment and company commander's name and the number of men that the property was to accommodate. If possible a regiment or company would be accommodated in a village or town to make training easier, although sometimes as few as two or three men might be quartered in a village in order to keep order. Unfortunately for the local population they had no say in the matter, and although they were paid for giving a soldier food and accommodation, most houses just had a couple of rooms, and probably only one bed. If the family were lucky then the soldiers might continue their march after just a night or two, but it could be several months over the winter or even years if they lived in a garrison town.

Moreover far from being paid for this inconvenience, while his regiment was soldiering in what is now modern day Poland in 1629, Peter Hagendorf recalls that the soldiers ran a sort of protection racket, demanding half a *taler* each from the head of the household in return for being able to keep their livestock.

In 1633 Peter Hagendorf records that Pappenheim's Regiment of Foot was quartered in Ravensburg, 'my quarters being near the Market Gate, with Johannes Stobel, a grocer. Good quarters.' Johannes Stobel not only had to billet Peter Hagendorf, but also his wife, Anna, who gave birth to a daughter Barbara. Unfortunately Barbara and then Peter' s wife died later that year.

Some accommodation was not as nice as that enjoyed by Peter Hagendorf. Father Drexel, when he saw the quarters of wounded soldiers, recorded in his diary for 21 August:

14 Ward, Book 2, p.32; Hexham, *The Prinicples of the Art Militarie*, part 2, p.4 (1642).
15 Wallhausen, *L'Art militaire pour l'Infantrie*, p.151.

> The condition of the patients was deplorable … In Linz there are now 1500. The bed of straw is filled with dung and lice which into their legs. Many lie on bare wood. Some did not get anything to eat for three or four days. Two or three dead are found every day … The misfortune of the patients in these stables is unimaginable.[16]

It would be not until the war ended that the misery of quartering soldiers ended for the inhabitants in Germany, even then it would be several more months before all the soldiers returned home.

16 Drexel, p.152.

9

Tactics

After mastering how to handle their designated weapons, the recruits would be taught how to manoeuvre in formation. For Catholic armies this has traditionally been seen as attacking in great lumbering formations which squandered their firepower by having the musketeers surround the formation; whereas the formations used by the Protestants, especially the Swedish, have been seen as modern and progressive. The 'Swedish brigade' formation had been developed by the Dutch during the Twelve Years Truce and adopted by the Danish, before Gustavus Adolphus introduced it to the battlefields of Germany. However, the Swedish infantry drew up six deep, whereas the Dutch were eight or 10 deep. This formation's 'progressive approach' appears to have been too complicated for inexperienced soldiers to manoeuvre with, so by the middle of the 1620s the Dutch had reverted back to their old system whereby the muskets drew up on each side of the pike block. Nevertheless, in the Swedish Army it appears to have been abandoned only after their defeat at the battle of Nördlingen in 1634. It did make a reappearance in 1642 at the battle of Edgehill during the English Civil War, when Prince Rupert insisted the Royalist infantry deploy in this fashion, although after this the Royalists adopted the Dutch formation, which they originally intended to do before Rupert's interference.

However, the large formations used by the Catholic armies, and some Protestant ones, had proved very effective since their introduction during the 15th century, when the Swiss pikemen ruled the battlefield, and up to the battle of Breitenfeld in 1632 the Catholics had swept all before them. These large formations are traditionally known as 'Tertios', but there is no contemporary evidence to confirm the name; when Johan von Wallhausen wrote a treatise on infantry tactics based on his experience during the sixteenth century, he never referred to them by that name nor in the French translation of his work. Instead they are referred to as regiments, and it is clear from Spanish sources, such as Barroso's *Teórica, Práctica y Exemplos* written in 1628, that when he refers to 'tertios' he is referring to the tactical unit, rather than the name of the formation.

Other contemporary writers refer to these large formations as 'battles', 'squadrons' or 'battalions'; in his book *A Discourse of Military Discipline* published in 1634 and dedicated to King Philip IV of Spain, Gerrat Barry mentions four types: a large

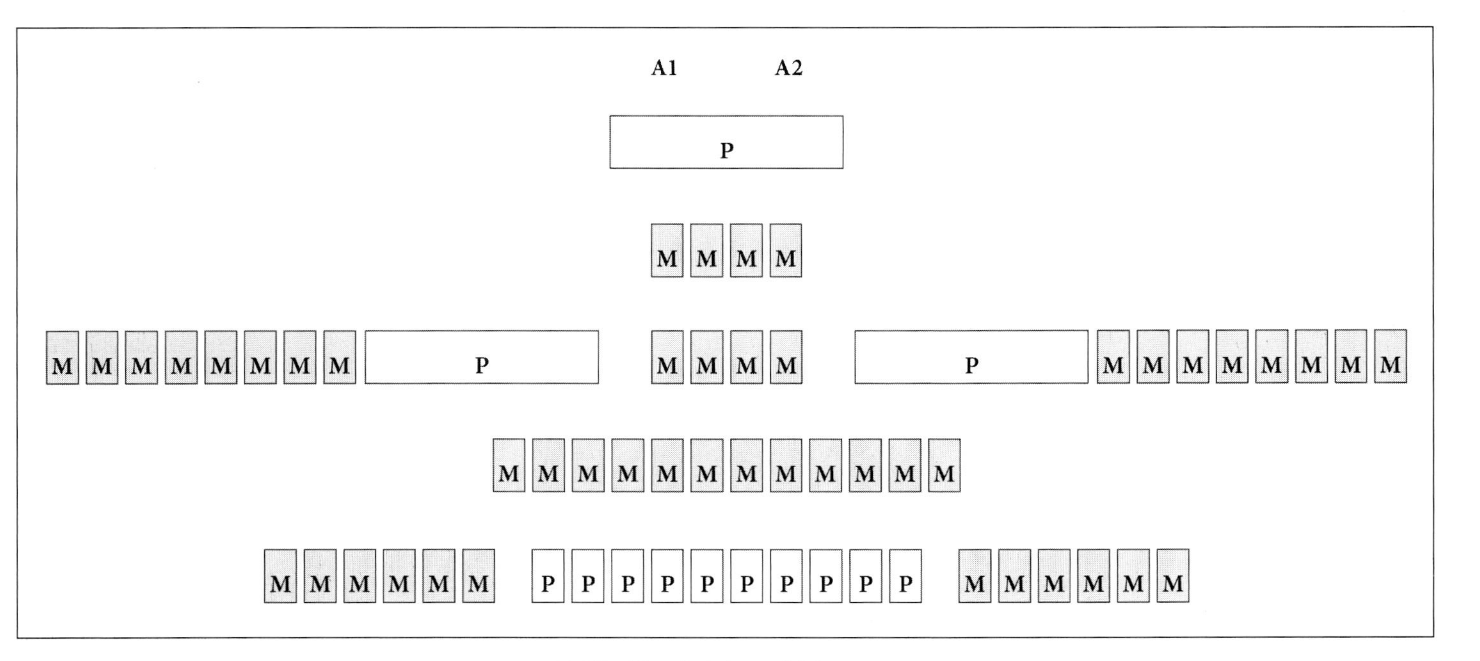

19. The ‘Swedish brigade’ formation.

'battle square' which could be composed of between 1,000 and 10,000 men, a smaller 'squadron square', which appears to be formed of fewer than 1,000 men, and a 'cross battle' which was formed by about 1,500 men divided into four and was formed in the shape of a cross. However, although Barry refers to them as squares some were more rectangular in shape having between 61–72 files by 26–31 ranks depending on how many infantry a general had and how many formations he required. The fourth formation Barry suggests is the 'triangle battle' whereby one man was in the first rank, three in the second, five in the third and so on. Unfortunately, he does not say why this formation should be used and it probably never was used on the battlefield. Extra musketeers could be drawn up in squadrons at the four corners of the formation and sometimes on its flanks. Barry also shows a 'squadron square' with a hollow centre, presumably where the musketeers etc. could retire if the formation was attacked by cavalry.[1]

Writing a few years after Barry, Raimondo Montecuccoli records that the infantry formations:

> [Have] customarily been formed in five different ways. 1. A square of men; 2. A terrain rectangle; 3. a double square; 4. an oblong rectangle; and 5. a rectangle the horizontal and vertical dimensions of which are determined according to a given ratio, the space which each soldier takes up marching in battle three feet in breath and seven in depth.

These formations are similar to those mentioned by Sieur Du Praissac in 1614, whose work was translated by John Cruso and published in English in 1639.

To form a regiment in a square formation, which was usually the job of the regiment's major, he had to know the number of men he had at his command and divide them by the square root, e.g. the square root of 100 is 10, which gives 10 ranks and 10 files. Any additional pikemen would be used to guard the colours.

However, Montecuccoli warns,

> A battalion can never fight effectively if it has more than six or seven ranks. This is because the pikes are eighteen feet long. The hands occupy three feet of the shaft and thus the remaining part extends fifteen feet beyond the first rank. The second rank in addition to the space.[2]

Praissac does not give a preference for which formation was best, just that 'the Spaniards often use double battalions. And the Hollanders broad fronted ones, that they make their files no deeper than ten men.' A double battalion had twice as many files as ranks, so a regiment of 2,000 men would have about 62 files and was 31 ranks deep, although he gives a square root table for commanders with up to 4,096 men. He also recommended that the formation should have a larger frontage than its opponent,

1 Gerrat Barry, *A Discourse of Military Discipline* (Brussels: 1634), p.125. He sometimes refers to these rectangular squares as 'squadrons on a broad front'.

2 Barker, p.90.

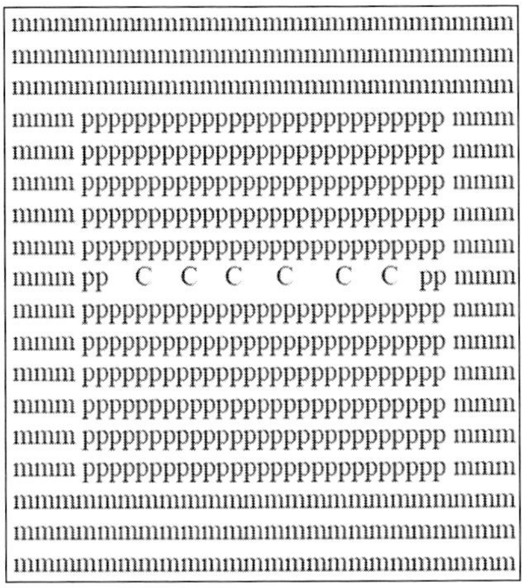

```
mmmmmmmmmmmmmmmmmmmmmmmmmmmmmmmmm
mmmmmmmmmmmmmmmmmmmmmmmmmmmmmmmmm
mmmmmmmmmmmmmmmmmmmmmmmmmmmmmmmmm
mmmm ppppppppppppppppppppppppppp mmmm
mmmm ppppppppppppppppppppppppppp mmmm
mmmm ppppppppppppppppppppppppppp mmmm
mmmm ppppppppppppppppppppppppppp mmmm
mmmm ppppppppppppppppppppppppppp mmmm
mmmm pp  C  C  C  C   C  C  pp mmmm
mmmm ppppppppppppppppppppppppppp mmmm
mmmm ppppppppppppppppppppppppppp mmmm
mmmm ppppppppppppppppppppppppppp mmmm
mmmm ppppppppppppppppppppppppppp mmmm
mmmm ppppppppppppppppppppppppppp mmmm
mmmm ppppppppppppppppppppppppppp mmmm
mmmmmmmmmmmmmmmmmmmmmmmmmmmmmmmmm
mmmmmmmmmmmmmmmmmmmmmmmmmmmmmmmmm
mmmmmmmmmmmmmmmmmmmmmmmmmmmmmmmmm
```

20. Left: A typical Spanish battalion used by the Bavarian Army at the beginning of the war (officers not included)

M = musketeer
P = pikemen
C = colours

Below: Arrangements of several Spanish battalions. Other formations might be drawn up in a straight line or in two lines.

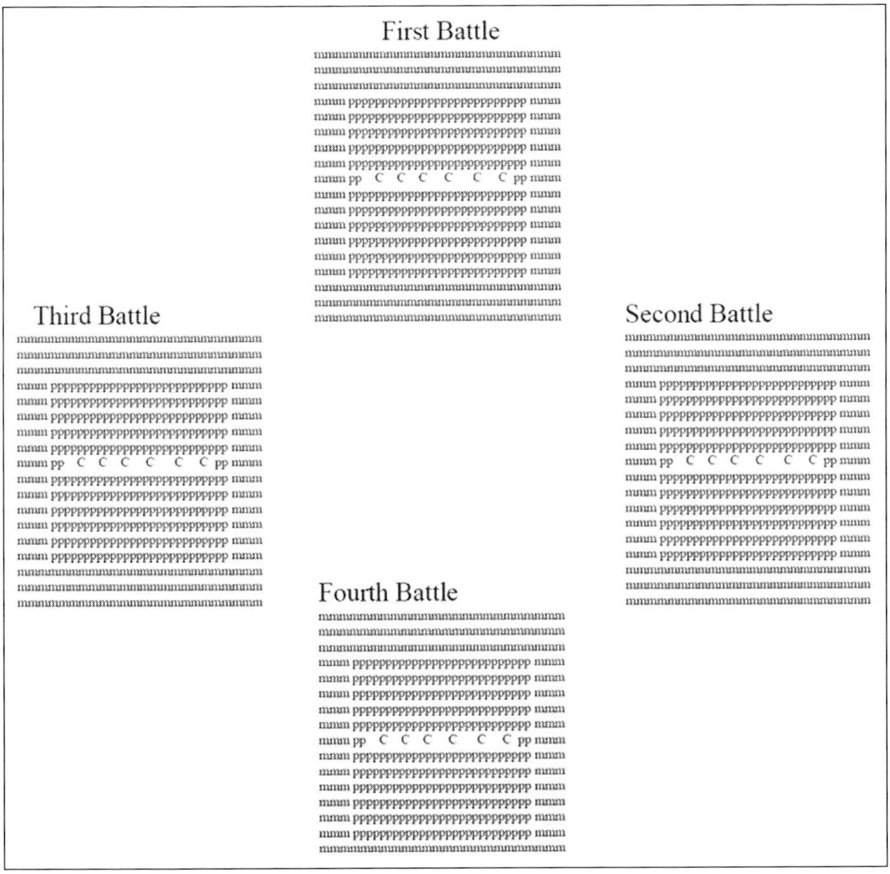

First Battle

```
mmmmmmmmmmmmmmmmmmmmmmmmmmmmmmmmm
mmmmmmmmmmmmmmmmmmmmmmmmmmmmmmmmm
mmmmmmmmmmmmmmmmmmmmmmmmmmmmmmmmm
mmmm ppppppppppppppppppppppppppp mmmm
mmmm ppppppppppppppppppppppppppp mmmm
mmmm ppppppppppppppppppppppppppp mmmm
mmmm ppppppppppppppppppppppppppp mmmm
mmmm ppppppppppppppppppppppppppp mmmm
mmmm pp  C  C  C  C   C  C  pp mmmm
mmmm ppppppppppppppppppppppppppp mmmm
mmmm ppppppppppppppppppppppppppp mmmm
mmmm ppppppppppppppppppppppppppp mmmm
mmmm ppppppppppppppppppppppppppp mmmm
mmmm ppppppppppppppppppppppppppp mmmm
mmmm ppppppppppppppppppppppppppp mmmm
mmmmmmmmmmmmmmmmmmmmmmmmmmmmmmmmm
mmmmmmmmmmmmmmmmmmmmmmmmmmmmmmmmm
mmmmmmmmmmmmmmmmmmmmmmmmmmmmmmmmm
```

Third Battle

```
mmmmmmmmmmmmmmmmmmmmmmmmmmmmmmmmm
mmmmmmmmmmmmmmmmmmmmmmmmmmmmmmmmm
mmmmmmmmmmmmmmmmmmmmmmmmmmmmmmmmm
mmmm ppppppppppppppppppppppppppp mmmm
mmmm ppppppppppppppppppppppppppp mmmm
mmmm ppppppppppppppppppppppppppp mmmm
mmmm ppppppppppppppppppppppppppp mmmm
mmmm ppppppppppppppppppppppppppp mmmm
mmmm pp  C  C  C  C   C  C  pp mmmm
mmmm ppppppppppppppppppppppppppp mmmm
mmmm ppppppppppppppppppppppppppp mmmm
mmmm ppppppppppppppppppppppppppp mmmm
mmmm ppppppppppppppppppppppppppp mmmm
mmmm ppppppppppppppppppppppppppp mmmm
mmmm ppppppppppppppppppppppppppp mmmm
mmmmmmmmmmmmmmmmmmmmmmmmmmmmmmmmm
mmmmmmmmmmmmmmmmmmmmmmmmmmmmmmmmm
mmmmmmmmmmmmmmmmmmmmmmmmmmmmmmmmm
```

Second Battle

```
mmmmmmmmmmmmmmmmmmmmmmmmmmmmmmmmm
mmmmmmmmmmmmmmmmmmmmmmmmmmmmmmmmm
mmmmmmmmmmmmmmmmmmmmmmmmmmmmmmmmm
mmmm ppppppppppppppppppppppppppp mmmm
mmmm ppppppppppppppppppppppppppp mmmm
mmmm ppppppppppppppppppppppppppp mmmm
mmmm ppppppppppppppppppppppppppp mmmm
mmmm ppppppppppppppppppppppppppp mmmm
mmmm pp  C  C  C  C   C  C  pp mmmm
mmmm ppppppppppppppppppppppppppp mmmm
mmmm ppppppppppppppppppppppppppp mmmm
mmmm ppppppppppppppppppppppppppp mmmm
mmmm ppppppppppppppppppppppppppp mmmm
mmmm ppppppppppppppppppppppppppp mmmm
mmmm ppppppppppppppppppppppppppp mmmm
mmmmmmmmmmmmmmmmmmmmmmmmmmmmmmmmm
mmmmmmmmmmmmmmmmmmmmmmmmmmmmmmmmm
mmmmmmmmmmmmmmmmmmmmmmmmmmmmmmmmm
```

Fourth Battle

```
mmmmmmmmmmmmmmmmmmmmmmmmmmmmmmmmm
mmmmmmmmmmmmmmmmmmmmmmmmmmmmmmmmm
mmmmmmmmmmmmmmmmmmmmmmmmmmmmmmmmm
mmmm ppppppppppppppppppppppppppp mmmm
mmmm ppppppppppppppppppppppppppp mmmm
mmmm ppppppppppppppppppppppppppp mmmm
mmmm ppppppppppppppppppppppppppp mmmm
mmmm ppppppppppppppppppppppppppp mmmm
mmmm pp  C  C  C  C   C  C  pp mmmm
mmmm ppppppppppppppppppppppppppp mmmm
mmmm ppppppppppppppppppppppppppp mmmm
mmmm ppppppppppppppppppppppppppp mmmm
mmmm ppppppppppppppppppppppppppp mmmm
mmmm ppppppppppppppppppppppppppp mmmm
mmmm ppppppppppppppppppppppppppp mmmm
mmmmmmmmmmmmmmmmmmmmmmmmmmmmmmmmm
```

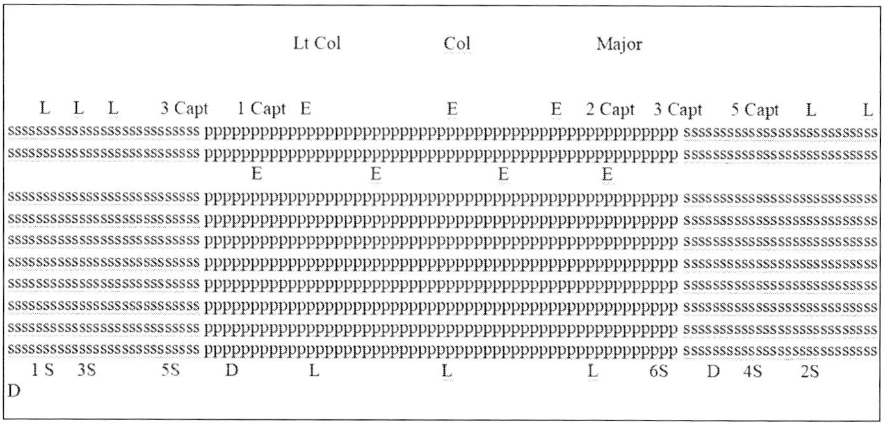

```
                                  Lt Col              Col                 Major

   L   L   L      3 Capt     1 Capt  E                      E              E   2 Capt   3 Capt     5 Capt    L      L
ssssssssssssssssssssssssssssssssssss pppppppppppppppppppppppppppppppppppppppppppppppppppppppppppp ssssssssssssssssssssssssssssssssssss
ssssssssssssssssssssssssssssssssssss pppppppppppppppppppppppppppppppppppppppppppppppppppppppppppp ssssssssssssssssssssssssssssssssssss
                                   E             E              E             E
ssssssssssssssssssssssssssssssssssss pppppppppppppppppppppppppppppppppppppppppppppppppppppppppppp ssssssssssssssssssssssssssssssssssss
ssssssssssssssssssssssssssssssssssss pppppppppppppppppppppppppppppppppppppppppppppppppppppppppppp ssssssssssssssssssssssssssssssssssss
ssssssssssssssssssssssssssssssssssss pppppppppppppppppppppppppppppppppppppppppppppppppppppppppppp ssssssssssssssssssssssssssssssssssss
ssssssssssssssssssssssssssssssssssss pppppppppppppppppppppppppppppppppppppppppppppppppppppppppppp ssssssssssssssssssssssssssssssssssss
ssssssssssssssssssssssssssssssssssss pppppppppppppppppppppppppppppppppppppppppppppppppppppppppppp ssssssssssssssssssssssssssssssssssss
ssssssssssssssssssssssssssssssssssss pppppppppppppppppppppppppppppppppppppppppppppppppppppppppppp ssssssssssssssssssssssssssssssssssss
ssssssssssssssssssssssssssssssssssss pppppppppppppppppppppppppppppppppppppppppppppppppppppppppppp ssssssssssssssssssssssssssssssssssss
ssssssssssssssssssssssssssssssssssss pppppppppppppppppppppppppppppppppppppppppppppppppppppppppppp ssssssssssssssssssssssssssssssssssss
   1 S   3S         5S       D          L               L                L      6S     D   4S      2S
D
```

21. Above: a regiment drawn up in the Dutch style. By the mid 1630s the Bavarian Army had abandoned the Spanish formation in favour of the Dutch system.

Key:
Col = colonel; Lt Col = lieutenant colonel;
Capt = captain; L = lieutenant;
E = ensign; S = sergeant D = drummer;
s = shot; p = pike

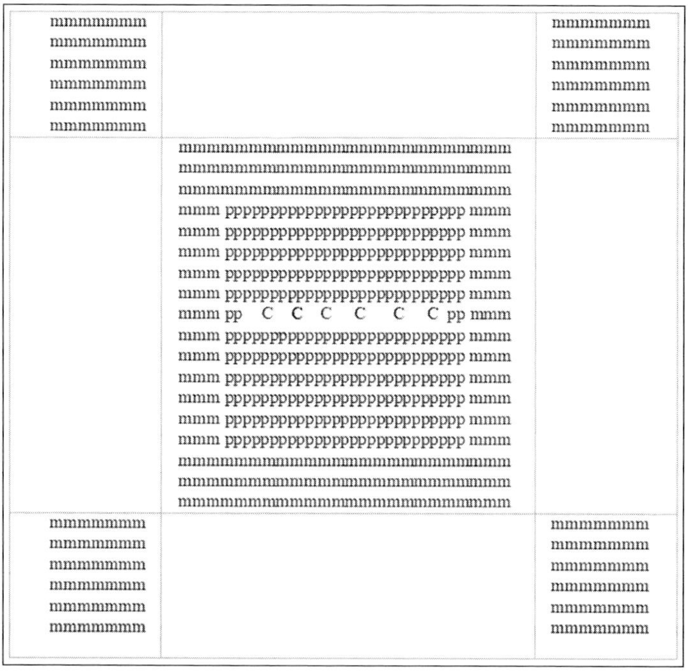

```
mmmmmmmm                                            mmmmmmmm
mmmmmmmm                                            mmmmmmmm
mmmmmmmm                                            mmmmmmmm
mmmmmmmm                                            mmmmmmmm
mmmmmmmm                                            mmmmmmmm
mmmmmmmm                                            mmmmmmmm
           mmmmmmmmmmmmmmmmmmmmmmmmmmmm
           mmmmmmmmmmmmmmmmmmmmmmmmmmmm
           mmmmmmmmmmmmmmmmmmmmmmmmmmmm
           mmm pppppppppppppppppppppppppppppp mmm
           mmm pppppppppppppppppppppppppppppp mmm
           mmm pppppppppppppppppppppppppppppp mmm
           mmm pppppppppppppppppppppppppppppp mmm
           mmm pppppppppppppppppppppppppppppp mmm
           mmm pp   C   C   C   C   C   C pp mmm
           mmm pppppppppppppppppppppppppppppp mmm
           mmm pppppppppppppppppppppppppppppp mmm
           mmm pppppppppppppppppppppppppppppp mmm
           mmm pppppppppppppppppppppppppppppp mmm
           mmm pppppppppppppppppppppppppppppp mmm
           mmm pppppppppppppppppppppppppppppp mmm
           mmmmmmmmmmmmmmmmmmmmmmmmmmmm
           mmmmmmmmmmmmmmmmmmmmmmmmmmmm
           mmmmmmmmmmmmmmmmmmmmmmmmmmmm
mmmmmmmm                                            mmmmmmmm
mmmmmmmm                                            mmmmmmmm
mmmmmmmm                                            mmmmmmmm
mmmmmmmm                                            mmmmmmmm
mmmmmmmm                                            mmmmmmmm
mmmmmmmm                                            mmmmmmmm
```

22. Above: a variant of the Spanish battalion, with sleeves of musketeers at each corner. These sleeves could be between 64 and 81 musketeers strong.

so if the infantry occupied three feet distance square then a formation of 2,000 men would be 186 feet long and 93 feet in depth.[3]

Montecuccoli continues:

> Large bodies of men are inconvenient because they require a very level battlefield: without the latter they cannot maintain good order. Nor can they function effectively on either their right or left flank; they can only fight frontally. Once they are routed, it is difficult to pull them together and repair the damage which is like that of a building that has collapsed and cannot be fixed unless it is completely reconstructed. Of course, it is quite true that to protect and salvage one's forces during a retreat or in order not to be attacked, such large solid and massive corps are quite useful. Since they are immobile and of little offensive value, yet are difficult to break, they do serve a purpose when one wishes to defend one's self.[4]

However, at the Battle of White Mountain the Catholic army did take the offensive against the Bohemians who were arrayed at the top of the hill. Amongst the Spanish–Catholic League's army was Verdugo's Regiment, which 'advanced with fine resolution up to four pike lengths' from the enemy before the musketeers gave fire. This, and no doubt the sight of the battalion, made the Bohemians 'take fright and began to retreat, and so the right platoon gained the crescent and the left the battery.'[5]

Christian of Anholt also recorded that the Bohemian Army panicked at the sight of the advancing enemy: 'As soon as the enemy arrived about 300 or 400 paces from Count Thurn's Infantry, our soldiers started to shoot without order or sense and, even against expressed ordered, shot in the air and immediately started to flee, seemingly in the grip of fear.'[6]

This is not the only account of these large formations of infantry advancing. In his account of the Battle of Breitenfeld, on 17 September 1631, the Swedish officer, General Horn, describes Tilly's infantry:

> The main battle of the enemy which comprehended the whole force of his infantry and was parted into four great Spanish Battalions (consisting of 16 regiments) marched down the hill with the cavalry which stood on the right and left hand thereof and being sorely galled with the artillery discharged from our left wing they changed their station, in such a manner as that the most of them fell upon the Elector's [of Saxony's] Army.[7]

True, other regiments met with mixed success at the Battle of White Mountain, and at Breitenfeld Tilly's army was routed, but these two accounts clearly show that these large formations did have an offensive capability. Moreover, Napoleon would

3 Sieur Du Praissac, *A short method for the easie resolving of any militarie question propounded, translated by John Cruso* (Cambridge: Roger Daniel, 1639), pp.28, 196–201.
4 Barker, p.90.
5 Louis de Haynin, seigneur du Cornet, *Histoire Générale des guerres de Savoie, de Bohême, du Palatinat & des Pays-Bas, 1616–1627* (Brussels: C. Muquardt, 1868), vol. 1, p.175.
6 Letter from Christian of Anhalt to Frederick V, quoted in Wilson, *The Thirty Years War: A Sourcebook*, p.65.
7 TNA: SP 95/3, f.121, General Horn's Account of the battle of Leipzig, 7/17 September 1631.

rely on dense columns when he attacked enemy positions during the Napoleonic Wars, which dwarfed those used during the Thirty Years War.

When these formations advanced upon the enemy's infantry, according to Gerrat Barry,

> Coming within reach of the musket then the first ranks of the wings of musketeers are to march in this manner; the first ranks stepping some two or three paces forward having cocked their matches, then with readiness and expedition all those of the first ranks (their muskets being upon their rests or forks) to discharge at once, permitting other ranks to proceed, then presently those of the second rank to step up before the first rank, as the battle or battalion do march, and so to discharge as their former fellows had done before, and then the third rank before the second and the four, before the third, and so all the other ranks consequently with this kind of double march and at the train of the last rank those of the first to follow up again, and so consequently the rest. But if chance that the squadron of pikes be distressed or constrained to retire, they are to discharge at the enemy, retiring back upon a counter march, and with speed fall back into their rank, to give place to the next ranks, and no time be idly employed.[8]

It is generally believed that Gustavus Adolphus, introduced the practice of firing by three ranks in a 'Swedish volley'. However the English writer Gervase Markham, in his 1625 drill book, also mentions this type of firing, describing it as an 'ancient and vulgar manner of discipline', because:

> In teaching to give volleys ... (which is that the whole volley shall be given of all the shot in one instant as well of them behind as before [in front] is utterly to be condemned for either the hindmost must venture to shoot their fellows before through the heads or else will over shoot and so spend their shot improfitably. Besides the volley being once given, the enemy comes on without impeachment or annoyance.[9]

He does not mention this type of volley in the first part of his *Soldiers Grammar*, but in the second part he does refer to it when repelling enemy cavalry, insomuch that it is better to fire single volleys when surrounded by the pikes:

> So that the volley is given entirely and without impeachment or trouble to one ... another. Whereas to shoot over one another's shoulder or by making the first man kneel, the second stoop, the third bend his body, the fourth lean forward and the fifth to stand upright and so deliver their volley both rude and disorderly, bringing great danger to the soldier and placing them in such a lame and uncomely posture.[10]

When advancing in a formation Praissac states that:

8 Barry, p.134.
9 Gervase Markham, *The Souldiers Exercise* (London, 1639), p.9.
10 Gervase Markham, *The Second Part of the Soldiers Grammar* (London: A Matthews, 1927), p.23.

> You must not give on so hastily … [by this] the Battalion be disordered … you are to use a marching pace until you come within a pistol shot by then to double your pace and to charge furiously the pikes being close to serried and the muskets continually playing on the flanks, having targeteers in front which may shelter the battalion and disorder the enemy pike.[11]

Unfortunately, when it comes to how the pikes performed in battle, there are few examples except that they were to protect the musketeers against enemy cavalry. Writing in 1591, William Garrard records that:

> When the soldiers are joined and closed in battle with their pikes and when they stand in term to fight … the battle is to close and join as straight together as is possible, in such sort as they may manage and bestir themselves with their weapons, without being an impediment one to another, to the intent that the ranks being straight in fighting, or that the soldiers be invaded by their enemies, or that they recoil by force of an onset, they need not to fall to the ground, but rather that they may by those ranks that be behind receive help, that under setting them with their breasts they may hold them straight up upon their feet.[12]

Sir John Smythe, writing in 1595, agrees with Garrard that the rear ranks should support the front ranks when it comes to 'push of pike':

> [When the pikes are] ready to encounter with another … letting fall the points of their pikes and carry them close breast high with both hands steadily and firmly, the points full in the faces of their enemies. And the second rank likewise straightening and closing themselves by rank and front and joining themselves to back of the first rank, and following them step with step carrying their pikes above hand over the shoulders of the first rank, the points of their pikes likewise towards the faces of the enemies.

Once the pikemen come into contact with the enemy then Smythe suggests that they make a 'pushing and foining [i.e. thrusting]' movement as they press forward without standing and 'give a puissant thrust into the faces of the enemy and so force the front ranks onto the rear ones.'[13] In 1627 Sir Thomas Kellie stated that, 'When battles [formations] come to push of pike, good commanders sayeth that your pikemen must not push by advancing and retiring their arm as commonly is done, but only go jointly on together without moving their arms.'[14]

Once the pikemen could no longer use their pikes, because the enemy had come within the length of their pikes, then according to Smythe they often resorted to their swords, although in 1627 during the landing of the Duke of Buckingham's Army at the Isle of Rhé one account records, the pikemen, 'fell to it with swords and push

11 Praissac, *A short method*, p.28.
12 Garrard, p.219.
13 Sir John Smythe, *Instructions, Observations and Orders Mylitarie* (London: 1595), pp.23–27.
14 Thomas Kellie, *Pallas Armata or the Art of Instructions for the Learned: and all generous spirits who effect the Profession of Arms* (Edinburgh, 1627), p.25.

of pike, until they were breathless on both sides. The French finding our pikes to be longer than theirs, threw away their pikes and went to it with stones and so did our men, but ours beat them out and made them fly.'[15]

Johann von Wallhausen suggested that in hand-to-hand fighting the musketeers not only use their muskets as a club, but also their bandoliers, musket rests, helmets and fists. During the English Civil War there were many references to musketeers 'falling on' with 'clubbed muskets'. An English volunteer in the King of Bohemia's army also recalls, 'our General gave command to draw out part of every company to be of the forlorne hope to give onset … [we] threw away our snapsacks, with all our provisions, both linen and woollen because it would be troublesome to us.'[16]

Having the musketeers surround the pikemen made it easier for them to shelter between the latter if attacked by cavalry, whereas the Dutch formations required the regiment to form a square, which took time. At the battle of Lützen the Swedish Blue Regiment was surprised by Imperialist cavalry on their flanks while engaging the enemy's infantry to their front, and were cut to pieces.

However, Breitenfeld was the beginning of the end of these large infantry formations. During the early 1630s Raimondo Montecuccoli recalls, 'In the Imperial army it is customary to make the battalions seven men deep placing the remainder in front. If the total is between 300 and 400 pikes Friedland [Wallenstein] made the number of ranks in even, so that the ensigns would be stationed exactly in the middle of the unit, i.e. the fourth row.'[17]

Curiously the publication *Theatrum Europaeum* shows Tilly's army in the Dutch formation at the Battles of Höchst and Wimpfen, although it was probably artistic licence as it was published in 1646 when this formation had been universally adopted.[18]

The Dutch formation usually drew up in 10 (later eight) ranks deep and divided the musketeers equally between both flanks of the pike block. Each soldier had his own place of importance in the following order:

File	Order of Importance
1	1 (leader)
2	5
3	9
4	8
5	4 (middle man)
6	3 (middle man or half file leader)

15 Smythe, pp.23-27; Mr. Gareston, *A Continued journal of all the Proceedings of the Duke of Buckingham on the Isle of Ree*(London: 1627), p.7.
16 John Bingham, *Tacticks of Aelian* (London: 1616), p.84; Johann von Wallhausen, *Kriegskunst zu Fuss* (Oppenheim, 1615); *A Relation of the passage of our English Companies from time to time…* (London: 1621).
17 Barker, p.90.
18 Abelin, vol 2., pp.635, 692.

File	Order of Importance
7	7
8	10
9	6
10	2 (bringer up)

When the order was given to 'double your ranks and files', the 10 ranks would become five with the half file leaders moving up to the file leader. As the English writer, John Bingham, points out, that this manoeuvre 'bringeth as many hands to fight as the proportion of the forces will allow.'[19]

The seniority (called a 'dignity') of the files was as follows:

Ranks	10	9	8	7	6	5	4	3	2	1
Order of Importance	2	6	10	7	3	4	8	9	5	1

Therefore a block of either musketeers or pikemen would consist of 100 men.

The cavalry were traditionally deployed on the wings of the army and for the cavalry officer they could turn to the works by Wallhausen, Giorgio Basta and Ludovico Melzo who were some of the leading tacticians of the day. Melzo first published his work on cavalry in 1611 and by 1626 it had been republished 16 times and translated into German and French as well as the original Italian.[20]

However, these tacticians disagreed on certain points, including how many ranks the cavalry were to draw up in: some advocated five for cuirassiers while others recommended six, which could be 'doubled to three deep on occasion', which predates Gustavus Adolphus' reforms; although according to Wallhausen harquebusiers should be drawn up in eight ranks and the cuirassiers 10. These ranks and files had the same seniority as the infantry, with the file leader being the most important and the bringer up the second.

As with the infantry there were various ways the cavalry could fight in battle. According to John Cruso, who studied the works by Wallhausen, Melzo and Basta, the cavalry:

> Must be exercised to give fire by ranks. The first rank, having given fire, is to wheel off to the left (unless the ground will not permit it, but that it must be to the right) making ready and falling into the rear, the second rank immediately gives fire upon the wheeling away of the first, and so the rest successively ... But others do utterly reject it, as too much

19 John Bingham, *The Art of Embattailing an Army, or,the second part of Aelians tacticks* (London: 1631), p.16.

20 Johann von Wallhausen, *Art Militare a Cheval*, Giorgio Basta, *Il Governo della cavalleria Leggera* (Bernardo Giunta, Giovanni Battista Ciotti & C. Venezia, 1612), and Ludovico Melzo, *Regole, Militari del Cavalier Melzo sopra il governon e servitio della cavalleria* (1611).

> exposed to danger. In their firing by ranks, the first rank advanceth some 30 paces before the body, first on the gallop, then in career (as some direct) and so to give fire; the second doth the same and so the rest.[21]

Although Basta and Wallhausen do not refer to it by this name, the manoeuvre is usually referred to as the Caracole, or Snail, and was usually performed when the cavalry were skirmishing. Wallhausen refers to the Caracole manoeuvre as when a body of cavalry splits in two allowing the enemy cavalry to charge through the newly made gap in the line, while being raked by pistol shot. However, it was a dangerous manoeuvre to perform because the cavalry unit might be caught while it was deploying and put to flight. It was during the pursuit of a regiment that it usually suffered the most casualties. It is said that the king of Denmark lost only 600 men during the battle of Lutter itself, but 3,000 were killed in the pursuit afterwards. Certainly it would be useless for the heavily armed cuirassiers to fire their pistols at anything less than point blank range since their armour was, in theory, pistol proof.

It has been said that Gustavus Adolphus introduced the cavalry charge into western Europe, when on the eve of the Battle of Breitenfeld he ordered that, 'only the first or at most the first two ranks, when near enough to see the whites of the enemy's eyes were to give fire, then to reach for their swords; the last rank however was to keep both pistols (or in the front ranks, one) in reserve for the melee.' Robert Monro records that during the battle the Swedish cavalry waited for the Imperialists to fire first, then after a volley of musketry, 'our horsemen discharged their pistols and then charged through them with swords.'[22]

Since the cavalry had to see the 'whites of the enemy's eyes' before they fired their pistols, the cavalry must have made contact at a walk. Moreover far from Gustavus Adolphus introducing the cavalry charge, Sir John Smythe suggested that a squadron:

> Should charge but 30 paces, that is 20 galloping … and 10 for their full career to give them the greatest blow and shock … [any further] they shall find themselves in so great a distance greatly disordered and confounded in their ranks and their horses out of breath and thereby the force of their blow and shock greatly weakened when the come to encounter with the squadron of the enemy.

He also suggests that about 10 paces from the enemy the cavalrymen should give a 'terrible shout' and that if they themselves are charged, then to advance to meet the enemy, which would then result in a general melee.[23]

In 1625 Gervase Markham records that on the word *Passe a Cariere* the trooper should:

21 Cruso, *Military instructions for the Cavall'rie*, pp.97–98.
22 Monro, part II, p.65; Chemnitz, quoted in Richard Brzezinski and Richard Hook, *The Army of Gustavus Adolphus 2: Cavalry* (Oxford: Osprey Publishing, 1993), p.23.
23 Sir John Smythe, *Instructions, Observations and Orders Mylitarie* (1595), p.169.

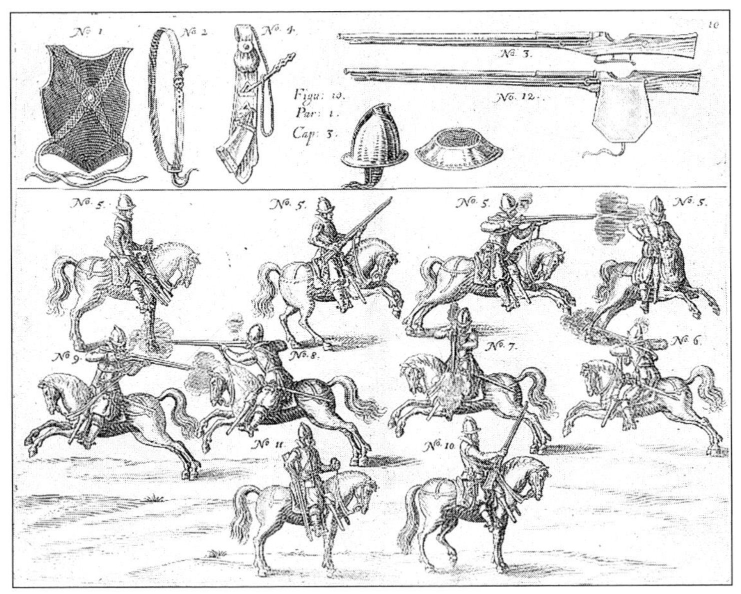

23. The 'caracole' tactic as depicted in a military manual. The tactic was an attempt to integrate firearms into cavalry operations, but its effectiveness is much debated.

> [Thrust the] horse violently forward both with his legs and body and giving liberty to his bridle. As soon as the horse is started into his gallop he shall give him the even stroke of his spurs, one or twice together and make the horse run to the height of his full speed … which will not be above six score or eight score yards.[24]

According to Montecuccoli, cuirassiers 'are the most suitable instruments of combat for creating stability, providing support and absorbing shock.' Sydnam Poyntz records that, at the battle of Lützen, Piccolomini's Regiment of Cuirassiers 'at the first coming made a wonderful breach through the King's Finlanders, who are light horsemen, but lighting upon a Brigade of the King's infantry, thinking to break throw them also, the foot received them with such a volley of shot they were constrained to retire.'[25]

In another incident during the battle an unnamed cuirassier officer mortally wounded Gustavus Adolphus, and as the Swedes tried to rescue him, 'the cuirassiers charged so fiercely in upon the Swedish; that they were not able to bring off the dying king.' True, Piccolomini's Regiment was forced to retreat, but these two accounts hardly suggest a slow plodding attack.[26]

24 Markham, *The Souldiers Accidence*, p.52.

25 Sydnam Poyntz, *A True Relation of these German Warres From Mansfeld's Going out of England which was in the yeare (1624) untill this last year of 1636 whereof my self was an eyewitness of most I have here related* (Tonbridge: Pallas Armata, 1992), p.73; Barker, p.108.

26 *The Swedish Intelligencer, the third part* (London: 1633), p.173.

On the other hand Melzo, Basta, and Wallhausen suggested that the cavalry should charge at the trot rather than the gallop in order to keep the formation tight, although even this had its problems, because if a horse was killed or stumbled then it would bring down the other horses behind it, killing or wounding their riders. As with the ranks of the infantry, the front and rear ranks were the most important because they would steady the rest of the squadron of cavalry; otherwise:

> Even though the brave soldiers (who are in the minority) proceed resolutely to the fray, the others (who have no desire to take the bit into their mouth) remain behind. And so, over a distance of 200 paces, one sees this long rank thin out and dissolve. Great breaches appear within it ... On many occasions only twenty or twenty five of a hundred horse actually charge. Then, when they have realized that they have no support or backing, after having fired a few pistol shots and after having delivered a few thrusts of their swords, they withdraw, assuming that they have not been immediately overturned themselves.[27]

Squadrons were made up of one or more troops of horse and varied between 200 and 300 troopers. When they deployed in battle order the squadrons were deployed in a chequer board formation so that the second rank could cover the intervals between those in the front rank, which according to Raimondo Montecuccoli:

> The foe would be showing great temerity if he were to dash into the gaps, passing by and offering his flanks to the two units posted behind the first line ... such a disposition is that since the troops cannot be attacked, they remain an unknown factor. The mere sight of them does not fail to make the foe suspicious and uneasy. They keep him intimidated because they can always advance when and if they want to.

However, the disadvantage of this formation is that if a squadron in the front line had to retreat then it usually wheeled to the right or left, then 'it is a matter of sheer luck if it happens to meet quite precisely that vacant space to its right or left.'[28]

As for harquebusiers, they could skirmish at a greater distance with their carbines than the cuirassiers with their pistols, but they lacked the weight in a charge. According to Montecuccoli, Tilly was 'accustomed to say that he would never have seriously considered using harquebusiers in a military engagement.' They also performed badly at the battle of Lützen which prompted Albrecht von Wallenstein to write to General Johann Aldringen that the harquebusiers had:

> Failed to injure the foe, even a little, but on the contrary these troops had either thrown the other [friendly] cavalry into disarray as a result of being thrust back upon it or else had

27 Barker, p.92.
28 *Ibid.*, pp.94–96.

24. Tercio deployed at Nördlingen behind earthworks, 1634.

> hindered the latter when it began to charge. Thus he unconditionally commanded all the commanders of horse to abolish the carbines and to supply such regiments with cuirasses.[29]

Certainly, when a colonel could afford to he usually re-equipped his harquebusier regiment to become cuirassiers, since the cuirassiers were seen as having a more important role on the battlefield and so were higher in status. However, despite the advantages in battle a cuirassier regiment was expensive to maintain, and by the end of the war many troopers had discarded their cuirassier armour in favour of that of a harquebusier.

During the sixteenth century the lancers would have led the way and forced open any gaps which had appeared, but by the beginning of the seventeenth century lancers were in decline and only appeared on the battlefield as a general's lifeguard. Certainly Matthias Merian in his Theatrum Europeaum shows the Cardinal Infante's Guard at the battle of Nördlingen armed with lances and Wallenstein's lifeguard also appears to have included lancers.

When lancers were used, Montecuccoli recommended that they should be drawn up in two ranks of 25 men each:

> Since they are effective only because of the fury which characterises their entry into the battle; the enemy is put to flight by the mad dash of the horses. Once the lance has torn

29 *Ibid.*, pp.108, 110.

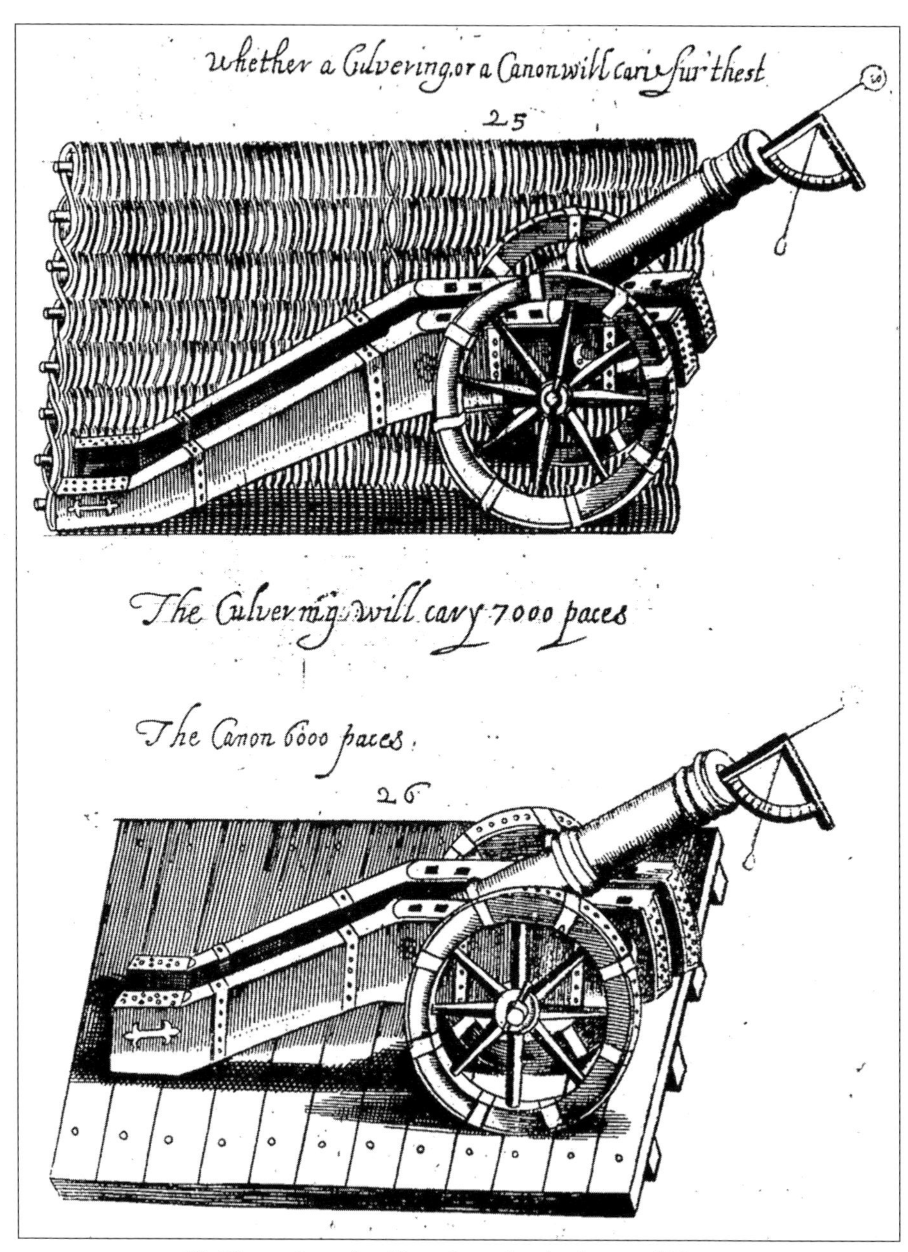

25. Illustration of artillery from the third part of Henry Hexham's *Principles of the Art Military*, 1643 edition.

> open a gap, it is seconded by the cuirassiers, arrayed in serried ranks. This weapon then proceeds to bowl over and rout all that it encounters.

Wallhausen suggested a similar tactic: that the lancers would make a gap in the enemy's ranks which was exploited by the cuirassiers.[30]

As lancers were declining in popularity dragoons were being introduced. Dragoons were mounted infantry and would ride to the battlefield on inferior horses to those of the cavalry, and then dismount and fight on foot. According to Wallhausen a company of dragoons should muster 200 men: 100 pikemen, who were to form up 10 ranks deep, and 100 musketeers divided into two bodies of 50 and also drawn up in 10 ranks by five files, and placed on each flank of the pikes.[31] As well as their role on the battlefield dragoons were ideal for ambushes, patrols and escorting convoys. Detachments from the foot regiments could also be mounted temporarily as dragoons. Sydnam Poyntz, who was then with Count Ernst von Mansfeld at Troppo, recalls 'our pikemen were made dragooners.' Why Mansfeld should just choose a detachment of pikemen as dragoons Poyntz does not say, although he does say that his musketeers were loaded into wagons some days later.[32]

Croats, being light cavalry, had little shock value when it came to a clash on the battlefield, but they were usually posted on the far end of the cavalry wing so that they could outflank their opponents, while the enemy's troops were engaged with friendly cavalry. This tactic met with great success and at the Battle of Breitenfeld Colonels Palant's and Saradetzky's Regiments captured several colours belonging to the Saxon regiments of Ernest von Starscheledel and Hans Casper von Klitzing, with little loss to themselves.

Praissac recommended in his *Arte of Warre* that, in battle:

> The artillery ought to be so placed that it hinder not the passage of the battalions, and that it may easily discover those of the enemy. For the most part the infantry is within the body of the army, in several Battalions, disposed chequer wise: the cavalry on their wings and rear in several squadrons, and the artillery according to the convenience of the place, so the Front of the Army or on the flanks of the Battalions … The artillery must play so soon as they begin to discover the battalions of the enemy; making the battery fully and speedily to disorder and scatter them before they come to give battle.[33]

The larger guns such as the culverin had a maximum range of 2,100 paces, so that they could probably hit the enemy forces even before they advanced, and would probably be able to fire several shots before the enemy came within point blank range of 400 paces. By now the smaller artillery pieces would have begun firing: the sakeret or minion had a range of between 280 and 1,400 paces and a falcon 260 and 1,200

30 *Ibid.*, p.106.
31 Wallhausen, p.55.
32 Poyntz, vol. 1, p.48.
33 Praissac, *The Arte of Warre*, p.27.

paces, so the battalions would be under constant fire. There are accounts of whole ranks being swept away, and Robert Monro who was serving in Colonel Donald Mackay's Regiment in the Danish Army, recalls that a lieutenant and thirteen soldiers had their heads shot off by one cannon bullet. While in another incident Monro, whose regiment by now had transferred to the Swedish service, recalls that at the crossing of the Lech, Gustavus Adolphus formed his artillery up in a large battery of 72 pieces of cannon. These 'played continually into the middest of Tilly's Army [all day], who were drawn up in Battle' on the opposite bank of the Lech, 'where many were made to lie dead by our cannon, for those that were not hurt by the bullets, they were lamed by branches and trees, cut by the cannon.'[34]

Whatever their tactics, many probably performed the following ritual that Father Fitzsimon observed just before the Battle of White Mountain on 8 November 1620:

> The chaplains were hearing confessions most zealously, and especially the Fathers of the Society [Jesuits], who shirked no labour or dangers in this campaign. Eight of these Fathers were carried off suddenly in the Bavarian Army alone. Many of the bravest soldiers were saying their beads, and kissing their crucifixes. Then they eat something and called out to be led to battle.[35]

The artillery pieces might also be blessed before they opened fire on the enemy.

After this Father Fitzsimons was ordered to recite the *Salve Regina* and was answered by Maximilian and General Bucquoy who commanded the Imperialist troops at that time. The commanders may have given their men a rousing speech before the trumpets sounded the advance, but for many their prayers to keep them safe would go unanswered.

The early seventeenth century soldier was more likely to take part in skirmishes, or form part of a garrison or besiege a town than take part in a large battle. The news sheet *More News from the Palatinate* for 5 June 1622 gives some advice concerning ambushes when fighting in wooded countryside with the defendant has the advantage over the assailant:

> That they need not fear either ambush or surprise, but the assailant is rather weary to enter those thicket for fear of falling himself into an ambuscado ... [by] an enemy in the wood, the enemy can have small use of his horse and the trees and bushes make his pikes mostly unserviceable too. As for the shot, they may go abirding if they please for any great good they can do for they shall be sure to hit more trees then men; whereas the defendants may better use their arms; for their body of pikes may be orderly ranged and may make a firm stand and are not encumbered with carrying and entangling them among the trees, but need no more but charge them upon the assailants and every tree again is as good as a tower for a musketeer from behind which he may at pleasure and in

34 Monro, part I, pp.65–66, part II pp.116–117.
35 Fitzsimon, p.97.

safety almost discharge and the tree serves him for a rest too: so then an army there fears nothing but firing the coppis about their ears.[36]

Newssheets often printed how many towns a general had captured, therefore for a general, knowing how to defend or attack a town was just as important as knowing the latest formations in the field.

The old medieval stone walls of towns and cities could no longer withstand the onslaughts of heavy siege artillery pieces of the sixteenth and seventeenth centuries, therefore they needed extra protection in the form of earthworks. Commanders had a large variety of military manuals which they could use to construct these earthworks, such as Pietro Sardi's *Corona imperiale dell'architettura militare divisa in due trattati. Il primo contiene la teorica. Il secondo contiene la pratica,*[37]which described the theory and practice of siege warfare in two volumes, including the purpose of fortifications, how to assault them, their form and the materials used to construction them. To illustrate the text it had 37 examples of bastions and other fortifications, and such was its popularity that it was translated into French and German at Frankfurt and published in 1622 and 1623. It was reprinted again in Italian in 1639. On the other hand Symon Stevin's *Nieuwe maniere van sterctebow door spilsluysen*,[38] which contained 38 diagrams and plans of fortifications seems to have been less popular being only translated into French the following year.

Whatever manual a commander or his engineer used, they all had a similar description of the fortifications to use and where to use them, so that an arrow-shaped bastion or 'horn work' might be used to guard the gates of a city and joined by a ravelin which was a curtain wall of earth. These ravelins might also be interspersed with additional earthworks and protected by a moat (where the earth came from) and pallisadoes, which were described by Sir Balthazar Gerbier as being 'high stakes of timber, set together like pales, shod on the top with iron forked heads', which were placed on the top, middle and/or the base of the work to make it harder for storming parties to get a foothold on these defences. Star-shaped earthworks might be used to prevent or delay the enemy from approaching the city too closely or to protect a strategic place, such as a bridge or river, or be placed in the vicinity of the town.[39]

An area within these fortifications would be allocated to artillery pieces and musketeers would line the rest of the fortifications, so many regiments raised for garrison duties were only armed as musketeers since pikemen were considered useless when it came to the defence of a town. However, even though it was usually the citizens of the town who were called upon to dig these fortifications, they could be expensive particularly if they were multilayered. Sienna is a good example: during the sixteenth century its government paid to fortify the city in the latest fashion, only to

36 *More News from the Palatinate*, 5 June 1622, pp.6–7.
37 Venice: Barezzo Barezzi, 1618.
38 Rotterdam: Ian van Waesberghe, 1617.
39 Sir Balthazar Gerbier, *The First Lecture being an introduction to the Military Architecture or fortifications, read publically at Sir Balthazar Gerbiers Academy* (London: Robert Ibbitson, 1650), pp.5–11.

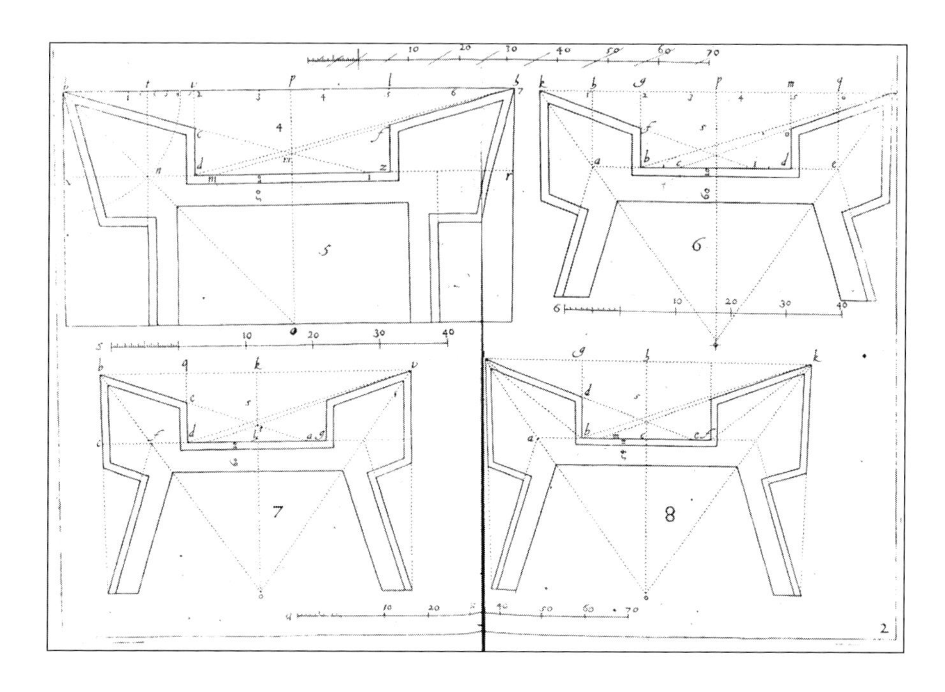

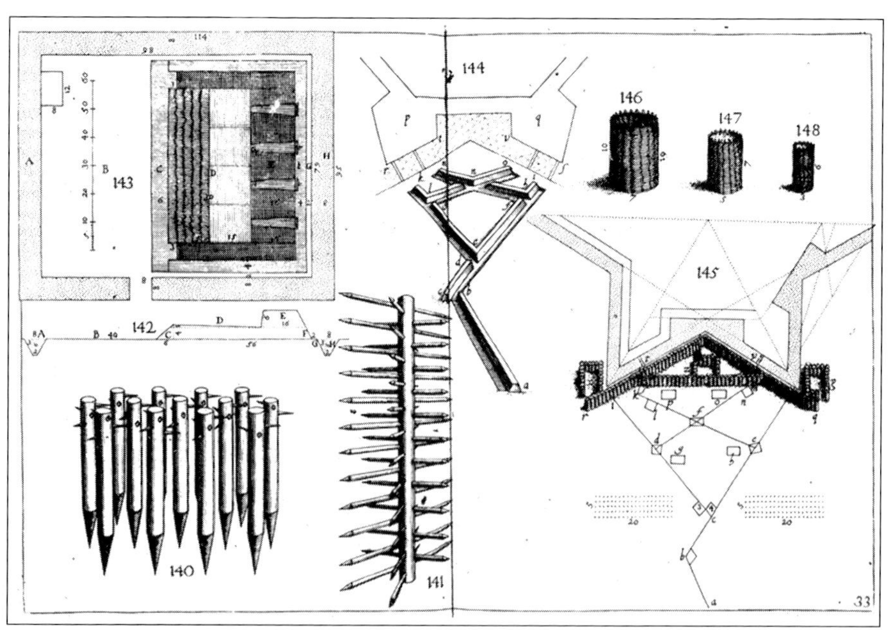

26. Diagrams from Samuel Marolois' *Art of Fortification*, 1638.

find that once that was completed it did not have enough money to hire soldiers to defend it. Therefore some smaller towns might only erect a star fort or similar type of fortification which might protect its approaches.

Since many large towns and cities were strongly fortified this gave the commander of an attacking force two options: either storm the town, which could be very costly to the besiegers, or starve it into surrender which might take many months to achieve. Either way there was no guarantee of success. True, a medieval commander had the same options, but since modern fortifications a storming party would not only have to overcome the new defences but the older medieval ones also. On the other hand, if the town was to be starved into surrender then the outcome would depend on whether the garrison's or the besiegers' food supply lasted the longest. On hearing of the approach of the enemy's army the garrison may have collected the supplies from the surrounding countryside, so forcing the besieging force to forage for supplies further afield.

Either way a besieging force would begin by digging their own fortifications to protect it from any sallies from the town and prevent any relieving force resupplying the garrison, but it would be impossible to resupply a large town or city in just one or two nights. According to Samuel Marolois' *Fortification ou architecture militaire tant offensive que defensive*, which was first published the Hague in 1615 and reprinted in 1628 and 1651, with an English edition in 1638, the town to be besieged was to be reconnoitred for any places of weaknesses before the besiegers began to set up their batteries, which were to be:

> In such a manner that they may beat upon the parapet of the ramparts and bulwarks of the town, to dismount the enemy's ordnance, and for this reason you must raise your batteries high according to the height of the ramparts, so that your cannon may play freely about two foot lower then the top of the parapet, according to which and in consideration of the distance, you must raise your said batteries, taking heed that your cannon be planted upon a plain superficies and elevated some 13 degrees, when the distance is far off. You must not raise them so as when the batteries are near unto the place.

Marolois continues,

> You [must] make your batteries and platforms according to the greatness and number of your pieces. For a demi-cannon being shorter then a whole [cannon] of necessity the platform of the one must be longer and deeper then the other, and seeing a cannon being mounted upon its carriage is some 16 or 18 foot long it is evident that the batteries ought to made for recoiling at the least 10 or 12 feet longer making 28 or 30 foot. Twelve or 15 of the first foot towards the parapet must be under laid with thick and strong oaken planks and the other with hurdles, when you have not planks enough. Upon the said batteries you [must] make a parapet 12, 16 or 20 foot thick or thereabouts with port-holes for your cannon.

> Sometimes you set up gabions six foot high and three foot broad filled with earth, for your ordnance to play out of leaving a little space between them to put out the mouth of your

> cannon, which space so soon as the cannon is discharged is presently stopped and blinded with a bundle of brush full of leaves that the enemy may not discover the portholes. But when you make your batteries upon the counterscharfe or upon the brink of a moat then the portholes as soon as your cannon is shot off, are shut with doors of thick oaken planks musket proof, that the said portholes may not be seen.[40]

A battery was usually formed of four cannons, which were to be at least 12 feet apart so that the entire battery covered about 58 feet and was under the command of a battery or quarter gunner. A short distance away a cellar was to be dug where the gunners could store their gunpowder, match and shot until they were required. The gunpowder was to be covered with animal skin to protect it from any loose sparks which might ignite the powder.

Once the batteries had been established, the besiegers might also erect similar fortifications to those protecting the town with the trenches and ravelins joining each battery. These were usually out of musket range, but once the trenches, batteries etc., had been established then the besieging force would start their 'approaches', which ran towards the weakest place or places within the fortification or town. Those digging the approaches would have to work quicklym since they came within musket range of the garrison and it was not until they had dug down at least a yard and piled the earth on the sides that they could feel comparatively safe. The garrison would also try to disrupt this work by sallying forth from the town. Since digging these trenches was considered to be extremely dangerous it was often suggested that these men should be paid extra.

Marolois suggests that these approaches were to be wide enough so that 'a wagon loaded with fagots brush or gabions may go in them', and deep enough so that the pioneers or soldiers could work freely. Fire steps were also cut into the approaches so that musketeers could fire at the garrison, or engineers could see that they were still digging in the right direction, since the banks of the approaches were higher than a person's height. Gabions or wicker baskets filled with stones and earth could also be set on top of the earthworks and approaches to protect the besiegers further. According to Marolois there were three types of gabions: 'ordinary' which were six foot high and three foot wide; 'middle' which were seven by five feet and 'double' gabions of 10 feet high and seven feet wide. These were usually made by the soldiers themselves.[41]

Since these approaches ran parallel with the town's fortifications, once they were considered close enough to the enemy's fortification a narrow sap would be dug from where an attacking force could launch an assault with scaling ladders etc. Needless to say the enemy would pour all the shot they could at this point to kill as many attackers as possible. It would not be until the end of the seventeenth century that Marshal Vauban suggested that an attack be launched from the nearest approaches so the garrison would have less of an idea of where it was to attacked.

If the ground was right then the besiegers might 'undermine' the town's fortifications by digging a tunnel, and once they reached the walls then barrels of gunpowder would

40 Samuel Marolois, *The Art of Fortification*, translated by Henry Hexham, (Amsterdam: 1638), p.37.
41 *Ibid.*, p.37.

be placed at the end of the gallery and the entrance blocked up to make the explosion more powerful. However if those in the town suspected that the besiegers were digging a mine then they would commence their own countermine in an effort to stop the besiegers springing their mine.

Usually before the siege began the garrison would be called upon to surrender, which was usually refused. Another summons would be given before an attack which the governor might also refuse. However, the governor had to be careful: if he surrendered too soon then he might be executed by his own side for treason, but if he held out without any hope of relief or beyond what was seen as an honourable then the garrison could expect to be slaughtered if the town was stormed, and its inhabitants would be plundered. The survivors were given no terms other than holding a white stick, the traditional sign for a safe passage, and had to swear not to fight again for a certain period of time.

If a town held out for an honourable amount of time before it surrender then the garrison might be able to march out with the 'full honours of war', i.e. with colours flying, drums beating, the musketeers with lighted match and the promise they would not be attacked for a certain period. Unfortunately for one Scottish officer, when he surrendered Loven Castle to Tilly's forces he forgot to include the colours of the two companies which formed its garrison in the terms of surrender: he was forced to give them up, which resulted in him being cashiered from the army in disgrace.[42]

42 Monro, part I, p.12.

10

Civilians and Soldiers

The Thirty Years War has traditionally been seen as an all-destructive war, where soldiers destroyed vast swathes of Germany and the population declined dramatically during this period. The war is also said to have stifled Germany's economic expansion for centuries to come. However, recently some historians have argued that these atrocities have been greatly exaggerated by those wanting relief from rents and taxation. This may be true in some cases, but there are far too many letters and diaries which mention that the soldiers of all armies committed crimes against the civilian population and references to whole areas being laid waste, such as Hesse-Kassel and Bavaria itself.

No matter what side the civilians were on, they inevitably suffered from the war. This could be by quartering soldiers and paying taxes. During the war the Bavarians alone paid 40,677,019 florins, which was 74 percent of the 58,828,799 florins raised by taxation or voluntary means towards Maximilian's war treasury. For taxation purposes property was divided into whole farms, half farms, quarter farms and so on down to an eighth of a farm.

Armies could also demand contributions from hostile lands, although Maximilian appears to have only collected 1,684,630 florins this way, but both Wallenstein and Gustavus Adolphus are known to have heavily relied on the 'contributions system', inasmuch they could finance a larger army than they would otherwise have been able to afford. However, this way of financing an army was fine when it was successful and controlled large areas of Germany, but when they began to lose land they would also lose its income and so would not be able to afford their war effort. Furthermore, although these contributions were usually a monetary payment, payment could also be made in kind, such as food and clothing, to save time purchasing these items. On 10 November 1631 it was reported from Swynfordt:

> Tis a great misery that befalls these countries and none without pity or compassion can either behold or hear of the ruins in these parts. Men have heavy taxations laid upon them, and great contributions must be paid, but especially by the clergy, which causeth

> both laity and clergy to abandon their residence, which is pillaged and spoiled by the soldiers in their absence.[1]

If a town or village were lucky they would only have to pay their tax to one side, but for lands which both sides fought over, then they would have to pay both sides.

Probably the most famous accounts of the atrocities committed against the civilians is Philip Vincent's *Lamentations of Germany*, which records among the violence against civilians, that:

> Some of Tilly's soldiers caused his [the Duke of Saxony's] subjects to be tortured by half strangling them and pressing their thumbs with wheels...
>
> They made the people by force to eat their own excrement and if they would not, they thrust them down their throats and so choked some of them...
>
> They have hung up some in smoke drying them with their fires, refreshing them sometimes with small drink or cold water. For these being such as were before overwhelmed with grief, they took care, left in their torment they should die too soon.
>
> Some they have put into hot ovens and so smothered or burnt them. Some they roasted with straw fires...
>
> To many they have bound so hard both hands and feet that the blood hath spouted out of the ends of their fingers and toes.

Then there are the medically impossible tortures which Vincent records, such as, 'Many have they trussed up on high hanging on their feet stones and weights to stretch out their bodies', or 'with chisels or like instruments they have gone about to plain the faces of some, pretending that they would make it equal or smooth.' Vincent also mentions that the soldiers thrust a knotted piece of cloth or string down a person's throat and once he had swallowed it the soldiers pulled the string so the poor individual is pulled inside out.

However, it would be unfair to blame only Philip Vincent for an exaggerated view of the atrocities of the war, and many of these supposed acts were repeated again and again without question. However, in the mid nineteenth century some historians began to question these events, such as the widespread cannibalism committed by Melchior der Schultz's band who it was said had eaten 500 human beings. The historian O. Mainardus looked into the archives and found that although Schultz's band had killed 251 people in 11 years, the only reference to cannibalism was that he had allegedly eaten the heart of an unborn baby whose mother he had killed. It is thanks to Mainardus and other historians that the 'fact' of widespread cannibalism

1 LR 263/C/6, *The continuation of our forraine newes...*, 29 November 1631.

27. 'La revanche des paysans' ('The peasants fight back'), from Jacques Callot's *Les misères et les malheurs de la guerre*, 1633.

28. 'Le pillage', from Jacques Callot's *Les misères et les malheurs de la guerre*, 1633.

during the war has been discredited. Even so, in 1962 a survey carried out in the state of Hesse in Germany found that the people believed the greatest catastrophe Germany had suffered throughout its history was the Thirty Years War, with the Second World War, which had ended just 17 years before, in second place.[2]

However it would be wrong to dismiss all atrocities as mere propaganda or hearsay. Certainly one of the most common abuses mentioned by Vincent as being committed by the soldiers, is known as the 'Swedish drink'. Despite its name it is said to have been used by all armies, whereby, 'the mouths of some have they opened with gags and then poured down their throats water [from a] stinking puddle, filthy liquids and piss itself, saying this is a Swedish draught, so growing sick and their bellies swelling like a tun, they have died by leisure with the greater torment.'[3]

Although at least some of Vincent's examples are almost certainly untrue, other examples appear to be based on some evidence, such as the case of soldiers 'drying' civilians in smoke: the inhabitants of the town of Sechene appealed to the Mayor of Brabant in 1625, complaining that soldiers had roasted some men to find out where their money was. True, these inhabitants were petitioning the mayor for extra time to pay their taxes, but Jacques Callot also shows soldiers hanging a civilian over a fire in his *Les Grandes Misères et Les Malheurs de la Guerre*, published in 1633.[4]

On 22 September 1620 Francis Netherole wrote from Prague, that the King of Bohemia's Army, 'cannot take Bautzen [but] hath pillaged and burned 40 villages thereabouts and they tell of strange and more than barbarous cruelties exercised by his soldiers which whether true or false being here believed to be practised on men.' Bautzen finally fell to Frederick, but as Netherole again wrote, 'it is said there are not above 130 houses remaining, the rest about a thousand being burnt.' Unfortunately there is no way of verifying these rumours, but whether true or not they must have spread fear among the population of a town or village that the same fate might await them if the soldiers came near them.[5]

On 10 April 1636 Peter Hagendorf recorded in his diary, 'we besieged the city of Liège … This bishopric had three hundred churches and cloisters, eighteen cities and eighteen hundred towns. All of these we, for the most part, plundered and robbed.' Hagendorf did not write this passage for propaganda purposes, so there is no reason to doubt it actually happened.[6]

Another event that does seem true is when some soldiers of Johan Sprinzenstein's Regiment of Foot broke into a house at Neumarkt at midnight on 4 December 1622. The head of the household was away in Nuremberg at the time, but the soldiers threw his wife on to the floor and she was badly beaten and a cushion stuffed into her mouth. The soldiers managed to steal 6,000 *fl* from the house. A Sergeant Syring was later court-martialled for this incident and was hung for this and other crimes, although

2 Ergang, pp.16–17; Steffan Davies *The Wallenstein Figure in German Literature and Historiography, 1790–1920* (London: Maney Publishing, 2010), p.6.
3 Philip Vincent, *Lamentations of Germany*, pp.6–8, 11.
4 TNA: SP 77/18, f.268.
5 TNA: SP 81/18, Francis Netherole, 22 September 1620, f.112; SP 81/19 f.37.
6 Helfferich, pp.292.

a Lieutenant Gunther who was also court-martialled was released due to lack of evidence. However, there is no suggestion the woman was raped, so it may be that the soldiers were more interested in pillaging the property than for any sexual pleasure. On the other hand she may have been concealing the abuse committed against her because she would lose respect from the other townsfolk, even though she was forced into it. Even so there are a surprisingly few first-hand accounts of rape, so either rape was not as common as people believe, or crimes against women of the lower orders were ignored.[7]

Far more common in letters are reports of the land being 'utterly wasted', especially the State of Hesse between 1623 and 1625. Sometimes newssheets reported atrocities being committed, such as in April 1627 when Tilly is said to have 'taken Northein and pillaged it with a general massacre', but the town was reported to be still holding out a month later.[8]

However, it was not just the soldiers who threatened the civilians with violence: the civilians, or boors as they were often called in contemporary sources, could be just as violent. On 2 May 1626 Sir Dudley Carleton wrote to Lord Conway, 'The Boors of Hessen have driven out soldiers of Tilly['s army] quartered upon them and cut in pieces the new regiment of Duke Adolph Holstein.' Sometimes civilians were actually encouraged to attack the occupying soldiers, such as when the Swedish invaded Bavaria between 1632 and 1634, but as Colonel Abraham Loyson pointed out on 22 February 1634, 'twelve thousand Boors in Lower Bavaria do more harm to the Duke of Bavaria than our men do to him.'[9]

The most serious outbreak of civil disorder happened in Upper Austria, when Maximilian tried to impose heavy taxation and the Catholic Reformation on its Lutheran inhabitants. In May 1625 the inhabitants of the town of Frankenburg besieged the castle after the appointment of a Catholic priest. Adam von Herbersdorf called upon the town leaders and committee members to negotiate with the promise of an amnesty; but Herbersdorf broke his promise and arrested the 38 leaders, who had to dice for their lives; 17 people were hanged as an example to the rest, which, not surprisingly, caused ill feeling and distrust towards the Bavarian occupiers. For those who refused to convert they would have to leave their property and become refugees. Thousands of white sticks, the traditional sign of safe conduct, were made and issued to those who refused to convert and wished to emigrate to another province. But this was not enough and in May 1626 the Upper Austria exploded into the revolt known as the 'Bauernkreig' or Peasants' War. Tens of thousands of people took up arms against their Bavarian oppressors, led by leaders such as Stefan Fadinger and Christoph Zeller. Their flags were black with a white skull and their war cry was 'Free us, Dear God from Bavaria's yoke and tyranny and its cruel oppression!' On 17 May the small garrison of

7 Stefan Helml, *Die Oberpfalz im 30jähriger Krieg, der Deutschland und Europa in seinen Bann zog* (Amberg: Scherer, 1990), p.37. The Depositions collected after the 1641 Irish Rebellion also mention very few cases of rape by the soldiers.

8 TNA: SP 101/47, ff.147, 200.

9 TNA: SP 101/46; SP 101/29, f.117; 81/42 f.37.

25 Bavarian soldiers at Lembach was massacred, before the population moved on to attack Herbersdorf at Peuerbach on 21 May.

On 24 June the People's Army, which by now had conquered most of Upper Austria, besieged Linz, the capital of Upper Austria, which refused to surrender. However, this was the high tide of the revolt, because when the people tried to storm the city they were repulsed with loss including Fadinger. With this failure the people laid siege to the city, but on 29 August Linz was relieved by an Imperialist force. Meanwhile there had been other engagements with Imperialist troops fighting them at Enns on 24 July, Neuhofen on 17 August, and at Ebelsberg on the following day, plus also Leofelden on 28 and 30 August and Schlagl on 13 October.

Pappenheim with a force of Bavarian troops was also sent to quell the rebellion, but at Kornrödt on 20 September 1626 the peasants attacked a Bavarian force and massacred three companies, Colonel Gottfried von Hubner's Regiment of Foot, which were estimated at 700 men, plus 800 men of Colonel Schmidt's Regiment. Hubner and other senior officers, including Major George von Planeck of Schmidt's Regiment, were killed.[10]

On 9 November 1626 at the battle of Eferdling the People's Army sang psalms with the battle cry, 'Come out, Pappenheim!' they charged the Bavarian's ranks, which wavered against this onslaught. It was only the threats and encouragements of Pappenheim himself which stiffened the Bavarians' resolve, but even so the peasants fought with religious fanaticism and were, with difficulty, overcome; but not before the Bavarians had suffered heavy casualties. There were further clashes at Vöcklabruck on 18 November and Pinsdorf on 15 November between Pappenheim and the People's Army, but the results were usually the same: the peasants were almost always defeated, but not before they had inflicted heavy casualties on their opponents. The Imperialists and Bavarians seized municipal leaders and hanged them as an example to the rest. The parish register of Lasberg records the death of 31 men and that of St Oswald 20, who went willingly to their deaths. With the deaths of their leaders and the large scale slaughter of the people the 1626 uprising was defeated. Although there would be further uprisings in the following years, none were as serious as that of 1626.[11]

The Upper Palatinate, which was also annexed by Maximilian in lieu of payment for his war expenditure, was a different matter. In April 1623 it was reported that 200 monks and Jesuits were ready at Munich to be sent to the Upper Palatinate as part of the Counter-Reformation, and by May 1625 the Protestants in the state were forced to go to an assigned church each day to be instructed in the Catholic religion by the Jesuits. True, some did leave, but many could not afford to do so or had no where to go so had to listen to these Masses, and in years to come the Upper Palatinate was one of the most ardent areas of Catholicism in Germany.[12]

10 Stadler, p.207.
11 George Heilingsetzer, *Der Oberösterreichische Bauernkrieg, 1626* (Vienna: Militarhistorische Schriftenreihe, 1976).
12 TNA: SP 101/28, f.291; SP 101/42, f.243.

However, one event which is infamous of all the atrocities during the Thirty Years War is the sack of Magdeburg on 20 May 1631. When Gustavus Adolphus landed in Germany, Tilly planned to confront him before he could consolidate his position. However, by the treaty of Bärwalde Bavaria was technically a Swedish ally along with France, therefore Maximilian ordered Tilly to besiege Magdeburg instead. Although technically also an ally since it had declared for Gustavus, it was an Imperial city which had challenged Ferdinand II's authority. At first Count Wolfgang von Mansfeld, who commanded the area around Magdeburg, began to blockade they city, but he was not strong enough to entirely surround it.

Magdeburg was divided into three, the old and new towns and the 'Sudenberg'. In 1572 the city was described as 'the noblest city in Saxony ... there are splendid houses, magnificent streets, large and richly decorated churches; the church of St Maurice built by the Emperor Otto is particularly handsome.' It was at St John's Church where Martin Luther is said to have preached his Reformation ideas.[13]

Magdeburg's alliance with Sweden had provided little benefit for the city either in money or troops, so it would have to rely mainly on its garrison of about 2,000 foot and 200 horse. Moreover many of the inhabitants of the city wanted to stay loyal to the Emperor, rather than support a foreign invader. To encourage the city, Colonel Dietrich Falkenburg arrived with promises of support from Gustavus Adolphus, and that his arrival was imminent; but he brought little else. Falkenburg was appointed governor of the city and began raising more troops and erecting new fortifications to protect its medieval walls, which were surrounded by a moat. The Heydrick fort was erected near the Sudenburg and two hornworks were placed in front of the city. Protecting the bridgehead on the other bank of the Elbe was a star fort known as the 'Zoll Schants'. There were further outlying earthworks, but these needed to be garrisoned, which weakened Falkenburg's force.

It was about now that, in a superstitious age, what was seen as a bad omen occurred. On 26 November 1630 a furious storm burst over Magdeburg which damaged many of the city's defences and the following month Pappenheim arrived before the walls. Although both his and Mansfeld's forces were still not strong enough to take the city by storm, this did not stop them from trying, and several attacks were beaten off. They even offered to promote Falkenburg to Field Marshal of the Imperial Army and give him 400,000 Rix-dollars if he would surrender the city, but to no avail. The lack of progress of the siege caused ill feeling between Mansfeld and Pappenheim, who both complained to Vienna about the situation. Unfortunately, their despatches were captured by a patrol from Magdeburg and published.

Meanwhile the siege went on through the winter with the besieging force freezing in their trenches and encampments, while the garrison of Magdeburg was quartered in houses within the city. On 3 April 1631 Tilly's main army arrived with his siege artillery, but far from being a precursor to storming the city, many believed that Tilly would abandon the siege altogether, since Gustavus Adolphus had taken Frankfurt on

13 Georg Braun and Franz Hogenberg, *Civitates Orbis Terrarum* (Cologne, 1572).

the Oder on 13 April and was believed to be marching to relieve Magdeburg. At about this time another ill omen occurred for the inhabitants of Magdeburg, when the wife of a captain within the garrison was dying in childbirth. She begged her husband to cut their baby out of her womb such was her agony, but on doing so it was said that the baby was as large as a three year old, 'with a headpiece and an iron breast plate upon him; great boots of the French fashion and a bag by his side', ready to defend the city. It was probably just a baby too large to be born naturally which possibly had a deformity.[14]

With Tilly's arrival the besieging force was able to press home its attacks with more force and several of the satellite forts fell to Tilly. According to Count Galeazzo Gualdo Priorato:

> Tilly kept his quartered about the sconce of Zoll; Count Pappenheim environed the ways that led to from the New Town; the Duke of Holstein enlarged his quarters almost to the Croken and Count Mansfeldt bound to the precincts of the camp with his station on the side of the Haydeck and the Fort Marsh. They had already made their approached on these four sides, even to the edge of the counterscarf; but their entrance thereupon was hindered by the continual playing of the cannon and muskets from the tower.[15]

Rumours were still rife in the city that Gustavus would shortly arrive. Tilly pressed forward with attacking the forts nearer to the city especially the Zoll Schants, which the Duke of Holstein and Colonel Wangler were ordered to take. After several days bombardment they attacked it but were beaten off, but finally it was taken along with several other forts so that the besiegers were now in close proximity to the walls of Magdeburg itself. At the beginning of May Neustadt fell to Pappenheim and Sudenburg to Mansfeld, leaving only the old city holding out.

With preparations for the storming of the city visible to the garrison on 18 May, Tilly sent a trumpeter to demand Magdeburg's surrender, but the city council would only agree that the Bishopric and city might still enjoy all their privileges, which Tilly rejected. The following day the garrison beat off an attack by Pappenheim and destroyed the besiegers' mines, nevertheless Tilly sent another trumpeter to negotiate the city's surrender. That evening the sentries observed movement in the besiegers' camp, which the garrison believed was Tilly preparing to raise the siege. With this in mind, according to the *Swedish Intelligencer*, the sentries got some sleep.

That day Tilly had held a council of war which decided that they should storm the city early the next morning on four sides. Spies within the city had informed Tilly's Army that few sentries were kept to man the fortifications, nevertheless the soldiers were given alcohol to encourage them in the assault. The firing of 30 pieces of ordnance before daybreak would be the signal to attack, although another source said just one piece was to fire the signal, but failed to do so. A third source suggests that

14 William Watts, *The Swedish Intelligencer* (London, 1633), p.115; L. Brinckmair, *The Warnings of Germany, By Wonderful Signs and Strange Prodigies* (London: John Norton, 1638), no page number.

15 Priorato, p.27.

Tilly had appointed a certain time when the main assault was to take place, although he delayed it for a further hour, but Pappenheim was not told of this revised timetable, so attacked an hour too early.[16]

Whatever the signal, the events that followed would send shockwaves around Europe, as one newssheet, *Continuation of our Foreign News*, put it, 'No pen is able to write, or tongue express the woeful and lamentable Tragedy lately happened at the taking of the city [of] Magdeburg.'

Pappenheim with his own regiment, and those of Wangler, Savelli and Gronsfeld, which on paper mustered about 5,100 men although was probably much weaker, was to attack from the new town. Count von Holstein would fall on a hornwork before the Crock Port, while Count Wolfgang von Mansfeld with Tilly's men would assault the Heydrick. Three Imperialist regiments with the remainder of the Tilly's soldiers would attack a new work on the marshes between the bridge and the river.[17]

In Pappenheim's quarter the companies of Captain Ackermann and Captain La Croy, both of Pappenheim's Regiment, appear to have formed a forlorn hope and the soldiers, who were given 'a good Rhinish wine' to encourage them, charged the defences. According to one anonymous pamphlet:

> Pappenheim had the best advantage, because he was to pass over a dry moat with his men and having no parapet or defence upon the wall and the wall itself hanging down stoop wise, in so much it was very mountable. Seeing then that the work was but slightly manned … [with] not above 30 men in this work and the most of them asleep he fell upon that work, and carried it easily without any great loss of men.[18]

However, Ackermann recalls there were 400 defenders waiting for them, but the attackers managed to uproot the wooden staves in front of the walls, and 'turfs and faggots' were thrown into the ditch to fill it in. All this time some musketeers were trying to keep the garrison's heads pinned down with their fire. Once the first line of defences had been breached Ackermann and La Croy's companies came to the walls themselves. 'There was such a thundering and crashing of muskets, mortars and cannon that nobody could neither see nor hear.' By now the main body of attackers were pressing forward, crushing the forlorn hope against the defences so that the 'whole rampart was filled, covered and black with soldiers and storm ladders.'[19] According to Priorato:

> It proving very hard for the soldiers to scale those high walls with their ladders, they being likewise so well flanked with opposite bulwalks, they were forced to give over with no little loss. Pappenheim notwithstanding … egged on his soldiers, assuring them of

16 *A Brief and True Relation of the taking in of Magdenburch by the Emperors' and the Catholic League*, 10 May 1631, British Library, C194a 836.

17 *Ibid.*

18 *Ibid.*

19 Volkholz, p.14.

> rich booties and threatening those that should give back [i.e. retreat]; and though many tumbled from off the ladders into the ditches; yet their places were continually supplied by fresh men, who enraged at the difficulty they met.[20]

Some of the ladders were found to be too short, but after a fierce struggle the League troops breached the walls and entered the city. They captured several pieces of ordnance and turned them on the city itself, while others pursued the fugitives of Count Falkenburg's Regiment through the streets. Falkenburg made a stand in Lakenmacher Street and the pikemen of the storming party were called up, but according to Ackermann they were too intent on plundering the city and had broken their pikes, so they arrived with only short pikes. Falkenburg led a counter-attack which drove Pappenheim's men back to the walls, but when he was struck down by a musket ball the attack soon petered out. It was probably about now that Peter Hagendorf, who was a musketeer in Pappenheim's Regiment, was wounded. 'There I entered the city by storm without incurring any injury', he recalls, 'But once in the city at the New Town Gate, I was shot twice through the body, that was my booty.'[21] By now Pappenheim's men had managed to open one of the city's gates to let more men into the city.

A Captain Schmidt from the garrison led a second counter-attack which beat the Imperialists back to a bulwark, but Schmidt was also seriously wounded and the attack lost momentum, and finally the garrison was driven back. These may have been Holstein's men who had broken through the defences after a stubborn resistance from the garrison, and with Pappenheim's men the garrison men were either killed or pushed back to the cathedral.[22]

What of Mansfeld's force? The anonymous pamphlet accuses Mansfeld of cowardice, having 'stayed a good while, thinking it was good sleeping in a whole skin'. Whether he did not hear the signal is unknown, but:

> He fell upon the Haydeck and gave not on until Pappenheim and other regiments had possessed themselves of more than half the town, but at last falling on, they [the garrison] resisted him valiantly, and he was twice beaten back, so that he was not able to enter there, but at last those of the town seeing that all was lost, their own men opened [for] him the Ulrick port of the city and so gave them entrance.[23]

However, other Imperialist troops also appear to have attacked late, and 'seeing the town was taken in, then they began to fall upon it, howsoever they found no less resistance, than the Mansfeldters had done before till at length they were let in willingly.'[24]

20 Priorato, p.28.
21 Peters, p.47.
22 *A Brief and True Relation of the taking in of Magdenburch…*
23 *Ibid.*
24 *Ibid.*

According to one Protestant newssheet:

> In this hot and furious assault they spared none, but slew all in their way, except only some of the soldiers which sheltered themselves for a while in the Cathedral Church. Most of the citizens were slain and burnt for the city was fired in divers places in so much that the whole city in a short space was in a blazing flame. The soldiers and the fire both alike cruel, devoured men, women, maidens and children. The women and maidens which were escaped from the heat of the fire … were preserved for the heat of these miscreants lusts, which they drew along with them into their army and even like beasts were sold and conveyed to the use of one after another, in a savage, barbarous, unnatural and inhuman manner.[25]

It was said that one woman to save her 'chastity' threw herself in a well and drowned, while two soldiers 'found an innocent child lying crying and sprawling in the street, the one took one leg and the other another leg and pulled it in pieces'. In another incident a soldier in Pappenheim's Regiment boasted that he had stabbed more than 20 children, and in one church the survivors found the remains of 53 people whom the soldiers had beheaded, then chopped the heads in two. One man was attacked by four soldiers; he begged for mercy but one soldier stabbed him, another struck him about the head before another soldier finally chopped his head off with an axe. Finally the fourth soldier cut off his penis. Unfortunately, we will probably never know whether these incidents were true or the imagination of a propagandist's pen in the war of words that followed the destruction of the city.[26]

Nevertheless, not all atrocities can be dismissed as propaganda. Otto Von Guericke was about 29 at the time and later recorded:

> Thus it came about that the city and all its inhabitants fell into the hands of the enemy, whose violence and cruelty were due in part to their common hatred of the adherents of the Augsburg Confession and in part to their being embittered by the chain shot which had been fired at them and by the derision and insults that the Magdeburgers had heaped upon them from the ramparts.
>
> Then was there nought but slaughter and burning, torture and murder. Most especially was every one of the enemy bent on securing much booty. When a marauding party entered a house, if its master had anything to give he might thereby purchase respite and protection for himself and his family till the next man, who also wanted something … It was only when everything had been brought forth and there was nothing left to give that the real trouble commenced. Then, what with blows and threats of shooting, stabbing and hanging, the poor people were so terrified that if they had had anything left they would have brought if forth if it had been buried in the earth or hidden away in a thousand castles. In this frenzied rage, the great and splendid city… [was] given over to the flames,

25 *The Continuation of our Foreign News* (London: 10 June 1631), no. 30, pp.7–11.
26 Mary Noll Venable, 'Evenius and the Siege of Magdeburg' in *Linking of Heaven and Earth*, ed. Emily Nicholson et al. (Farnham: Ashgate, 2012) p.118; *A Brief and True Relation of the taking in of Magdenburch…*

29. The sacking of Magdeburg, 1631.

> and thousands of innocent men, women and children, in the midst of a horrible din of heartrending shrieks and cries, were tortured and put to death in so cruel and shameful a manner that no words would suffice to describe.[27]

Hearing that Tilly's army had entered the city many civilians shut their doors hoping that the soldiers would pass them by: among them was the Friese family. Daniel, who was then a young boy, records that the victorious soldiers were hammering on the doors of the house demanding to be let in, saying they would kill everyone in the house if they were not:

> We had to let them in; they soon attacked father and mother and craved money; they were only two musketeers. Father and mother gave them the money they had with them, as well as some clothes and utensils. They were satisfied with this, and only asked for shoes and went away again. We pleaded that they help us get away … but they didn't listen because they said they had to find booty first.[28]

However, more soldiers arrived and threatened Daniel's parents, until they also were paid to go away. Daniel's family decided to flee to a nearby stable, but this did

27 Helfferich, pp.108–109.
28 Quoted in Wilson, *The Thirty Years War: A Sourcebook*, p.158.

not stop the soldiers. Hearing a commotion outside Daniel's father rushed out into a yard to see what was happening followed by the rest of his family. They found about seven musketeers, who 'spoke a foreign tongue and no one understood what they said. They kept putting out their hands for money'. By now the family had no more money to give so the musketeers fired at Daniel's father. Fortunately they missed and so the soldiers chased the family back into the house and proceeded to ransack it for any valuables which might have been missed by the previous soldiers. Once these soldiers had left in search of more plunder the family once more hid, this time in the attic. However, a soldier spotted their maid running into the house and followed her and found the family's hiding place. He was about to hit Daniel's father when Daniel's younger brother intervened with a promise that he would give the soldier his pocket money which he received on Sundays if he let his father live. This brought the soldier to his senses, and he agreed to help them, but first he needed to find some plunder and told the family that he would return to help them. The family remained hidden not knowing whether the soldier would keep his promise or not.

The intervention of a wife or child saved many from the soldiers' lust for blood. Among them was Christopherus Theodaenus who was the pastor of St Katherine's church. When soldiers burst into his house demanding money, but when he said he had no more money to give, 'one who looked like the Devil himself having two muskets and in his mouth a ball in each side', was about to fire one of his muskets at the pastor when his wife struck the musket upwards so that the ball missed her husband and she held the soldier so that he could not move. She then remembered that the hooks that fastened her bodice were made of silver, so she offered them to the soldiers. Once she had cut them off and given them to the soldiers, they left.[29]

Meanwhile the soldier who had promised to return for the Friese family was as good as his word and returned to their house. He led them through the streets of Magdeburg,

> As we went through a couple of alleys, we saw various dead laying atop each other, and often in the great crowd we had to step over the corpses. Amongst others we saw a peasant jump out of a gable, who was scalded by hot water, and he was smoking mightily. He lay in the alley writhing and crying piteously. Farther along the alley lay a maid, who had been carrying meat in a basket. She had been shot, and a dog was standing nearby eating the meat… We saw very many dead in the alleys and a number of women lying totally naked, with their heads in a large beer barrel, which was standing full of water in the street. They had been pushed in and drowned, but half their bodies and their legs were hanging out, which was a wretched spectacle.[30]

Daniel Friese and his family eventually arrived at the army's encampment and the soldier took him to his hut, where his reward for helping the family was to be scolded

29 Hans Medick, 'The Destruction of Magdeburg' in *Historical Workshop Journal* (Oxford University Press, Autumn 2000), p.39.

30 Quoted in Wilson, *The Thirty Years War: A Sourcebook*, p.162.

by his wife for bringing back so little plunder. The Friese family watched Magdeburg in flames and Daniel records that 'you could have read a letter by the glow of the fire'.

Even the officers joined in the plundering of the city. Jürgen Ackermann, who was a captain in Colonel Pappenheim's Regiment of Foot and who had lost 72 of his company during the storming, records that in one house near the old market he found a shopkeeper who in return for his life showed Ackermann a locked iron chest. After Ackermann and several of his soldiers hacked a hole in the side they found some gold and silvery cutlery and a gold chain with a jewel.[31]

Leaving her husband recovering in the army camp with their sick child, Peter Hagendorf's wife went in search of plunder and some cloth to make bandages; but while he was lying in his hut he recalls, 'there came a great outcry in the camp that the houses of the city were all collapsing on top of each other so that many soldiers and their wives who had wanted to loot were trapped. But I was more concerned about my wife … yet God protected her. She got out of the city after one and a half hours with an old woman from the city.'[32]

The old woman was a widow who had probably agreed to help carry Peter Hagendorf's wife's plunder in return for safe passage. This is how Simon Printz, who was a constable and gunsmith of Magdeburg, was saved. With no money or valuables he could do nothing but offer to carry the soldiers' booty away for them.

Some inhabitants sought sanctuary in the cathedral and churches, but soldiers burst into St John's Church, which according to one Swedish account, 'was full of womenfolk, whom they locked in from the outside, thereafter throwing burning torches through the windows. The Croats and Walloons behaved mercilessly, throwing children into the fire.'[33] Another account records that the preacher of St John's Church tried to protect himself with a Bible which seems to have saved the pastor Andreas Krammer as he died in 1640. However, this 'Blood Bible' still shows signs of a sword cut where a soldier is said to have slashed at the preacher.

Another newssheet continues:

> Murdered all there and this continued three hours in which time the city was set afire in four or five places, and it is yet unknown whether it was done by treason or by the immediate hand of God, but the sudden increase and fierceness thereof was such by reason of a wonderful wind, that in a short time all the fires met, and the spoilers that plundered were forced to leave the most part of the women, maids and children were smothered and stifled in vaults and cellars, where they had hid themselves. Some part of them driven into the fire by violence. Many others thrown into the fire and part of the beautiful young women and maids carried into the camp, there forced, spoiled and carried away in the meanwhile, yea even on that very day was the whole city, with all the inhabitants so wasted by the fire and sword that on the Wednesday morning their remained no more standing, but the cathedral church and a very few houses standing

31 Volkholz, pp.16–17.

32 Quoted in Helfferich, p.283.

33 Quoted in Gerhard Benecke, *Germany in the Thirty Years War* (London: Edward Arnold, 1978), p.35.

about it. All the rest, both men and beasts, consumed to ashes, that the sword left. And none escaped except some very small number that were here and there which with very great peril ran away…

In this manner as is set down that brave city of Magdeburg, by fire and sword, was in one day consumed with many thousands of Christian poor souls therein.[34]

According to Guericke the plundering by the soldiers lasted just two hours:

But in this time the fire, which had originally been ordered by Count Pappenheim in order to perturb and fright the citizens and inhabitants, but which had afterward been used by the common soldiery without discretion or pause, took the upper hand by means of the sudden appearance of the wind, so that by ten o'clock in the morning everything was afire; and by ten o'clock in the evening the entire city, including the beautiful courthouse and all the churches and cloisters, had been reduced to ashes and heaps of stone.[35]

In his *History of the World*, which was published in 1640, Alexander Ross records that the weather also played its part:

The Garrison and townsmen fought stoutly so long as they were able, till the Caesarians [Imperialists] to quiet them set the City on fire, which proved as prejudicial to the besiegers, who thereby lost their plunder, as to the townsmen who lost their habitations; for the fire was so violent by reason of the wind.[36]

Who started the fire is not known. Pappenheim is said to have ordered a house to be set on fire so that the smoke would cover his soldiers' movements, whereas Captain Ackermann of Pappenheim's Regiment of Foot said that two houses were set on fire to drive the defenders from the walls. While Count Galeazzo Gualdo Priorato blamed it on, 'the carelessness of a soldier who throwing aside his musket with the match lighted to get up the stairs in a drugster's house, the match set fire to a barrel of Brimstone and this taking hold of other combustible matters, the fire did so dilate itself, as the houses being built of wood all was destroyed.'[37]

However, according to *The Continuation of our Foreign News*:

Those few that are escaped, related that the whole city is almost quite burnt down, and there are not above three citizens' houses standing whole in the city except only about the cathedral there stand some 70 houses, which the fire hath not consumed. The cruelty of the soldiers was so great that the citizens with their wives and children, (as it is reported)

34 'A true information what manner the city of Magdeburg was overthrown', in *The Continuation of our Forraine Newes* (London: May 1631), pp.9–11.
35 Helfferich, p.109.
36 Alexander Ross, *The History of the World the second part in six books being a continuation of famous history of Sir Walter Raleigh knight…* (1640), pp.384–385.
37 Priorato, p.28.

> would rather suffer death, then stand to the cruel mercy of these barbarous soldiers, and fall into their hands; which was the cause that they fired their own houses.[38]

Alexander Ross continues:

> This great and stately City was in a space of four and twenty hours burnt down to the ground, in which six parish churches were consumed in the same fire, all the churches, streets and high ways were covered with dead bodies, in the Cathedral of St Catherine were found three and fifty murdered, the governor being wounded in his head and thigh is carried away prisoner with most of the chief men and Ministers; the barbarous soldiers spares neither sex nor age, abusing even young girls to death; yet the High church and the monastery of St Mary were saved from the fire, and so were 139 houses, but all the inhabitants were either slain or taken, the number of slain is not certain, but it is reported that two and twenty thousand were flung into the River Albis which flows by the city; six hundred townsmen were chained, though they were able to ransom themselves.[39]

On 22 May Tilly entered the ruins of the city and the following day forbid any more pillaging, and on 25 May held a *Te Deum* was held in the cathedral for his victory. However, it was a hollow victory as he had wanted to capture the city with all its provisions intact. Moreover he and Pappenheim would go down in history as having destroyed Magdeburg.

However, large fires in towns and cities were common in the seventeenth century with their narrow streets and houses mostly made out of wood, the great fire of London being one example. Therefore the *Swedish Intelligencer* is probably correct when it recalls that while the battle and plundering raged, 'a mighty fire breaks out (how, none knows) and it being a great windy day, all was on the sudden become one great flame: the whole town was in twelve hours space, wholly turned to cinders, excepting 139 houses. Six goodly churches are burnt; the cathedral together with St Mary's church, were by the Monks and soldiers' diligence preserved.'[40] Some of these six churches may have included St Jacob's, which would not appoint a new pastor until 1659, and a new pastor was appointed to St Catherine's in 1679. It was not until 1690 that St Patrick's appointed one. On the other hand St John's and St Ambrose's still held services after the sack of the city. Whoever was to blame, it is estimated that of the 1,900 buildings within the city 1,700 are said to have been destroyed.

It was said that over 20,000 people perished in Magdeburg that day, the city's population having been swelled by the inhabitants of the surrounding countryside who sought protection within its walls. Pamphlets claimed that Tilly had all the corpses thrown into the river, while his soldiers had a Christian burial. A pamphlet reported on 28 May, 'All the dead carcases are now almost conveyed out of this city, which have sorely pestered and annoyed us hitherto [by the smell] … and are cast into

38 *The Continuation of our Foreign News* (London: 10 June 16310, no. 30, pp.7–11.
39 Ross, pp.384–385.
40 Watts, part 1, p.114.

the River Elbe. There were many of them so disfigured that it was impossible any way to discern who they were'. Many of these bodies had been burnt and there were too many to bury, so throwing them into the Elbe was seen as the best way of disposing of them before disease broke out.[41]

On 22 February 1632 commissioner Christoph Schultz held a census of the remaining inhabitants of the city and found that in the old city there were just 239 men, 117 widows and a single burgomeister; in the Sudenburg and the borough of St Michael were 15 men and 7 widows and in the new town 39 men, 30 widows and a burgomeister, which according to Friedrich Hoffmann, who wrote a history of the city, gives a total of 449 inhabitants in all. This figure has been widely repeated ever since by historians. However, there are no wives or children mentioned in this census, therefore the figures must show the heads of households rather than people, which increases the remaining Magdeburg population considerably. Furthermore, it also gives a greater number of houses that survived the fire or had been repaired than previously thought.[42]

Nevertheless, in the war of words that followed 20 newspapers, 205 pamphlets and 41 illustrated broadsheets were published in Germany about the sack of Magdeburg in 1631 alone, some accusing Tilly of the destruction of the city, while others exonerated him. However, even the Protestant pamphlets admit that the population had several times refused terms of surrender, so according to the laws of war any town and city stormed by an army could be plundered by the victorious soldiers.[43]

However, if the survivors of the sack of Magdeburg thought their war was over they were mistaken. On 3 June Tilly broke camp and marched to Hesse, but left a garrison within the city, which was quickly besieged by the Swedish Army. It was not until January 1632 that Pappenheim withdrew the garrison to reinforce his own army. In 1636 the city would again be besieged, this time by John George of Saxony's forces. During this time some of the city's former inhabitants began to return, among them Otto von Guericke, in February 1632. However, in 1639 only 450 households were charged with a tax to pay the garrison of 1,500 men. In 1668 William Carr first published his book on his 16 year long Grand Tour and recorded, 'I had the curiosity to go from Lübeck to see the Ancient city of Magdeburg, but found it so ruined and decayed by the Swedish War, that I had no encouragement to stay there. I therefore hastened to Berlin.' Unfortunately he did not say when he visited Magdeburg, but since he dedicated it to King William III he may have left Britain about the time of the Restoration in 1660.[44]

Among the survivors of that fateful day was John Neesing, a burgher and councillor, who in September 1633 petitioned the English government on behalf of 'his wife, children and kindred (to the number of 33 persons) [who] made an escape and saved

41 *The Continuation of our Weekly News from Forrain Parts* (London: 25 June 1631), no. 31, p.5.
42 Friederich Hoffmann, *Geschichte der Stadt Magdeburg* (Magdeburg, 1885), vol. 2, p.215.
43 Parker, *The Thirty Years' War*, p.112.
44 Hoffmann, vol. 2, p.270; William Carr, *The Traveller's Guide and historians faithful Companion* (London, 1600).

their lives from the bloody slaughter and fire but lost all their goods and estates.' They had maintained themselves through the charity of foreigners, but now asked King Charles I to grant a 'royal licence for a collection of charity in your city of London and such other shires and places as your Majesty please'. The petition was passed to the Lord Keeper who rejected it since there were too many other petitions needing his attention. Nevertheless, at the beginning of March 1634 John Neesing did received £5 for his and his family's upkeep. What became of him and his family is unknown, but he must have been one of many displaced families who wandered around Europe looking for help.[45]

One young woman was luckier, according to Patorius Kurte: while the plundering was going on she dressed in her brother's clothes and hid in an empty wine barrel until she was discovered by a cavalryman. The cavalryman befriended her and she, still in men's clothing, became his servant, attending his horses until his death three months later. At which point she was captured by the Swedish Army and served for five years as a musketeer, taking part in several duals until she was betrayed by a miller and so forced to give up her life as a soldier.

Unfortunately, the destruction of Magdeburg changed nothing and the civilian population would go on suffering from the soldiers' brutality. When Tilly was defeated at the battles of Breitenfeld and the Lech, the Swedish Army invaded Bavaria itself. Although Wallenstein had quartered his soldiers on Maximilian's territory which had brought strong complaints to Ferdinard II, for 15 years the people of Bavaria had been spared the horrors of war within its borders. This changed on 16 April when Gustavus Adolphus crossed the Bavarian border and advanced on Donauwörth, which quickly fell to him.

On 24 April, the Bavarian garrison of Augsburg also surrendered to him. After attempting to capture Ingoldstadt, which was too strongly fortified and garrisoned by the remnants of Tilly's Army, Gustavus marched on Munich, which he entered on 17 May. Among his entourage was Frederick V, which must have been a further blow to Maximilian. On 9 June 1632 the Protestant pamphlet *The Continuation of Our Forraign News* reported that the Duke of Bavaria had 'cowardly fled his country', and that the inhabitants of Bavaria, found 'so much favour at the hands of so great and gracious a conqueror as the King of Sweden, all people show great joy and to profess they will do anything for him.' In reality Gustavus had ordered his army to devastate the country and demanded 400,000 Rixdollars.[46]

Munich itself was spared the worst excesses of the Swedish brutality, since Gustavus had ordered the majority of his army to remain outside the city, except for Sir John Hepburn's Brigade which was to act as its garrison. This is not to say that the inhabitants did not live in fear, because a chronicler records, the citizens were 'often warned that the city would suffer the dire fate of Magdeburg' if they did not

45 TNA: SP 16/246, f.126, Petition of John Neesing, 24 September 1633 and Report of the Lord Keeper; John Fortescue et al (eds.), *Calendar of State Papers Colonial*, vol. 8, 1630–1634 (London: Her Majesty's Stationary Office, 1892), p.529.

46 British Library Burney MS, LR 263/C6/19, *The Continuation of our Forraign News*.

pay their contribution money. Moreover, 'all citizens had soldiers quartered on them', the chronicler continues, 'according to their wealth and income.' The houses where the owners had fled were plundered, but for the wealthier citizens and monasteries who could afford to pay for protection, or a *Salva Guardia*. Two or three soldiers would be posted there to protect the property from other soldiers, and it was punishable by death to break into a house protected by a *Salva Guardia*.

The chronicle continues:

> Whatever the soldiers bought in the way of beer, bread, etc., they conscientiously paid for. They twice moved camp from the meadows of Schwabing to those in front of the Neuhauser Gate, which was burnt down after their departure. But neither pillows nor bolsters nor any other articles of bedding were left in the city. Often victuals had to be carried out to the camp. A number of Swedish sutlers carried out the March ale casked by the farmers and sold it to the soldiers…
>
> In the daytime the Swedish soldiers brought all manner of things into the city and sold them, large numbers of oxen, many horses, many more pigs, women's veils, all sorts of linen, flax and yarn, oats, tin plates and jugs, a great number of copper saucepans, stolen goblets, wax tapers and many other things for use in the kitchen; they even brought the iron hoops from cart wheels, they brought whole carts, locks taken from doors, coats, women's skirts; all of which things were bought up by the inhabitants of this city at an extremely low price. In those days you could buy an ox for a gulden and pay the same for a pound of dripping.[47]

Therefore for the inhabitants of Munich, who still had money, they could obtain some very good bargains from the soldiers, whereas the soldiers might only receive a tenth of the value of their plunder, as they did at Magdeburg.

The chronicle continues:

> 'And so we have lain for three whole weeks under the enemy's yoke and bondage. May Almighty God grant that we may find joy to compensate for this great harm we have suffered, and may he gladden our hearts with an enduring peace, and protect us as a father from such ravages of war.'[48]

Munich was lucky that it was only occupied for just three weeks; some towns and villages were not so fortunate and for the next three years would be occupied by soldiers of one side or the other. In 1632 the Swedish would occupy Landsburg, Regensburg, Moosburg and Freysing and Albert, Maximilian's brother with his wife and children and Maximilian's wife fled to Salzburg. Maximilian believed that God had forsaken

47 Chronicle quoted in Carl J. Burckhardt, *Richelieu and his Age* (London: George Allen and Unwin Ltd, 1965), vol. 2 p.395.

48 *Ibid.*, p.397.

him, and the *Swedish Intelligencer* recorded sarcastically that he was 'much troubled with sore eyes caused by smoke of his own country.'[49]

About 29 miles west of Munich is the town of Erling, with the nearby monastery of Ansbach, where Father Maurius Friesenegger lived. He recorded in his diary that the Swedish all the time 'devastate, burning and killing … every night in the distance four, five and even more' villages could be seen burning. The inhabitants sought shelter in the forests whenever the Swedish occupied the town, after two of its inhabitants had been killed. On one occasion when the townsfolk returned they found their church was 'full of stench and horse manure … all the donation boxes broken, [as well as] the tomb of the founder. However, the altars and the images were all undamaged, except for the portrait of St Rasso.' In the monastery they found 'a horrible devastation, no door, no lock, no box, no closet, no window, which was not broken.' Only one bed was found to be unbroken and to make matters worse the Swedish and their horses had defecated in the rooms and corridors. 'More miserable than the monastery,' Maurius Friesenegger continues, was the village, 'the upper inn, the beautiful Richter House, the new school building, in all 43 houses, almost the whole upper village lay in ashes … [There were] no wagons, no ploughs throughout the village. From 140 horses were only three left, of 400 head of cattle only four, sheep, pigs and the whole poultry was lost entirely.' This was the choice of the civilian in lands occupied by foreign, and sometimes friendly, soldiers: do they flee to the forest to save themselves, knowing their home might be plundered or destroyed by the soldiery, or do they remain to protect their possessions knowing they might be beaten or even killed?[50]

There was a third choice, to fight back as people in other states had done, and the Bavarian population are known to have waged a guerrilla war on the occupiers; but this could lead to reprisals. One newssheet recalls that the priests and Archduke Leopold encouraged the Bavarian peasants to:

> Give no quarter to any Swedish soldiers but either kill them in [a] cruel and scornful manner or cut … off [their] ears, noses and hands. To some they pull out their eyes and their tongues … the Swedish troops began likewise to forget their wonted moderation and use their enemies in like manner, so that in one day there were seen 200 fires, so many villages and small towns being laid in ashes.'

It was even said that Maximilian had armed his subjects for this purpose.[51]

However, this widespread looting did not bring any riches to the soldiers themselves, as one soldier with the Swedish Army records:

> We do daily obtain great store of booty, but we cannot sell them, for they will yield us but little money or none at all, a good fair horse may be bought for four Rixdollars, a cow for own [sic] florins, and a hog for a very small value, poultry and geese and the like bare

49 Watts, part 1, pp.167–168.
50 Maurus Friesenegger, *Tagebuch aus dem 30jährigen Krieg* (Munich: Allitera, 2007), pp.16–18.
51 TNA: SP 101/30, ff.211, 228, 230, *Advise from several places in Germany*, May 1632.

no price, bedding, linen, cloth, copper-work and pewter is of no estimation at all neither any manner of household stuff. Money is that which is here looked after. And in the Palatinate they are in the very same case.[52]

Fortunately for the people of Bavaria Gustavus needed to seek out and destroy the armies of Bavaria and Wallenstein. Leaving strong garrisons in Nördlingen and Augsburg, he led the Swedish Army into Saxony and was killed at the battle of Lützen on 17 November 1632. In early December a Bavarian Army drove the remnants of the Swedish Army out of most of Bavaria. Father Maurus Friesenegger recalls, 'the beginning of this year, [1633] we lived a little quieter, but always in fear because of the Swedes in Augsburg and other Imperial cities; in Erling there was nothing in the houses but misery, half of the houses lay in ashes, the others had no roofs.'[53]

Efforts were made to send food from Munich and bakers from other towns to feed the populace, but too few provisions came to satisfy all their hunger, which implies that not all of Bavaria was as badly affected as Friesenegger's village. On 19 April 1633 Landsberg surrendered to the Swedish, who burnt the city gates and plundered the city. On 9 July news was brought to the village of Erling that the Swedish were in the neighbourhood, which made the villagers prepare to flee, but the Swedish retired to Landsberg again, 'woe to the future', records Friesenegger in September 1633,'many fields were already barren ... What bitter prospect for extreme hunger!'[54]

Unfortunately for Erling and the surrounding villages, what the Swedish had started the Croats continued, inasmuch that Friesenegger declared that the Croats were 'more hated than the Swedish because of their thieving.' The Croats were meant to stop the Swedish raiding parties, while the main Bavarian Army was away. Then, 'On 30 September [1633] another troop of 1,000 Spanish cavalry passed through. Although as new recruits they understood no military discipline, they did understand blackmail and robbery, whereat the inhabitants once more left their houses and homes and fled into the woods.'

If this were not enough the Spanish had brought plague with them which killed about a tenth of the population of Deggendorf. Some inhabitants managed to bury their valuables before the soldiers arrived. A hoard of 3,829 coins dating from this time were found in 1986; whether their owner succumbed to the brutality of the soldiers or to the plague is not known.[55]

Meanwhile the Swedish garrison of Augsburg continued its raids into Bavaria. At the beginning of October Friesenegger again wrote, 'In the night one could see first two, then six fearful fires burning in the Lechrain towards Augsburg ... from which it was concluded that the Swedes from Augsburg were laying waste everything as they thought there were no more soldiers to resist them.' This party was ambushed on their way back to Augsburg, but in vengeance the garrison 'burnt down 140 houses in

52 *The Continuation of our Forrain Avisoes* (London: 28 April 1632), no. 20, p.6.
53 Friesenegger, p.24.
54 *Ibid.*, p.40.
55 *Ibid.*, p.31.

the parish of Prittriching; in Bergen all but two small houses; 40 in Mering; nine in Kissing and an unknown number of thatches and houses.' The diocese within this area of Bavaria had to issue tin vessels and chalices to its churches to replace the silver ones that had been plundered, but 'there was often a shortage of wine, wafers and other necessities so that the Mass had to be cancelled, especially as the parish clergy often had no supplies and not even enough black bread to eat.'[56]

Unfortunately, winter brought no respite for these Bavarian villages and throughout December enemy raids continued. To keep warm the villagers sought sanctuary in Friesenegger's monastery, which they barricaded themselves into. They set up their own Salva Guardia to protect them, but they were no match for the veteran soldiers. Neither were the Spanish soldiers any better and with the inhabitants sheltering in the monastery, as Friesenegger records in his diary for 21 December,

> The village, where the [Spanish] soldiers found only empty houses and no people, became a terrible sight. The whole village seemed to be aflame. They took chairs and benches out of the houses, removed roofs, filling the streets with dangerous camp fires and the whole village echoes to their shouts and screams that could only have been brought on by hunger and despair. Not a single villager who looked on from afar had any hope of seeing his house again when the next day dawned.[57]

The following day he adds, 'these monsters burnt down the beautiful castle of Muhlfeld.' The villagers could not wait until 23 December when they had been told the Spanish would leave, but they were disappointed when the 23rd came and went and still the soldiers remained, and it would not be until 17 January 1634 that they finally marched away, their commander taking five cows with him. By now:

> Soldiers and peasants were now to be seen half clothed and pale with misery, emaciated with hunger and walking about with bare feet in the great cold. What would happen in the long term? The soldiers were eating dogs, cats and any stolen meat. For days on end the peasants had not even a crust of bread. Many searched our monastery gardens for greens, winter lettuce, roots and herbs, which they ate raw or stewed.[58]

Worse still they ate their seed crop for the following year, so they would have to buy in more seed if there was to be a harvest in 1634. One villager who had died of starvation was found to have gnawed at her fingers. Wagons carrying bread continued to arrive from Munich but still there was not enough food, and by now there were 1,000 people sheltering in the monastery. 'All rooms were crammed, one leaning against the other,' Friesenegger continues, 'Imagine the misery, the cries of children, the wailing of the parents, the hunger, the stench!'[59]

56 *Ibid.*, p.32.
57 *Ibid.*, p.35.
58 *Ibid*, pp.36–37.
59 *Ibid.*, p.43.

With the soldiers now gone they could return to their village, but they found it in ruins, the soldiers having burnt anything combustible for firewood. In all the occupation of the Spanish had cost them 9,072 *fl* 34 *kr*, but their ordeal was not over: some Burgundian soldiers soon arrived who would cost them a further 1,008 *fl* 30 *kr*.[60]

Another Bavarian pastor, Johann Renner, records that between 1632 and 1634 the village of Vach had been raided 61 times, and in the parish register for Eldersdorf, about 10 miles north of Nuremberg, is recorded the burial of Hans Gursing in 1632, who was 'formerly a shepherd, who was ridden down by a cavalryman and died from his injuries.' Also Georg Reusch, 'who received two shot wounds three weeks before during the plundering by Forchheim soldiers died in the hospital at Nuremberg and the following day 29 May [1634], he was taken out and buried.' Which side these soldiers were on is not recorded, although one entry for 1631 records that 'Margareta, Hans Stuber's wife, who was terrirized and beaten by soldiers from Tilly's Army'.[61]

It was not just villages that were affected. In April 1633 Eichstadt had been captured by Swedish troops, who in return for not plundering the city demanded a substantial ransom. In October 1633 the Swedish were expelled, but wanting vengeance they set fire to the city, burning 444 houses, seven churches and two cloisters. They also destroyed the city's famous garden.[62]

In 1632 both Nördlingen and Augsburg had been captured by the Swedish after a short siege, but shortly after Gustavus' departure they were besieged by Bavarian and Imperialist forces, although they were not strong enough to completely blockade the cities. Nevertheless between 1627 and 1640 Nördlingen's population fell by 793 households or nearly half, mainly between 1633 and 1636, the largest drop being in 1634 when a larger besieging force was able to blockade the city more thoroughly. Coupled to this there was an outbreak of plague.

In January 1633 all non-residents of the city were ordered to leave, unless they were prepared to help with its fortifications. Soon it was reported that there was great hunger within the city and a pound of horsemeat cost three *batzen*, a pound of donkey meat two *batzen*, and a calf 18 *fl*. These prices were too expensive for the poor within the city, who had no choice but to starve. It was said that the inhabitants consumed 'horses, dogs and mice and people with atrocities in the mouth fell dead in the street (it is said that they ate even children and human flesh).' Even if they had meat there was no wood to cook it, and anyone who ventured from the city to forage was attacked by the Croats.

If starvation was not enough, plague and typhus broke out; the inhabitants demanded the city's council should offer terms to the besieging force, but they refused. Although there is no way of knowing the exact population by the time the city finally surrendered on 24 March 1635, its population is said to have been reduced from 70,000–80,000 to about 16,000–18,000. On the other hand the parish records only record 2,467 burials between 1632 and 1634, with 1,549 being recorded between May

60 *Ibid.*, p.51.
61 Quoted in Geoffrey Mortimer, 'The Thirty Years War in Eyewitness Personal Accounts' in *German History*, vol. 20, no.2 (2002), pp.149, 152.
62 Joseph Schlecht, *Tagebuch Der Augustinernonne Klara Staiger* (Eichstätt: 1889), pp.90–91.

and December 1634. In the same period there were 1,127 baptisms, with an additional 176 in 1635.

However, before this time the average number of births per year was about 300 and afterwards about 200, only rising to its pre-1632 levels in 1718. So many of the city's inhabitants may have fled rather than succumbed to the effects of the siege or plague. Nevertheless, such was the misery within the city during this time that one eyewitness, Johannes Mayer, recorded, 'It was considered a blessing in these times to die of the plague. Many might have been healed of this evil if they had taken steps against it at its onset, but they preferred to take on the sickness than to live [in] such times of punishment.'

It was during the siege of Nördlingen that the combined Swedish Armies of Bernard of Saxe-Weimar and Marshal Horn were defeated by an Imperialist–Spanish Army on 7 September 1634. With no hope now of relief the city surrendered, and the garrison was able to march out with the full honours of war and with safe passage to Erfurt. Augsburg had surrendered shortly before.[63]

However, this scorched earth policy was having an effect on the Bavarian war effort: at the beginning of 1633 when Erling was charged with a 'prohibitive [high] tax on the farms', and when the Andechs Monastery was charged with supplying four horses for the Bavarian cavalry it could only supply, 'two very old and frail' ones because the better four had been stolen on the way to Munich.[64]

At the end of 1634 Maurus Friesenegger records that the Andechs monastery had just four cows and the village of Erling five or six, but there were no sheep, pigs, geese or hens.[65] Six miles from Erling is the schloss of Seefeld, which records a similar picture:[66]

Types	1632 Census	1635 Census	Losses
Whole farms	78	29	-
Half farms	75	52	-
Salaried	342	200	-
People	2,915	979	1,936
Horses	2,915	146	690
Cattle	2,915	92	2,823
Pigs	1,346	6	1,340
Sheep	1,572	0	1,572
Geese	1,784	0	1,784
Chickens	1,897	58	1,839

63 Friesenegger, p.56; J. N. Hays, *Epidemic and Pandemics: their impact on human history* (Santa Barbara, Calif.: 2005), p.98; Christopher R. Friedrichs, *Urban Society in an Age of War: Nördlingen, 1580–1720* (Princeton: Princeton University Press, 1979) , pp.30, 43, 302–311.

64 Friesenegger, p.24.

65 *Ibid.*, p.56.

66 Alex and Volker Buchner, *Bayern im Dreissigjährigen Krieg* (Dachau: Bayerland, 2002), p.79.

To make matters worst there was a severe winter which caused the death of many half-starved and naked villagers, and in 'many village communities which had previously counted 1,000 souls, [there were] now scarcely 20 or 30 left.'[67]

The battle of Nördlingen and the surrender of Augsburg not only brought France into the war but ended the systematic destruction of Bavaria, since the seat of war moved to the Rhineland and Hesse-Kassel once more. However, the population of Bavaria still lived in fear of enemy raids and in the neighbourhood of Andechs 200 villagers had died, buried in shallow graves so that the survivors could smell their decaying bodies. According to Philip Vincent, 'In the confines of Bavaria the living were nothing near able to bury the dead. But the rats and mice devoured their carcasses most horrible to behold.'[68]

But life had to go on. The people of Andechs rebuilt their houses and tried to sow their fields as best they could, but the cost of a farm horse was between 40 and 50 *fl*, a cow 20 to 30 *fl*, a calf 5 to 7 *fl*; wheat was 25 *fl*, Rye 14 *fl*, and barley 15 *fl*, which the villagers could not afford. On the other hand by August 1636 Erling could boast 47 horses and 26 cows and a November harvest produced a bumper crop. The following year 3,000 people made a pilgrimage to Andechs Monastery as a thanksgiving and since there were fewer labourers their wages increased from between eight and 10 *fl* to about 20 to 30 *fl*.[69]

As the situation in Bavaria improved Maximilian was able to impose taxes once more, depending on the size of the property. In 1643 each whole farm had to pay 2 *fl*, half farms 1 *fl*, the quarter farms probably had to pay 30 *kr* and eighth farms 15 *kr*, which in Erling raised 136 *fl* 52 *kr*, although Maurus Friesenegger added, 'How gladly would everyone give the same again, if he had peace.' Even so the income was nowhere near the income before the Swedish occupation, which was 31,779,253 *fl* from 1619 to 1634, but only 8,897,766 *fl* from 1635 to 1649. Maximilian had to weaken his field army in order to garrison various town in Bavaria which varied greatly in size: in 1637 the town of Heidelberg contained a garrison of 152 men, while Hassmersheim and Bretten had just one soldier each. However, the civilians' suffering would go on until the war was over and most of the soldiers were disbanded.[70]

67 Friesenegger, p.57.
68 Vincent, p.61.
69 Friesenegger, pp.58–59, 65.
70 Friesenegger, p.76; Kasper, p.285; *The current to this week from Holland*, 29 May–8 June 1639; Franz Meier, *Die bayerische Unterpfalz im Dreißigjährigen Krieg*, pp.340–341.

11

Death in the Army

A soldier usually enlisted to that one day after making his fortune he could enjoy a better life, but for the majority death awaited them, either a violent death in battle or more likely from disease. Until then he might have to march thousands of miles across Europe: it is estimated that Peter Hagendorf of Pappenheim's Regiment of Foot marched 22,500 km (around 14,000 miles) or an average of 900 km (559 miles) per year. This was not unique during the seven years he served with the Danish, and then the Swedish Army. Robert Monro traveled 6,385 km (around 4,000 miles) or on average about 1,198 km (744 miles) per year. At times this might be pleasant, Monro recalls, as on sunny days a soldier had 'a variety of pleasures in marching softly without fear or danger, through fertile soils [i.e. land] and pleasant countries.' On the other hand Father Pietro Drexel records a less romantic view in his diary on 29 July 1620 while marching through Upper Austria, where 'here and there were still burning villages to see and everything stank.'[1]

Nothing had changed 17 years later in 1637, when General Johann von Werth warned Maximilian that his men were so exhausted that a quarter were sick or were straggling from their line of march, and that the regiments would be ruined before they had made contact with the enemy. He had to pay his 'poor starving men' himself, who had gone 10 or 12 days without bread and were living on horseflesh.[2]

It was said that the Croats' lifestyle was such that, 'few [are] likely to get grey hairs'. A a soldier who died on campaign would usually be buried in an unmarked grave which history forgets about until discovered accidentally centuries later. One of these mass graves was found on the battlefield of White Mountain near Prague in 1974. It contained 44 skeletons, of which 40 can be positively identified as men and two as women. Seventeen were between the ages of 20 and 40, 15 between 40 and 50 and four were approximately 60. Three were about 20, while one is estimated as being just

1 Monro, part II, pp.7, 89, and unnumbered pages; Father Drexel's diary in Sigmund Riezler, *Kriegstagebucher Aus Dem Ligitischen Hauptquarter, 1620* (Munchen: G Frans'chen, 1908) pp.147–149.

2 Redlich, p.513.

15 years old. Of the women, one was between 20 and 30 and the other was 40 to 50 years old.[3]

Another mass grave was discovered in 2007 on the battlefield at Wittstock and contained 125 skeletal remains, although there were only 88 complete skeletons. In 2010 three pits were found at Stralsund, containing a total of 25 skeletons, although the majority appear to have died from disease with only a few having signs of battle injuries. Only in one of the three pits can archaeologists say for certain that they were soldiers. They were buried where they fell, possibly when part of the fortification of the town collapsed. In this grave was also found six pikes, three muskets and three swords. The last grave was discovered in 2011 on the battle site of Lützen and contained the skeletal remains of 47 soldiers who are believed to have fought with the Blue Regiment in the Swedish Army.[4]

Some skeletons in these graves bore signs of more peaceful pursuits, such as smoking, a pastime said to have been introduced by the English; the English General, Sir Charles Morgan, said that smoking and cards kept his men happy. However, by always smoking a clay pipe in the same position in their mouths they had worn away part of their front teeth, forming a round groove.

The 'Lützen grave' contained the remains of soldiers aged between 16 and 45, although the majority were 21 to 35 years old. The youngest soldier in the Wittstock grave was about 18 years old, although the average age was 28. The average height was 1.70 metres (5 ft 7 in.) and the tallest was about 1.82 metres (5 ft 11 in.). By the examination of the skeletons' teeth 11 are known to have come from Scotland and a further 33 possibly being Scottish, although the tests were inconclusive. The remainder came from central Europe or Sweden.[5]

Twenty of the skeletons from the Wittstock grave had signs of head traumas with slash marks caused either from a blow from a pole weapon, such as a halberd, or sword slash from a cavalryman. One 17 to 20 year old soldier from Finland had five slashes to his head, although only one of these is believed to have caused the fatal blow.

A further 24 skeletons showed signs that they were either killed or wounded by a gunshot either from a pistol or musket, since lead balls were found among their bones. These shots were found in the pelvic area, the area of the right shoulder or the knee region of the leg and since they were buried on the battlefield they probably bled to death, unless they were killed by another method. Several skeletons appeared to have been cut down while they were running away, since they bore signs of being attacked from behind; one had a hole in his vertebrae probably made by a sword blade.[6]

3 TNA: SP 101/2 unfolio, Miscellaneous newsletters and correspondence for Flanders, 1603–1637; Vaclav Matousek 'Archaeological Erforschung der Schlachtfelder des Dreissigjährigen Krieges' in Janos Stekovics, *Die Blut'ge Affair bei Lützen: Wallensteins Wende* (Wettin-Löbejün Stekovics, 2012), p.283.

4 Don McNair, *The Struggle for Stralsund, 1627–1630* (Farnham: Pike and Shot Society, 2012), p.45.

5 Eickhoff, Anja Grothe and Bettina Jungklaus 1636, *Ihre Letzte Schlacht, leben im Dreissigjährigen Kreig* (Brandenburg: Archaeologisches Landesmuseum, 2013) p.178; Sabine Eickhoff 'Das Massengrab der Schlacht von Wittstock', in *Militargeschichte*, February 2013, p.49.

6 Eickhoff et al., pp.152–163; Eickhoff, 'Das Massengrab der Schlacht von Wittstock', p.49.

The skeletons from the Lützen grave showed similar wounds to the Wittstock burials. The Blue Regiment was overrun by Imperialist cavalry and so the majority showed signs of head wounds, including 21 having been shot in the head. Tests on the skeletons' teeth show that only one came from Sweden, possibly Erich Sirerson, who was one of the few Swedish soldiers serving in the regiment. The rest are known to have been German, which is confirmed by the regiment's muster roll. These skeletons also show signs of disease, such syphilis and a vitamin D deficiency, and it is estimated that they were on average between 1.65 and 1.80 metres (5 ft 5 in. and 5 ft 11 in.) tall. Some showed signs that they had been wounded before and some bore marks to their forearms from a desperate bid to save themselves from a sword slash.

A sixteenth century writer estimated that for every soldier killed by a firearm a further four were wounded, although this ratio was dismissed by Sir John Smythe, who does not give his own figure for casualties caused by firearms. However, a casualty return for 16 July 1621 shows the following casualties:[7]

Infantry regiment	Dead	Wounded	Killed in Action
Anholt	10	21	20
Bauer	15	32	18
Herliberg	3	12	2
Florinville	4	12	4
Schmidt	8	64	51 (incl. 12 missing)
Rouville	9	30	3
Mortaigne	3	4	4
Gaisberg	-	-	-

Moreover at the Battle of Breitenfeld, Tilly is said to have lost about two thirds of his infantry and half his cavalry, and Geleen's Regiment of Foot is said to have mustered on paper 2,000 men before the battle, but only 400 that evening. Likewise at the Battle of Wittstock only 30 men of Wendt's Regiment of Foot were with the colours after the battle.

At the battle of Nördlingen the Bavarian Army suffered the following casualties:[8]

Regiment	Strength	Sick and Wounded	Prisoners
Fugger	1,234	86	285
Reinach	1,270	109	246
Pappenheim	1,000	172	153
	6,357	664	1,494

7 BL Harl MS 135 f50; Heilmann, 1868, p.102.
8 Jacob, Carl, *Von Lützen nach Nördlingen: Ein Beitrag zur Geschichte des Dreissigjährigen Kreigs in Süddeutschland in den Jahren 1633 und 1634* (Strassburg: Ed. van Hauten, 1904), p.108.

Regiment	Strength	Sick and Wounded	Prisoners
Ruepp	1,017	150	35
Puck	836	73	426
Harttenberg	750	74	99
Salis	250	-	250
	6,357	664	1,494

Unlike today a surgeon would usually treat his patients in the sitting position, rather than lying down, because this was seen as the position of a corpse. In his bag or chest he would have razors, trepans, head saws, dismembering saws and nippers, cauterising irons and even a hammer and chisel. His tools for the extraction of teeth would include forceps and a small file. The surgeon also had various potions divided into Aqua [water], oils, syrups, and Opiats and such 'purging' medicines. Despite the unhygienic conditions soldiers did survive surgery. During the storming of Madgeburg on 20 May 1631, Peter Hagendorf was wounded and records that:

> I was taken to the camp and bound up. For I had been shot once through the stomach (shot right through from the front) and a second time through both shoulders, as that bullet was caught in my shirt. The army doctor bound my hands behind my back so he could use the gouge (forceps) on me.

Operations were performed without anaesthetic and the surgeon would not sterilise his instruments before he probed a wound. In fact he would pride himself on how bloody his apron was, nor did he see the need to wipe his instruments between operations. Many patients probably passed out due to the pain, as Hagendorf did, because he records 'thus I was brought back to my hut half dead.' On 24 May he was taken to Halberstadt, where 300 men from Pappenheim's Regiment were lodged in nearby villages to recover. It would take seven weeks before he was fit enough to rejoin his regiment.[9]

Fortunately for Hagendorf he does not seem to have developed an infection, which was a real danger after surgery, especially if the surgeon had left a piece of cloth or bone in the wound. Although writing in 1578, the Spanish nobleman Don Juan de Silva records what must have been familiar to many soldiers during the Thirty Years War. He was wounded at the beginning of August by a harquebusier which caused a 'considerable' wound in his left arm. His wound appears to have become infected so that he was operated on again, but by probing the wound the surgeon had caused seven wounds in his arm rather than the one he originally had. Five months later he was still suffering so much that he was bedridden through the pain: four of the wounds had almost healed but the others still festered, two of which caused him 'so much trouble

9 Quoted in Helfferich, p.283. The German words for 'tent' and 'hut' at this time are interchangeable, so I have used 'hut'.

and are so sore and painful'. A further six weeks or so went by and Don Juan noticed a piece of bone sticking out of the wound. The following day a surgeon pulled it out: according to Don Juan it was 'an inch thick and the length of three fingers; it was God's great favour to reveal it and remove it with so little damage – though with a lot of pain.' Later that day another bone appeared, which although it left a large wound was not as painful as the first, and once these had been removed the wounds quickly healed. Don Juan was lucky in that he could afford good surgeons to treat him, but most soldiers would succumb to their wounds.[10]

Some progressive surgeons put forward the idea that wounds should be bandaged, but in the heat of battle where operations had to be performed quickly then cauterising was seen as the only solution. Such would be the 'terror' to the patient who saw the red hot iron in front of him that several men would have to hold him down while the iron was applied to his flesh.

However, it was not just the ordinary soldiers who risked their lives. At Breitenfeld Tilly received two or three wounds from musket balls and pistol shots and a bruise on the neck from a butt of a carbine. Pappenheim was wounded on many occasions and it is said that at Breitenfeld he was wounded six or seven times. He was finally killed at the Battle of Lützen a year later. Officers like Tilly and Pappenheim would probably have brought their own doctors on campaign, who were better qualified in their profession than the ordinary regimental or company surgeons.[11]

However, the biggest killer for soldiers was disease. There are countless references to diseases spreading through an army during the war. On 8 October 1620 Father Fitzsimons records in his diary that 'The most serene Duke of Bavaria, made up his mind to go home. His army and nearly [all of] his whole staff got sick. All his councillors, secretaries, courtiers, and servants had been torn from him by death or disease.'[12] In September 1622 Tilly was said to be at Heidelberg with 'above 6,000 fighting men for there is great sickness in his army and no less want of victuals'. On 22 December 1631 one observer claimed that Tilly 'hath brave cavalry but very poor and impotent foot forces. In their march from Ansbach to Guntsbach they left behind them in the streets and ways above 1,500 sick and dead soldiers.'[13]

The destruction of armies from disease is usually blamed on typhus, which in the seventeenth century had many names: 'the burning ague', 'the Hungarian disease' or 'the Swedish disease'; as well as 'camp fever' and 'gaol fever'. It is caused by the *Rickettsia prowazekii* bacteria which thrives in filthy conditions and is highly contagious, being spread by lice faeces. If the lice bites its host who then scratches the itch, the faeces may be rubbed into the wound and so enter the bloodstream. About 10 days later the person develops a high fever, muscle pains, delirium, severe headaches and nausea. Five days after these symptoms a rash appears and the person has a flushed appearance.

10 Quoted in Lorraine White, 'The Experience of Spain's Early Modern Soldiers', in *War in History* (2002), vol. 9, no. 1, pp.23–24.
11 Harte, part 2, p.40.
12 Fitzsimon, p.89.
13 TNA: SP 101/28 unfolio, miscellaneous correspondence and newsletters for Germany, 1620–1625; BL Burney MS, 263/C6/5, *The continuation of our Forraine News since 2 this present to 12 January 1632.*

The next two weeks is crucial, because if the fever breaks then they are likely to survive, but if not then they may slip into a coma and death soon follows. The suffer may also have complications such as pneumonia and possibly organ failure.

During the twentieth century it was estimated that up to 15 percent of 15 to 30 year olds who suffered from typhus would die if their condition remained untreated, which rose to 60 percent for older people. Even if they survived, the person would have a long convalescence before they recovered fully.[14]

In July 1620 the Catholic League's army began the campaign with 32,000 men, but only 10,000 of these men were left by November of that year, during which time they had spread typhus throughout Austria and Bohemia. The survivors would carry it back to Upper Bavaria and Württemberg. This is not to say that measures to prevent the spread of the disease were not made. In Munich infected travellers were shut up in pest houses on the outskirts of the city and money from infected areas was washed in vinegar.[15]

However, it was not just typhus which was the 'killer of armies': typhoid was also common. The symptoms are similar to typhus and spread in the same way, although typhoid is caused by different bacteria. The symptoms develop in about seven days rather than 10 for typhus, spots may appear on the body, diarrhoea has a green appearance, and the liver and spleen become enlarged. After about four weeks death occurs in 10 to 20 percent of cases.

Strict rules for cleanliness were imposed when the army camped for a long time, since unhygienic conditions might lead to the third disease that a soldier could contract: dysentery. There are several types of dysentery, or as it was known, 'the bloody flux' which is caused by bacteria or parasitic worms find their way into food or water contaminated by human faeces. Symptoms include a high fever, fatigue, headaches, nausea or vomiting, abdominal pains and severe diarrhoea, which sometimes contains blood, hence the name 'bloody flux'. If untreated it can lead to death through dehydration or organ failure.

However, even before he contracted one of these diseases the soldier was my no means healthy. Tests on the skeletons in the Wittstock grave shows that three quarters suffered from malnutrition during childhood, which caused rickets or scurvy due to a lack of vitamin C, while a large proportion had osteoarthritis in the hips and knee joints, and over half had tooth decay. Many were missing teeth as well as suffering from inflammation of the maxillary sinuses or oral mucosa. A large percentage were also suffering from syphilis, tuberculosis or periosteal inflammation, and were infested with lice and other parasites. If they were suffering from syphilis the regimental surgeon might recommend mercury mixed with other ingredients to form a paste, which was rubbed into the sores which would appear all over their body. Alternatively,

14 R. N. Mazumder et al., 'Typhus Fever; an overlooked diagnosis', in *Journal of Health, Population and Nutrition* (Dhaka: Centre for Health and Population Research, June 2009), pp.419–421.

15 Dr F. Prinzing, *Epidemics Resulting from Wars* (Oxford, 1916), p.29, quoting J. C. Rhumelius' *Historia Morbi* (1621); Julius Krebs, *Die Schlact am Weissen Berge bei Prag* (Breslau: Wilhelm Koebner, 1879), pp.195–199.

the mercury might be taken orally or injected; either way, the long term effects of this chemical could cause madness and damage to the nervous system.

However, one disease which targeted both healthy and sick people alike was bubonic plague, which was spread by the fleas on black rats (*Rattus rattus*). Once bitten by an infected flea a person would develop buboes, usually on the neck, armpits and groin. If it spread to the lungs, then by coughing or sneezing they would spread the infection to others since the bacteria was present in their breath. This 'pneumonic plague' had the same symptoms as bubonic plague, and death would almost certainly follow.

In September 1622 plague spread through the ranks of Colonel Sprinzenstein's Regiment so that in just a few weeks its eight companies had to be reduced to four or five. An outbreak of the 'pestilence' in Dillenburg on 18 December 1625 quickly killed 378 people, and by the time the last victim died on 30 October 1626 it has been estimated that about a third of the population had died.[16]

In 1634 soldiers are said to have caused a severe outbreak of plague in Munich, with the occupants of between 200 and 250 houses having to be 'shut up' to await their fate. This was the usual way of dealing with the occupants of a house infected by the plague. A guard would be put on the building to make sure none of the occupants escaped until their sickness had run its course. It is estimated that during the Munich outbreak 15,000 people died by the time it subsided in December, ceased the following February. The dead were buried in mass graves, about 40 at a time. In September 1635 the plague again broke out in Munich and raged until February 1637. In all, 80,000 Bavarian families are said to have been wiped out by the plague during the war, although estimates of the Bavarian population beforehand suggest about one million, so the number of fatalities has either been greatly exaggerated, or there were more people living in Bavaria than previously thought.[17]

16 Helml, p.38.
17 Prinzing, pp.31, 55–56, 77.

12

Conclusion: Peace at Last

Many had seen the comet in the skies above Germany in 1618, the traditional sign of an impending disaster. In 1635 when the Peace of Prague was signed many believed that the comet had been seen for 15 days and so the war would last 15 years, taken from 1620, and so with the signing of the Peace, peace was now at hand. Unfortunately, they were disappointed and the war continued; but with the signing of the Peace of Westphalia in 1648 a pamphlet commented that few could remember such a beautiful day.

However, the Peace did not lift the civilians' burden from the soldiers, who continued in their garrisons, and they still had to quarter them and pay the taxes for their upkeep. There was even a fear that the fighting would start again, and certainly Spain and France would continue to fight for the next 10 years before they also made peace. This Franco-Spanish War would continue to be fought on German, as well as Flemish soil, and involved German and even English soldiers; the latter fighting on both sides, with former Royalists fighting for Spain and elements of the republican army fighting for France. This war was finally brought to a close by the Peace of the Pyrenees on 5 November 1659.

However, for many 1648 was the beginning of the end of their sufferings, On 13 November 1648 the city of Ulm heard the news and cerebrated as if it were Christmas Day with 'sermons, communions and diligent prayers,' records Hans Herberle, even though the day before he had fled to the city because of French troops marching through the countryside. News reached Memmingen on 16 November, where Peter Hagendorf was stationed with his regiment, which by now was commanded by Major General Winterscheid. He recalls that a 'joyous festival' was held, 'as if it were Easter or Whitsunday.' Three sermons were held in both churches, the lesson being from the first book of Moses chapter 8, in which Noah gave thanks after the flood subsided.

However, it was not until October 1649 that the Bavarian Army was finally disbanded, Colonel Ners' Regiment on 1 October at Augsburg, and Winterscheid's on 5 October at Memmingen; it was not until 11 July 1650 that Neven's Regiment was disbanded at Freiburg.[1]

1 Heilmann, 1868, vol. 2, p.908.

30. The swearing of the oath of ratification of the Treaty of Westphalia, 1648.

It was not until May 1649 that Peter Hagendorf finally was discharged from the army. He was given some money so that he could return home, but with his daughter he journeyed to collect his son from Altheim, where he had left him safe. History does not record what happened to him afterwards, nor how his diary found its way to the Berlin State Library, to be discovered centuries later by Jan Peters in 1988.

Unfortunately, no in-depth study had been made as to what became of the soldiers once they were discharged from the army, although of the 230 men from the Swedish village of Bygdeå who served in the war, 215 died during service and five returned home disabled, leaving just 10 able-bodied men. At the end of the war the population of Bygdeå was about 1,500 women to 1,000 men. This decrease of the male population led to a sevenfold increase in women running farms. True, these figures relate to a Swedish village, but there must have been a similar depopulation throughout Europe, with women outnumbering the male population.[2]

2 Parker, *The Thirty Years War*, p.193; Jan Lindegren, Utskrivning och Utsugning, Production och Reproducktion I Bygdeå, 1620–1640 (Stockholm: Almqvist & Wiksell international, 1980), pp.300–301.

Appendix I

Regiments of the Bavarian Army

Albert's Regiment of Foot
See Jung Tilly's Regiment.

'Alt Kolb Regiment'
See Binder's Regiment.

'Alt Tilly's Regiment'
See Eisenbeck's Regiment.

Colonel Johann Aldringen's Regiment of Foot
Raised in 1622, eight companies strong, but disbanded in 1623.[1]

Colonel Johann Jakob Freiherr von Anholt's Regiment of Foot
Raised 25 November 1619, and in 1620 mustered 3,150 strong in 14 companies. On 21 February 1631 Count Johann Baptist von Lodron took over the regiment before being succeeded by Colonel Gottfried Count Huyn von Geleen later that year. Geleen had been a captain in the regiment in 1621. Another captain, Beck, was cashiered on 3 October 1621 because of negligence, having surrendered the town of Pfreimd to Mansfeld. However, at his court martial the charge was disproved and he became a captain in Cratz's regiment of horse.

By 23 November 1638 Colonel Johann von Ruischenberg was commanding the regiment. He was succeeded by Generalzeugmeister Hans Wilhelm Bogt von Hunolstein on 8 April 1648. However, he only commanded it for a short period of time, as on 25 August 1648 Fieldmarshal Adrian von Enkefort (or Enkenvoirt) took over the regiment and commanded it until it was disbanded in 1649.

Present at the battles of Wiesloch, Wimpfen, Höchst, Stadtlohn, Werben, Lutter, Zusmarshausen, Breitenfeld (where it is estimated to have lost about 1,600 of its

1 Goetz, 1904, p.122.

2000 strength), Werben, Hessich Oldendorf, Wittenweier, Tuttlingen, Freiburg, Herbsthausen, Jankow, Freiburg and Allerheim.

Colonel Johan Bartl's Regiment of Dragoons
See Wolf's Regiment.

Colonel Jacob Bauer von Eisenbeck's Regiment of Foot
Raised 1619 in Würzburg about 1,500 strong in 6 companies and commanded by Colonel Johann Bauer von Eiseneck. On 11 April 1621 Bauer was killed at Frawenberg and his regiment passed to Colonel Wolf Dietrich von Truchsess von Waldburg. In 1624 Lieutenant General Tserchas von Tilly became the commander and it is often referred to as 'Alt Tilly's Regiment'. The following year it mustered 2,686 men in 11 companies. However, it was almost completely destroyed at the Battle of Breitenfeld in 1631, where it lost most of its colours. In 1632 it was brought up to strength again mustering 1,600 strong in 10 companies. A detachment of 400 was at the crossing of the Lech and three companies were garrisoning Göttingen and Minden. On 20 April 1632 the regiment passed to Generalfeldzeugmeister Duke Franz Rudolf von Saxon Lauenburg and was then known as the 'Saxon Regiment'.

However on 30 December 1632 the regiment passed to Generalfeldzeugmeister OttoHeinrich Graf von Fugger. After Fugger's death in 1634 it passed to Colonel Ferdinand Depp, then from 22 August 1637 to De Puech. Colonel Miehr succeeded De Puech and then on 15 September 1644 it passed to Colonel Cobb, who commanded it until it was disbanded in 1649.

Present at the battles of White Mountain, Wiesloch, Wimpfen, Höchst, Stadtlohn, Lutter, Madgeburg, Werben, Breitenfeld, Rain (detachment 400 strong), Nurnberg, Nördlingen, Tuttlingen, Wittenweier, Freiberg, Herbsthausen, Allerheim and Jankow.

Colonel Wilhelm von Beldin's Regiment of Foot
Raised in 1642 and disbanded in 1649.[2]

Bock's Regiment of Cuirassiers (ex Neu Cratz's Regiment)
Raised 1621 and in 1625 mustered 529 men in 5 troops.

Present at the battles of Dessau and Lutter.

Colonel Stephan Binder's Regiment of Cuirassiers
Raised 1634 by Colonel Stephan Binder, who commanded the regiment until 9 May 1637, when he was succeeded by Colonel Andreas Kolb, when it became known as 'Alt KolbRegiment'. In 1638 it mustered 9 companies. In 1648 it was garrisoning Schmutter and the following year was disbanded.

Present at the battles of Rheinfelden, Wittenweier, Wolfenbüttel, Tuttlingen, Freiburg, Herbsthausen, Allerheim and Dachau.

2 *Ibid.*, p.123.

Colonel Kaspar Blarer's Regiment of Foot
Raised 1623 and disbanded 1631.

Colonel Engelbert Bonninghausen's Regiment of Cuirassiers

Raised May 1619. In 1622 Lorenzo Maestro took over the regiment and commanded it until it was disbanded in 1629.

The regiment was present at the battles of White Mountain, Wiesloch, Wimpfen, Lorscher Heide, Höchst and Stadtlohn.

Colonel Bracciolini's Regiment of Horse
Raised 1631 and was present at Geltolfing and Nördlingen.

Colonel[?] Buck's Regiment of Foot
Raised 1620. In 1635 it mustered 839 strong in 5 companies. At the Battle of Nördlingen it lost 73 casualties and 426 taken prisoner.

Busch's Regiment of Cuirassiers
Raised 1633 and mustered 6 companies. It was present at the Nattle of Nördlingen.

Colonel Johann Franz von Caffoy's Regiment of Foot
Raised and disbanded in 1645.[3]

Comargo's Regiment of Harquebusiers
Raised 1632, in Bavaria and Würzburg. By 1635 the regiment had been taken over by Metternich and mustered 10 companies, although was just 300 strong.

Present at the battles of Rheinfelden and Wittenweier.

Colonel Cordenbach's (or Courtenbach's) Regiment of Horse
At the start of August 1624, his regiment of '5 cornets' was reported to be with Tilly.[4]

Present at Efferding, Rossing, and Lutter.

Cosalky's Regiment of Harquebusiers
See Nevenheim's Regiment.

Colonel Jakob Fürstenberg Cratz's Regiment of Cuirassiers
Raised in 1620. The regiment was later commanded by Ludwig Graf von Fürstenberg. In 1625 Phillip von Cronberg took over the regiment and then, from 8 August 1634, Colonel Heinrich Keller. On 20 September 1635 Heinrich von Gayling zu Altheim took over the regiment and commanded it until it was disbanded in 1649.

3 *Ibid.*
4 *A Continuation of the former news*, 9–10 September 1624; Weber, pp.406–407.

In 1638 it mustered 9 companies and in 1640 was 880 strong, although 111 were dismounted.

Present at the battles of Rakonitz, White Mountain, Lorscher Heide, Höchst, Stadtholm, Rossing, Lutter, Werben, Breitenfeld, crossing the Lech, Nurnburg, Nördlingen, Rhinefelden, Wittenweier, Wolfenbüttel, Tuttlingen, Herbsthausen, Allerheim, Zusmarshausen.

Colonel Johann Phillip Cratz's Regiment of Cuirassiers

Raised 1620 by Johann Phillip Cratz, mustering 823 in 8 companies. In 1623 Matthais von Bock took over the regiment and commanded it until 1627 when he was succeeded by Colonel Frederich Waldeck. Disbanded in 1629?

The regiment was present at Wimpfen, Haguenau and Lutter.

Colonel Johann Phillip Cratz's Regiment of Horse

Raised 1620. Later commanded by Jakob Ludwig von Fürstenberg, then Adam Philip von Cronberg's regiment. In 1632 it mustered 1,145 strong in 13 troops and was disbanded in 1634.

Colonel Cratz's Regiment of Horse

Raised 1631 and disbanded in 1633 when Cratz was captured by the Swedes.

The regiment served at the battles of Bamberg, Rain and Nurnberg.

Cronberg's Regiment of Cuirassiers

See Jakob Fürstenburg Cratz's Regiment.

Colonel Nicholas Desfour's Regiment of Harquebusiers

Raised in 1622 and disbanded in 1624.

It served at the battles of Wimpfen, Lorcher Heide, and Stadtholm.

De Puech's Regiment of Foot

See Colonel Johann Bauer von Eiseneck's Regiment.

Colonel Nicola Desfour's Regiment of Horse

Raised 1622, but despite mustering five troops it was disbanded in 1624.[5]

Edlinstellen's Regiment of Foot

See Ruepp's Regiment.

Colonel Dietrich Ottmar von Erwitte's Regiment of Cuirassiers

Raised 1619 in Bavaria and Neuberg by Colonel Dietrich Ottmar von Erwitte, and composed of 858 strong in 10 companies. In 1631 Colonel von de Horst took over

5 Goetz, 1904, p.121.

the regiment until 1639 when it passed to Kaspar Mercy. Then on 11 August 1644 Flechenstein took over command.

In 1638 it mustered 8 companies and in 1640 it mustered 576 men, of which 180 were without horses. In 1648 the regiment was at Schmutter and then disbanded the following year.

The regiment was present at the battles of Prag, Lorscher Heide, Höchst, Stadtholm, Rossing, Lutter, Werben, Breitenfeld, Hessich Oldendorf, Rheinfelden, Wittenweier, Ziegenhain, Wolfenbüttel, Tuttlingen, Freiburg Jankau, Herbsthausen, Allerheim, and Zusmarshausen.

Colonel Dietrict Ottmar von Erwitte's Regiment of Foot

Raised 28 April 1625 and mustered 1000 men in four companies, however later that year Colonel Matthias Gallas, took the regiment into Imperial, rather than Bavarian service. From 1629 Colonel Joachim von der Wahl, who had been the lieutenant colonel, took over the regiment. Colonel von Beauneau became the next *inhaber* on 16 September 1644, followed by Colonel Marimont on 14 May 1645. In 1649 the regiment was disbanded.[6]

Present at the battles of Dessau, Lutter, Magdeburg, Wervben, Breitenfeld, Bamberg, Rain, Rheinfelden, Wolfenbüttel, Herbsthausen, Allerheim and Zusmarshausen.

Colonel d'Espaigne's Regiment of Horse

Raised 1631, before transferring to Imperial service in 1634.

The regiment served at the battles of Bamberg, Rain, Nurnberg and Nördlingen.

Colonel Winandt von Eynatten's Regiment of Cuirassiers

Raised 1619 by Colonel Herman von der Lippe in Cologne. However, by June 1620 it had been taken over by Colonel Winandt von Eynatten and by 1624 a Colonel de Grana. On 9 September 1631 it mustered three companies of cuirassiers and two of harquebusiers, a total of 500 men. In 1632 Salis took over the regiment and commanded it until 1634, when it passed to Johann von Werth. In 1647 it became Johann Jakob Kolb's (or 'Alte'; or 'Alt Kolb's') Regiment and was disbanded in 1649.

The regiment was present at the battles of White Mountain, Wiesloch, Wimpfen, Lorscher Heide, Höchst, Stadtholm, Geltolfing, Nördlingen, Wittenweier, Wolfenbüttel, Tuttlingen, Herbsthausen, Allerheim and Zusmarshausen

Falkenburg's Regiment of Horse

His lieutenant colonel was Trost, who commanded the regiment at Magdeburg, where it mustered 800 strong.[7]

6 Heilmann, 1868, vol. 2, part II, p.904; Weber, pp.406–407.

7 Antonie Charles Hennequin Villermont, *Tilly: oder Dreissigjährige Krieg von 1618 bis 1632* (Schaffhausen: Fr Hurterschen, 1860), p.227; Weber, pp.406–407.

Fleckenstein's Regiment of Cuirassiers
Raised 1620 and in 1642 mustered 9 companies.
Present at the Battles of 2nd Breitenfeld and Jankow

Colonel Franz von Florenville's Regiment of Foot
Raised 1620 and disbanded 1622.[8]

Colonel Wilhelm von Forstenau's Regiment of Foot
Raised and disbanded in 1645.[9]

Franz Graf von Fugger's Regiment of Foot[10]
In 1638 it mustered 8 companies. At Nördlingen the regiment lost 150 men as casualties and 35 were taken prisoner.
Present at the Battles of Nördlingen, Wittenweier, Jankow, Freiberg and 2nd Nördlingen, Zusmarshausen.

Colonel Jakob Fugger's Regiment of Horse
Raised 1631 and disbanded 1634.

Colonel Otto Heinrich Graf von Fugger's Regiment of Foot
Raised 10 May 1631 by Colonel Otto Heinrich Graf von Fugger. From 10 December 1632 Colonel Johann von Troiberz took command and the regiment became known as the 'Saxon Regiment'.
Troiberz was succeeded by Colonel Hardenberg on 16 August 1634, and then by George Rudolf an Haslang. The final *inhaber* was Ferdinand von Puech who took over the regiment on 15 September 1644 and commanded it until it was disbanded in 1649.[11]
The regiment was with Pappenheim in 1631 and 1632 and present at the battles of Nördlingen, Rheinfelden, Wittenweier, Wolfenbüttel, Tuttlingen, Freiberg, Herbsthausen, Allerheim, and Zusmarshausen.

Colonel Egon Fürstenberg's Regiment of Cuirassiers
The regiment was raised in 1619 under Fürstenberg, before becoming Virmond's and later von der Nerssen's regiment, Nerssen had been Fürstenberg's lieutenant colonel in 1621. The regiment was reported to have been disbanded in 1628. However according to Die Kriegskosten Bayern, Jakob Ludwig von Fürstenburg, then Adam Philip von Kronenburg took over the regiment.
The regiment was present at Lorscher Heide, Höchst and Stadtholm.

8 Goetz, 1904, p.123.
9 *Ibid.*
10 Heilmann, 1868, vol. 2, part II, p.904; Weber, pp.406–407.
11 *Ibid.*

Colonel Egon Fürstenberg's Regiment of Foot
Raised 1621, but the following year it was reduced into Hohenzollen's regiment.
Present at the battles of Wiesloch and Wimpfen.

Colonel Friedrich Rudolf Fürstenberg's Regiment of Horse
Raised 1632. In 1635 Colonel von der Horst took over the regiment, and reduced it into his other regiment of horse. A Colonel Punder took over the regiment and commanded it until 1636 when it was disbanded.
The regiment served at the battles of Maastricht and Nördlingen.

Fürstenberg's Regiment of Cuirassiers
See Jakob Fürstenberg Cratz's Regiment.

Colonel Friedrich Rudolf Fürstenberg's Regiment of Foot
Raised 1631, continued until 1633.

Fürstenberg's Regiment of Foot
See Mortaigne's Regiment.

Colonel Friedrich von Gaisberg's Regiment of Foot

Raised April 1621. Gaisberg commanded the regiment until 1622, when Graf Hohenzollern took over the regiment and commanded it until it was disbanded in 1623. It was present at the battles of Wimpfen and Höchst.
Gallas' Regiment of Foot
See Erwitte's Regiment.

Colonel Heinrich von Gayling's Regiment of Cuirassiers
See Colonel Jakob Fürstenberg Cratz's Regiment.

Geleen's Regiment of Foot
See Anholt's Regiment.

Colonel Heinrich Christopher von Gelling's Regiment of Horse
Raised 1639 and disbanded in 1649.[12]

Generalwachtmeister Gil de Haas' Regiment of Foot
Raised 1640 by Generalwachtmeister Gil de Haas. He was succeeded possibly by Ludinghausen, then in 1642 by Gold, on 27 October 1646 by Koderitz, and then Colonel Burkhard von Elter, and on 26 June 1649 Colonel Johann Wilhelm Suler.[13]
In 1642 it mustered 590 men in 8 companies, but by 1645 this had risen to 1,064 men.

12 Goetz, 1904, p.121.
13 Heilmann, 1868, vol. 2, part II, p.904; Weber, pp.406–407.

Present at the battles of Wolfenbüttel, Ziegenhain, Tuttlingen, Freiburg, Herbsthausen, Allerheim and Zusmarshausen.

Generalwachtmeister Gil de Haas' Regiment of Foot
Raised 1644 and mustered 2,000 men in 10 companies, by Generalwachtmeister Gil de Haas, who was succeeded on 11 July 1646 by Colonel von Elter. On 27 October 1646 Colonel Beltin, who had been the regiment's lieutenant colonel, took over the regiment and commanded it until it was disbanded in 1649.

The regiment was present at the battles of Jankau and Allerheim.

Gold's Regiment of Foot
See Gil de Haas' Regiment.

Feldmarshal Götz's Regiment of Cuirassiers
Raised 1635.

Götz's Regiment of Foot
See Herliberg's Regiment

Colonel Gouschenitz's (or Guschenitz's) Regiment of Croats
Raised 1645 and disbanded in 1649.[14]

Gronsfeld's Regiment of Foot
See Herliberg's Regiment.

Colonel Theodor von Haimhausen's Regiment of Foot
Raised 1619 and composed of 8 or 9 companies. From 22 October 1624 Count Werner von Tilly took over the regiment and it became known as Jung (or Young) Tilly's Regiment.

At the Battle of Lutter it was 2,877 men strong in 12 companies. On 20 June 1633 its lieutenant colonel, Stefan Alber, took over the regiment which was garrisoning the towns of Minden, Bremen and Osnabruck. Colonel Marshalt or Marschalk succeeded Alber on 10 May 1635, who was killed at the Battle of Wittenweier. He was succeeded by Generalwachtmeister Hans Wilhelm Vogh von Hunoltstein on 2 February 1639. Finally Colonel Franz Rouyer commanded the regiment from 19 August 1642 until 1649 when the regiment was disbanded.

Present at the battles of Wiesloch, Wimpfen, Höchst, Stadtlohn, Lutter, Madgeburg, Maastricht, Rintelm, Hessich Oldendorf, Wittenweier, Breisach, Wolfenbüttel, Freiburg and Allerheim.

14 Goetz, 1904, p.122.

Colonel Bartholomew von Hardenberg's Regiment of Foot
Raised 1631. In 1635 it mustered 1270 men in 10 or 11 companies. At the Battle of Nördlingen it lost 74 casualties and 99 taken prisoner. It was later taken over by Heinrich von Metternich, then Johann von der Horst, Heresheim and finally Mercy. It was disbanded in 1649.[15]

Present at the Battle of Nördlingen.

Harthausen's Regiment of Cuirassiers
Raised 1634. At Wittenweier the regiment's colonel was killed.

Present at the Battle of Wittenweier.

Colonel Alexander von Haslang-Sulz's Regiment of Foot
Raised 1620 composed of 20 companies of 2,000 strong, but cashiered in January 1621.

Present at the Battle of White Mountain.

Haslang's Regiment of Foot
See Fugger's Regiment.

Colonel George Rudolf Haslang's Regiment of Foot
Known to have existed between 1633 and 1647 and was commanded by Haslang, Johann von Werth and Karl von Marimont.[16]

Colonel Hans Heinrich Haslang's Regiment of Cuirassiers
Raised 1632, mustering 5 troops. Later Hans Ludwig von Lowenstern and then Johann Heinrich von Lapierre took over the regiment. It was disbanded in 1649.[17]

Present at the battles of Wittenweier, Wolfenbüttel, Tuttlingen, Jankow, Herbsthausen, Freiburg, Allerheim and Zusmarshausen

Baron Adam von Herbersdorf's Regiment of Cuirassiers (1585–1629)
Baron Adam von Herbersdorf had seen service in the Count Palatine Wolfgang Wilhelm von Neuburg's Regiment, before raising a regiment for Maximilian of Bavaria on 8 October 1619. It mustered 5 troops of cuirassiers and among its captains was Gottfried von Pappenheim, who was Herbersdorf's stepson. In 1620 the regiment mustered 622 strong in 7 companies, however this had risen to 1,000 men in 10 troops the following year.

When Herbersdorf became governor of Upper Austria in 1621 the regiment was reorganised, although five troops were placed under Pappenheim's command. In

15 *Ibid.*, p.123.
16 *Ibid.*
17 *Ibid.*, p.122.

1625 the regiment was 1,946 strong in 10 companies. It was disbanded following Herbersdorf's death in 1629. At that time it mustered 16 troops.[18]

Present at Wiesloch, Wimpfen, Lorscher Heide, Höchst, Stadtlohn and Lutter.

Baron Adam von Herbersdorf's Regiment of Foot

Raised on 18 September 1621, in Upper Austria and part of Breisgau. It was disbanded in February 1629.

It was present at the battles of Wimpfen, Höchst and Lutter.

Colonel Hannibal von Herliberg's Regiment of Foot

Raised 1619 composed of 10 companies of about 1250 strong. In 1627 it was taken over by Colonel Jodok Maximillian Graf von Gronsfeld, and from 2 May 1635 by Generalwachtmeister Schellhammer. On 11 July 1636 Feldmarshal Johann Graf von Götzen took command of the regiment and then, on 7 December 1638, Generalfeldzeugmeister Franz Freiherr von Mercy. After Mercy's death at the Battle of Allerheim on 3 August 1645, his son Maximilian Leopold Mercy ('Young Mercy') took command ten days later.

Present at the Battle of White Mountain, Lutter, Wittenweier, Jankow, Freiberg and 2nd Nördlingen, Zusmarshausen.

Colonel Franz von Herzelles' Regiment of Cuirassiers (Würzburg Regiment)

Raised 1620 in Bavaria and Würzberg by Bishop Johann Gottfried and known as the Würzburg Regiment. In 1623 Schonberg took command of the regiment and then in 1634 Billehe. However the following year it became the lifeguard regiment of the Duke of Lothringen. In 1635 it mustered 9 troops rising to 13 by 1638.

Present at the battles of White Mountain, Wiesloch, Wimpfen, Lorscher Heide, Nurnberg, Nördlingen, Rheinfelden (though not the second battle), Wittenweier, Wolfenbüttel, Tuttlingen, Herbsthausen, Allerheim, and Zusmarshausen.

Colonel George Ernst Graf Hohenzollern-Sigmaringen's Regiment of Foot

Raised by the summer of 1621 and disbanded in 1623.[19]

Holz's Regiment of Foot

See Mortaigne's Regiment.

Colonel George Fredrich von Holz's Regiment of Foot

Raised 1639 and disbanded in 1647.[20]

Horst's Regiment of Harquebusiers

See Erwitte's Regiment.

18 Wertheim, vol. 2, pp.337, 573, 578; Weber, pp.406–407.
19 Goetz, 1904, p.123.
20 *Ibid.*

Generalwachtmeister Johann von der Horst's Regiment of Foot
Raised in 1640 by Generalwachtmeister Johann von der Horst, it later became Caspar Mercy's and then Martin Moderspachs' Regiment, before being disbanded in 1649.[21]
The regiment was present at the Battle of Tuttlingen.[22]

Colonel Kobbich's Regiment of Foot
Raised and disbanded in 1647.

Kolb's Regiment of Cuirassiers
See Binder's Regiment.

Kurnreuter's Regiment of Dragoons
Raised 1644, although Kurnreuter enjoyed his command only briefly, because later in the year the regiment passed to 'Jung Kolb', who in 1647 reduced his two regiments into one.
Present at the battles of Freiberg and Allerheim.

Landsberg's Regiment of Foot
Raised 1620 in Cologne and known as the Cologne Regiment. In 1623 Ott Ludwig von Plankhart took over the regiment, followed by Reven in 1635.
The regiment was present at White Mountain, Höchst, Stadtlohn, Magdeburg, Werben, Breitenfeld, Bamberg, and Rain.

Lapierre's Regiment of Cuirassiers
See Haslang's Regiment, although it may possibly have been Götzen's.

Limbach's Regiment of Dragoons
Raised 1633 and consisted of 10 companies.
Present at the Battle of Wittenweier.

Colonel Thimon von Lintelo's (or Lindlo's) Regiment of Cuirassiers
Raised 1620, 625 strong in 6 troops. In 1625 it mustered 830 men in 8 troops and was disbanded in 1632. Despite being a cuirassier regiment at least one troop was composed of Croats. However, this troop was transferred to Colonel Herbersdorf's regiment in 1622.
Present at the battles of Lorscher Heide, Wimpfen, Höchst, Stadtlohn, Efferding, Lutter, Breitenfeld, Maastricht, with Pappenheim in 1631–32, and Lützen.[23]

Colonel Rabe Wolf von der Lippe's Regiment of Horse
Raised and disbanded in 1645, but despite this it appears to have had three commanders: Lippe, Claus Dietrich von Sperreith and Hans Fredrich Pisinger.[24]

21 *Ibid.*
22 Weber, pp.406–407.
23 Wertheim, vol. 2, p.577; Weber, pp.406–407.
24 Goetz, 1904, p122.

Lohn's Regiment of Harquebusiers
Raised 1621. By 1638 it had been taken over by George Truckmuller. In 1648 it was at Schmuller.
Present at the battles of Wittenweier, Freiburg and 2nd Nördlingen.

Colonel del Maestro's regiment of Harquebusiers
See Bonninghausen's Regiment.

Marcussary or Marcosey's Regiment of Horse
The Lothringian Regiment was five troops strong but was disbanded on 31 May 1621.[25]

Meissinger's Regiment of ?
Raised 1635 and mustered 5 companies. At Wittenweier the regiment's colonel was killed.
Present at the Battle of Wittenweier.

Metternich's Regiment of Cuirassiers
Raised 1636 mustering 10 companies and was present at the Battle of Wittenweier.

Metternich's Regiment of Harquebusiers
See Comargo's Regiment.

Metternich's Regiment of Dragoons
Raised 1634 in Würzburg and mustered 5 companies.
Present at the Battle of Nördlingen.

Modersbach's Regiment of Cuirassiers
Raised 1645 and was composed of 5 companies.
Present at the Battle of Zusmarshausen.

Colonel Levin von Mortaigne's Regiment of Foot
Raised 18 February 1620 and mustered 2,279 strong in 13 companies. In 1635 it had 10 companies. In 1626 Jacob Ludwig von Fürstenberg succeeded Mortaigne and then Theodore Comargo on 20 May 1629. He was succeeded by Gabriel Comargo on 24 December 1632. The next commander was Puech in 1634, then Metternich in 1637, then on 29 May 1639 Colonel and Quartermaster General Frederick von Holz.
In 1645 it mustered 998 men in 8 companies and had been taken over by Holz.
Present at the battles of Wiesloch, Wimpfen, Höchst, Stadtlohn, Dessau, Lutter, Magdeburg, Werben, Breitenfeld, Maastricht, Rain, Nurnberg, Lützen, Nördlingen, Wittenweier, Rheinfelden, Tuttlingen, Jankow, Freiberg, Allerheim, Herbsthausen and Zusmarshausen.

25 Wertheim, vol. 2, p.578; Weber, pp.406–407.

Colonel Munch's Regiment of Horse
Raised 1632 by Colonel Munch. In 1633 it was taken over by Johann von Werth and mustered 18 troops, but by 1638 it had been reduced to 9 troops. It was known as 'Alt-Werth Regiment' but when he was captured at the Battle of Rheinfelden the regiment passed to Hans Jacob Kolb, known as 'Jung Kolb'. However, Kolb does not seem to have been the regiment's colonel until 19 July 1647. In 1640 it mustered 803 men of which 210 were without horses.

Present at Rain, Nurnberg, Geltolfing, Nördlingen, Rheinfelden, Wittenweier, Ziegenhain, Tuttlingen, Freiburg, Jankau, Herbsthausen, Allerheim and Zusmarshausen.[26]

Colonel Constantine von Nivenheim's Regiment of Horse
Raised 1623 and disbanded in 1624.[27]

Colonel Johann Birmont von der Nersen's Regiment of Horse
Raised 1620. It was taken over by Witzleben before being disbanded in 1629.[28]

Colonel[?] Von der Nersen's Regiment of Foot
Known to have existed in May 1645.[29]

Colonel Adrian Birmont van der Nerssen's Regiment of Foot
Raised 1645 and mustered 10 companies, although it was disbanded later that year.

Present at the Battle of Zusmarshausen.

Neuenheim's Regiment of Harquebusiers
Raised 1634. The regiment was either raised or taken over by Truckmuller or Neuenheim. On 21 December 1643 the regiment had been taken over by Colonel Cosalki. The regiment also seems to have had a detachment of dragoons attached to it.

By the time of Jankow, it mustered 689 men in 9 companies.

Present at the battles of Wittenweier, Zieggenhain, Wolfenbüttel, Tuttlingen, Freiburg Herbsthausen, Allerheim and Zusmarshausen.

Neuneck's Regiment of Harquebusiers
Raised 1633, and mustered 8 troops. In 1635 it mustered 400 men in 5 troops and in 1640 it mustered 441 men in 8 troops, of which 164 were dismounted.

It became Johann von Sporck's and then Heinrich Zunken's Regiment before being disbanded in 1649.[30]

Present at the battles of Rheinfelden and Wittenweier, and soldiered in south-west Germany.

26 Redlich, p.378; Weber, pp.406–407.
27 Goetz, 1904, p.121.
28 *Ibid.*
29 Weber, pp.406–407.
30 Goetz, 1904, p.122.

Nussbaum's Regiment of Dragoons.

Raised 1638 or 1644. In 1645 it mustered 857 men in 6 companies and had been taken over by Schoch. However according to Wrede Colonel Caspar Schoch's regiment was raised in 22 July 1647 entering Bavarian service in 1648. In 1647 it took part in the conquest of Rothweil and other actions for which Schoch and his lieutenant colonel, Flettinger received a gold chain. The following year the regiment was in Holzapfel's army at Donauwörth.[31]

Present at the battle of Jankow and many skirmishes.

Pappenheim's Regiment of Cuirassiers

In April 1622 the regiment was formed from five companies from Herbersdorf's regiment, plus two new troops of Croats. However, in 1624 the regiment entered Spanish service and later became Octavio Piccolomini's Regiment of Horse in the Imperialist service.

The regiment was present at the battles of the White Mountain, Bruschsal, Wiesloch, Wimpfen, Lorscher Heide, Höchst and Stadtholm.[32]

Colonel Gottfried Heinrich von Pappenheim's Regiment of Foot ('Alt Pappenheim's Regiment')

Raised 1625, mustering 1,800 strong in 7 companies. Later Caspar Schnetter's then Hans Ulrich Golt's Regiment. In 1644 it was disbanded.[33]

Present at the battle of Lutter.

Colonel Gottfried Heinrich von Pappenheim's Regiment of Foot ('New Pappenheim's Regiment')

Raised in 1627. On Pappenheim's death the regiment passed to his son Adam Wolfgang von Pappenheim (or 'Young Pappenheim'). However, he was too young to take up his position and the regiment was commanded by its lieutenant colonel. When Wolfgang was killed in a dual, Lieutenant Colonel Gunther finally took command and then from 17 April 1641 Colonel Johann von Winterscheid. Although according to Franz Weber, Wolfgang Pappenheim took over the regiment in 1632, then in 1646 Elter, until 1649 when Culer took it over.

At the Battle of Breitenfeld the regiment suffered heavy losses and at the battle of Nördlingen it suffered 172 casualties and 153 prisoners out of 1,000 men.

Present at the battles of Höchst, Stadtholm, Efferding, Magdeburg, Werben, Breitenfeld, Rain, Bamburg (9 March 1632), the crossing of the Lech, Nördlingen, Rheinfelden, Breisach, Wittenweier, Wolfenbüttel, Freiburg, Tuttlingen, Herbsthausen, Allerheim and Zusmarshausen.

31 Wrede, vol. 3, part 2, page 409; Weber, pp.406–407.
32 Wertheim, vol. 2, p.578; Weber, 406–407.
33 Goetz, 1904. p.123.

Colonel Gabriel Pechmann's Regiment of Foot
Raised 1622 and disbanded 1623.[34]

Colonel Johann von Rauschenberg or Rusischenberg's Regiment of Foot
Raised 1640. It later became Wilhelm von Hunolstein's, then Adrian von Enkenfort's, before being disbanded in 1646.[35]

Redetti's Regiment of Cuirassiers
Raised 1635 and in 1638 mustered 6 troops. At Wittenweier the commander of the regiment was killed.

Present at the battle of Wittenweier.

Reinach's Regiment of Foot
See Schmidt's Regiment.

Rouyer's Regiment of Foot
See Haimhausen's Regiment.

Colonel Franz von Royer's Regiment of Foot
Raised 1642 and disbanded 1647.[36]

Colonel Nichola Rouville's Regiment of Foot
The Lothringer regiment was commanded by Colonel Nichola Rouville which in January 1621 mustered 4 companies. However in August 1621 it was reduced into Anholt's Regiment.[37]

Colonel Hans Christopher von Ruepp's Regiment of Foot
Raised 1632. On 20 April 1635 Colonel Hans Jacob von Edlinstellen took over the regiment and from 19 April 1643 Colonel Frederick Von Puech. Disbanded 1649.

Salis' Regiment of Harquebusiers
See Eynatten's Regiment.

Salis' Regiment of Horse
Raised 1645 then from 1647 became Württemburg's Regiment.
Present at the battles of Herbsthausen and Allerheim.

34 *Ibid.*
35 *Ibid.*
36 *Ibid.*
37 Wertheim, vol. 2, p.590.

Salis' Regiment of Foot
Raised 1628 and mustered 1000 men in 5 companies in 1632. It was with Pappenheim in 1632. Possibly commanded by Werth up to 1634.
Present at the battle of Nördlingen.

Colonel Valentine Schmidt von Wellenstein's Regiment of Foot
Raised 18 August 1620 in Upper Austria and composed of 10 companies of about 1,800 strong. In 1626 Hans Heinrich von Reinach succeeded Schmidt as commander. Then on 22 August 1637 Melchior Reinach took command. The next commander was Hans Phillip von Hagenbach on 22 October 1640, followed by Josef Rupert Enschering on 27 June 1644. However, he only commanded the regiment for a short time: the following year Fieldmarshal Graf Geleen took over. On 9 November 1645 Geleen was succeeded by Graf Gronsfeld, and then by Karl Reveu de la Folie on 12 July 1648, who commanded it until 1649 when the regiment was disbanded.
In 1634 it mustered 1,270 strong in 18 companies and by 1645 it was 529 strong in 10 companies.
Present at the battles of White Mountain, Wiesloch, Wimpfen, Höchst, Stadtholm, Lutter, Madgeburg, Werben, Breitenfeld, Nördlingen (where 109 men were casualties and 241 taken prisoner), Rheinfelden, Wittenweier, Wolfenbüttel, Tuttlingen, Freiberg and Allerheim and Zusmarshausen.[38]

Schnetter's Regiment of Foot
Raised 1633 and mustered 10 companies. However it was disbanded in 1638.
Present at the battles of Rain, Nördlingen, Wittenweier and Breisach.

Schoch's Regiment of Dragoons
See Nussbaum's Regiment.

Schonberg's Regiment of Cuirassiers
See Herzelle's Regiment.

Colonel R. de la Spagna's Regiment of Horse
Raised 1631. It was later commanded by W. Casselky, until 1648.[39]

Sperreuter's Regiment of Harquebusiers
Raised 1639 in 10 companies. By 1648 it Heinrich Zink von Glesch had taken over.
Present at the battle of Zusmarshausen.

Generalwachtmeister Klaus Dietrict Freiheer von Sperreuter
Raised 1645. On 11 July 1646 it was taken over by Colonel Waldbott.[40]

38 Heilmann, 1868, vol. 2, part II, p.903; Weber, pp.406–407; Wertheim, vol. 2, pp.591–592.
39 Goetz, 1904, p.121.
40 Weber, pp.406–407.

Colonel Johann von Sporck's Regiment of Harquebusiers

Raised 1638, although another source says 1635. It consisted of 10 troops and on 19 July 1647 the regiment was taken over by Zink von Glesh. In 1644, while the regiment was quartered in Schwabisch Hall, several of its horses died in suspicious circumstances for which Sporck put several soldiers' wives on trial for witchcraft. These women were found guilty and burned.[41]

Present at the battles of Wolfenbüttel, Tuttlingen, Freiburg, Jankow, Allerheim and Zusmarshausen.

Colonel Johann Ernest von Sprinzenstein's Regiment of Foot

Raised 1622 and composed of 10 companies. On 19 March 1624 Lieutenant Colonel Gottfried Hubner was promoted colonel and commanded the regiment until 1634.

In May 1622 the regiment mustered 874 musketeers and 400 pikemen.[42]

Colonel Stahl's Regiment of Horse

Raised 1645, and in 1647 it became Württemburg's regiment

Present at the battles of Herbsthausen and Allerheim.

Colonel Albing Count von Sulz's Regiment of Foot

Raised 1619 and disbanded in 1623.[43]

'Alt Tilly's Regiment of Foot'[?]

See Colonel Truchsess' Regiment of Foot.

'Jung Tilly's Regiment'

See Haimhausen's Regiment.

Colonel Truchsess' 46
Regiment of Foot.

See Colonel Bauer's Regiment.

Colonel George Truckmuller's Regiment of Harquebuisers

See Colonel Neverheim's Regiment.

Vehlen's Regiment of Cuirassiers

Raised 1635 mustering 7 companies.

Present at the battle of Wittenweier.

41 K. Bussmann & Heinz Schilling (eds.), *1648 War and Peace in Europe* (Munich: Westfalisches Landesmuseum für Kunst und Kulturgeschichte, cop, 1999), p.127; Weber, pp.406–407.

42 William P. Guthrie, *Battles of the Thirty Years War, from White Mountain to Nördlingen, 1618–1635* (London: Greenwood Press, 2002) vol. 1, p.35; Weber, pp.406–407; Wertheim, vol. 2, p.590.

43 Goetz, 1904, p.122.

Waldott's Regiment of Cuirassiers
Raised 1642 in 8 companies.
Present at the battle of Zusmarshausen.

Colonel Hans Jakob von Waldbott's Regiment of Horse
Raised 1634 and later commanded by George Heinrich von Fleckenstein until it was disbanded in 1648.[44]

Colonel Albrecht von Wartenberg's Regiment of Horse
Raised 1621 and disbanded the following year.[45]

Johann von Werth's Regiment of Harquebusiers
See Eynatten's Regiment.

Neu Werth's Regiment of Dragoons
Raised 1634 and mustered 6 companies.
Present at the battle of Wittenweier.

Colonel Joachim Christian von Wahl's Regiment of Foot
Raised 1624 and mustered 11 companies. Formerly Matthais von Gallas' regiment. In 1635 it mustered 2000 men, but by 1642 this had been reduced to 800 men in 8 companies. In 1644 it was disbanded.
Present at the battle of Rheinfelden.

Wartemberg's Regiment of Cuirassiers
Raised 1632 and mustered 10 companies.
Present at the battle of Wittenweier.

Colonel Johan Wolf's Regiment of Dragoons
Raised 1638 by Colonel Wolf from several companies of dragoons. In 1645 it was taken over by Kreuz and then on 19 July 1647 by Colonel Johann Bartls who commanded it until 1649 when the regiment was disbanded. In 1640 it mustered 581 men in 6 companies, although 287 were dismounted.
Present at the battles of Rheinfelden, Wolfenbüttel, Wittenweier, Tuttlingen, Freiburg and Allerheim, Herbsthausen, and Zusmarshausen and many skirmishes.

Duke Ulrich von Württemberg's Regiment of Horse
Raised 1645 and disbanded in 1649. It became Jakob von Salis' and then Johann von Stahl's Regiment.[46]
Present at the battles of Jankow and Zusmarshausen.

44 *Ibid.*
45 *Ibid.*
46 *Ibid.*

Appendix II

Captured Protestant Colours

Regimental Colours Captured at the Battle of White Mountain by the Imperialist-Catholic League Army[1]

An arm coming from a cloud towards a cannon, drum, muskets and pikes with the motto, *Nori Fine Causi* on the other side a hand holding a sword with the motto, *Non dormit, qui custodit nos.*

A colour with the motto *ETSI* in gold thread.

A white and red colour with the motto *Cum gaudio incipis cum felicitate.*

A black colour with starred silver flames and a man riding a white horse bearing a sword in his mouth and three crowns in his hand, with the motto *Deus fortitude mea.*

A centurion in mail treading on a green, purple and turquoise Medusa with the motto *Justurn Dei indicium.*

A purple colour with two crowns, without inscription.

A colour with the motto *Si prudantia non desit Fortunae Satia.*

Small flames five rows with the motto *Virtute.*

A similar colour but with the mottos *Post rhubila phoebus* and *Vincit Constantia mentis.*

A Maltese cross with the motto *Si Pruentia non digit.*

1 Lobkowitz, pp.400–424.

A turquoise colour with a crowned gold lion holding a heart with the motto, *Pro conscientia et Patriae Liberate.*

A white colour with gold flames with a hand emerging from a cloud holding a pair of scales and weighing the world and the Imperial Diadem, with the motto *In honore requiem.*

A red colour with a naked Jesus with the motto *Considite Ego Vici.*

A prancing crowned lion with the motto *Abissima Fortundo.*

A woman holding a sword in her left hand and a pair of scales in her right, with the motto *Ich liebe Gott und dit gerechtigen.*

An angel holding a cup, with the year '1619'.

A hand emerging from a cloud holding a sword with the motto *Von domit qui cupodit.*

A ball with turquoise bands with the motto *Contero.*

A green arc behind a golden orb with the motto *Florebo prospiliate Deo.*

A yellow colour with an anchor and a turquoise world with the motto, *Spefirmus.*

A colour with a red orb and a crowned lion in the middle with the motto *Honestuin pro Patria mori.*

A colour bearing the image of Justice in Damascene purple, holding a pair of scales, with the motto *Utra?*

Regimental colours captured from Mansfeld's army at the battle of Stadtholm in 1623

Colours of double thickness taffeta.

Three red colours with blue flames

A gold colour and there in of the Virgin in armour with the motto *Revirescrit.*

A mounted cuirassier with the motto *Pro partria mori dulce & decorum est.*

Two hands holding a ring with a large diamond with the motto *Nec ignit nec ferro cedo.*

A torn colour with the image of Fortuna surrounded by four crowned virgins.

A pelican tearing at its breast and the motto *Quod in te est, est pro me.*
A large wreath. therein the motto *Chacun Chancon.*

An armoured hand with a naked sword coming out of the clouds with the words *Fiat Iustitia & pereat mundas.*

An olive branch and the words *Montour viendra.*[2]

Regimental colours captured from the Imperialist Army at the battle of Wittenweier in 1638

The cornet of the Guard company of Goetz, made of blue damask with a cross of Burgundy, silver embroidery with the motto *Pro Imperatore et Fide.*

A red standard of the Goetz's Guard regiment with a cross of Burgundy with the motto *Pro Imperatore et Fide.*

A white standard of a company of Savelli's Guard with a gold arm holding a sword and the other side an eagle, all embroidery gold with the motto *Viva Austria and Spanya.*

A white standard with the knight of St George on one side with the motto Audents Fortuna Junat, and on the other side the image of the Virgin Mary with the motto *Sperans in Deum Mortem non vereor.*

A Red standard with the motto *Pro Imperatore et Rege.*

Two red standards with the motto *Alacriter aggredere honoratus abibes.*

A red standard with the mark of the Jesuits and the motto *Sape insperata Veniunt.*

A green standard with an armoured arm and a naked sword and the motto *Audebo Deus Efficiet.*

A white standard with the motto *Contre variable Fortune bon coeur.*

A green standard with the motto *Patientia aimis lasa fit furor.*

2 Nicholaus Bellus Ostreichischer Lorberkrantz oder Kayserl, *Victori. Das ist: warhafftige, eigentliche vnd aussführliche historische Beschreibung aller ... Sachen vnd Händel, so sich in geistlichen, politischen auch Kriegssachen bey Regierung weyland Keysers Matthiæ ... vnd der jetzigen regierenden ... Majestät Ferdinando II. in diesem noch werenden sechsjährigen ... Krieg ... in- vnd ausserhalb des H. Römischen Reichs von dem 1517. Jahr bey gewesener Union zugetragen vnd verlauffen, biss auff dieses 1625. Jahr continuirt, etc.* (Franckfurt am Main: Durch E. Kempffern, 1625), p.50.

A white standard with the Jesuits' mark embroidered in gold on one side, and on the other the letter 'M'.

Infantry

A white ensign with a eschelle and the Eschelons marque of the name of courage and the motto *Nemo vepits ad patrem nisi per me.*

A white ensign with the image of the Virgin Mary with the motto *Martis Dei Memento Mei.*

A white ensign with an armoured arm and a hammer and two nails and the motto *Malleus Hareticorum*, and on the other side *Flaves Confixerunt Eum.*

A white ensign, with a white cross without a motto.

A white ensign with the image of the Virgin Mary, a red cross of Burgundy and an armoured arm with a sword and the motto *Pro Rege et Lege* and in the middle *Subtuum prasidium Confupinus*, and on the other side Fortuna and the motto *Non omnibus aqua.*

A white ensign and the motto *Vivat Ferdinandus III et Ferdinandus IIII.*

A white ensign with the letters 'F III'

A blue ensign and in the middle a rooster with the motto *Gallus Excitat Jacentes* and on the other side *Extollit Fortes in Bello.*

A blue ensign with a game bird and a hen with chicks and the motto *Evaserunt*, and above the hen *Congregasti nos Domine Sicut Gallina pullos suos.*

A blue ensign with the motto *Qui tuos destruere volunt Mare exhaurire Conantur nam forsan petri Naviculam Fluctuantem, nunquam submergentem videbunt.*

A blue ensign which has an armoured arm coming out of a cloud, with a balloon and the motto *Qui Ceridisse nocet.*

A white ensign and a square and the motto *Effundam Super vos Aquam Mundam*, and on the other side *Lavabit manus suas in Sanquin Peccatoris.*[3]

3 TNA: SP 81/45 Colours captured at the battle of Wittenweier, f.125–126.

Bibliography

Primary Sources

Bavarian State Archives

BayHStA 2274 Correspondence from Bavarian Army officers, 1620–1622
BayHStA 2255 Correspondence from Counsellors and Army officers, 1619–1931
BayHStA 2296 General and other Commissaries, 1621
BayHStA 2329 Incidental, Mustering and other war commissioners, 1622–1632
BayHStA 2301 Die Generalkriegskommissare Ferdinand von Muggenthal, Hans Jakob von Starzhausen, Christoph von Lerchenfeld und Hans Christoph Ruepp
BayHStA 2296 General and other Kommissäres, 1621
BayHStA 2304 Field Marshal Pappenhiem, 1621–1628
BayHStA 2883 Volume including references to providing clothing to soldiers, 1645, 1646

LVR Archivberstung und Fortbildungszeitum, Pulheim, Germany

Correspondence of Field Marshal Count Melchior von Hatzfeldt

Schonst 4 Correspondence from Torquato Conti to Hatzfeldt
Schonst 35 Correspondence from Landgrave Georg von Hessen Darmstadt to Hatzfeldt
Schonst 49 Correspondence from Maximilian I of Bavaria to Hatzfeldt
Schonst 172 Correspondence from Count Rudolf von Colleredo to Hatzfeldt
Schonst 206 Correspondence from Dietrict von Steinheim to Hatzfeldt
Schonst 357 Correspondence from Franz Mercy to Hatzfeldt
Schonst 386 Correspondence from Johan Pluckhardt to Hatzfeldt

Bibliothèque Nationale, Paris

FR14166 *Drapeaux et Etendant pris depuis le commencement du regne de Louis 14 jusqu'en 1688*

Swedish Army Museum

ST Museum artefacts, including captured regimental colours

National Archives, London

SP 9/-	State Papers, Williamson Collection, pamphlets and miscellaneous
SP 16/-	State Papers of Charles I
SP 77/-	State Papers, Flanders
SP 78/-	State Papers, France
SP 80/-	State Papers, Holy Roman Empire
SP 81	State Papers, German States
SP 82/-	State Papers, Hamburg and Hanse Town
SP 83/-	State Papers, Holland and Flanders
SP 84/-	State Papers, Holland
SP 94/-	State Papers, Spain
SP 95/-	State Papers, Sweden
SP 96/-	State Papers, Switzerland
SP 101/-	State Papers, Foreign Newsletters
E403/-	Exchequer Records
WO49/57	Debenture books, 1626

British Library, London

Add MS 39,288	Transcripts of State letters and papers, 1521–1631
Add MS 18,981	Sir William Vavasour: Letters: 1643–1648
Harl 390	Collection of letters of Joseph Mead, Jan 1626–Apr 1631
Harl MS 6,344	A short military treatise concerning all things military.
Harl MS 7,364	A book of tactics in Charles I's time.
Ref. no. 30000 (5)	Plan of Magdeburg, 1631

House of Lords Record Office

HL/PO/JO/10/1/27

National Archives of Scotland

GD406/1/234 Alexander Leslie and other generals, Brandenburg, on behalf of the marquis of Hamilton, ordering the provision of 500 suits of cloth and shoes and stockings in proportion, for the soldiers, 1 Nov 1631

Shakespeare Birthplace Trust Library

DR762/332 Fragment of a banner taken by Gustavus Adolphus during the 30 Years War, from his tomb in the cathedral of Stockholm

Printed Sources

Primary

A Brief and True Relation of the taking in of Magdenburch by the Emperors' and the Catholic League, 10 May 1631 (Holland, 1631), British Library C194a 836

A Continuation of the former newes (London: 9–10 September 1624), no. 23

A Courante relating divers particulars concerning news out of Italy, Germany and Turkey (London: 1 November 1622)

A Relation of the passage of our English Companies from time to time since their first departure from England to the parts of Germanie, and the united Provinces. Sent from Frankendale in Germanie, by a souldier of those colonels, to his worshipfull (London, 1621)

A True and perfect Relation of a Great and Bloudy Battell fought the 23 October [1642] (London?) Thomason Tract E127/30

A true information what manner the city of Magdeburg was overthrown (1631)

A True relation of all such battles as have been fought in the Palatinate since the king's arrival there until the present day of 24 May (London, 1622)

A True Relation of the Affairs of Europe, 4 October 1622

Copies of Letters, 30 May to 11 June 1622 (transcribed, BL SP 101/28)

More Newes from the Palatinate (London, 5 June 1622)

More news, 30 May to 10 June 1623

News from Foreign Parts (London, 28 February 1623; July 1642)

The Continuation of our Forraine Newes (London, May 1631; 29 November 1631, no. 1; 2–12 January 1632, no. 6; 24–30 January 1632; 15 March 1632)

The Continuation of our Forraine Avisoes (London, 9 August 1631; 28 April 1632, no. 20)

The Continuation of the Weekely Newes (London, 27 September 1622; 29 July 1623, no. 24; 30 May 1625)

The Continuation of Our Weekly Newes from Forrain Parts (London, 25 June 1631), no. 31

The current to this week from Holland, 29 May–8 June 1639

Weekly News (London, 20 January 1623, no. 14; 28 January 1623, no. 15; 11 February 1623, no. 18; 14 March 1623, no. 23)

Abelin, Johann Philip, *Theatrum Europaeum* (Frankfurt, 1643)

Barry, Gerrat, *A Discourse of Military Discipline* (Brussels, 1634)

Basta, Giorgio, *Il Governo della cavalleria Leggera* (Bernardo Giunta, Giovanni Battista Ciotti & C, Venezia, 1612)

Bellus Nicholaus, *Ostreichischer Lorberkrantz oder Kayserl, Victori. Das ist: warhafftige, eigentliche vnd aussführliche historische Beschreibung aller ... Sachen vnd Händel, so sich in geistlichen, politischen auch Kriegssachen bey Regierung weyland Keysers Matthiæ ... vnd der jetzigen regierenden ... Majestät Ferdinando II. in diesem noch werenden sechsjährigen ... Krieg ... in- vnd ausserhalb des H. Römischen Reichs von dem 1517. Jahr bey gewesener Union zugetragen vnd verlauffen, biss auff dieses 1625. Jahr continuirt, etc.* (Franckfurt am Main: Durch E. Kempffern, 1625)

Braun, Georg and Hogenberg, Franz, *Civitates Orbis Terrarum* (Cologne, 1572)

Carr, William, *The Traveller's Guide and historians faithful Companion* (London, 1600)

Bingham, John, *Tacticks of Aelian* (London, 1616)

Bingham, John, *The Art of Embattaling an Army, or, the second part of Aelians tacticks* (London, 1631)

Brinckmair, L., *The Warnings of Germany: By Wonderful Signes and Strange Prodigies* (London, 1638)

Crosfield, Thomas (ed. Frederick Boas), *Diary of Thomas Crosfield* (London: Oxford University Press, 1935)

Cherbury, Edward, Baron Herbert of, *The Expedition to the Isle of Rhe* (London: Whittingham and Wilkins, 1860)

Cruso, John, *Militarie instructions for the Cavall'rie* (being a facsimile to the edition of 1632, ed. Brigadier Peter Young; Kineton: The Roundwood Press, 1972)

Cruso, *Arte of Warre*, translated from the French (Cambridge, 1639)

Drexel, Father Pietro, his diary, in Sigmund Riezler, *Kriegstagebücher aus dem ligistichen Hauptquartier, 1620* (Munich: G Frans'chen, 1908)

Fitzsimon, Father Henry, 'Diary of the Bohemian War of 1620', in *Words of Comfort to Persecuted Catholics* (Dublin: Gill & Son, 1881)

Friesenegger, Maurus, *Tagebuch aus dem 30jährigen Krieg* (Munich: Allitera, 2007)

Gareston, Mr., *A Continued journal of all the Proceedings of the Duke of Buckingham on the Isle of Ree* (London, 1627)

Garrard, William, *The Art of Warre. Beeing the onely rare booke of Myllitarie profession* (London, 1591)

Gerbier, Sir Balthazar, *The First Lecture being an introduction to the Military Architecture or fortifications, read publically at Sir Balthazar Gerbiers Academy* (London: Robert Ibbitson, 1650)

Heath, John, *Observations upon military and Political Affairs written by the Most Honourable George, Duke of Albemarle* (London: Henry Mortlocke, 1671)

Hexham, Henry, *The Principles of the Art Militarie*, part 2 (1642)

Hoppe, Israel, (ed. Dr M. Toeppen), *Burggrafen zu Elbing, Geschichte des Ersten schwedisch-polnishen Krieges in Preussen nebst Anhang* (Leipzig: Duncker and Humblot, 1887)

Kellie, Thomas, *Pallas Armata or the Art of Instructions for the Learned: and all generous spirits who effect the Profession of Arms* (Edinburgh, 1627)

Khevenhueller, Franz, *Annales Ferdinandi* (Leipzig, 1722)

Lobkowitz, Juan Caramuel de, *Caramuelis Dominicus hoc est, Venerabilis P Dominici a Jesu-Maria* (Vienna: Apud Matthaeum Cosmerovium, 1655)

Markham, Francis, *Five Decades of Epistles of Warre* (London, 1622)

Markham, Gervase, *The Souldiers Accidence* (London: John Bellamie, 1625)

Markham, Gervase, *The Second Part of the Soldiers Grammar* (London: A. Matthews, 1927)

Markham, Gervase, The Souldiers Exercise (London: Lawrence Blaiklock, 1643)

Marolois, Samuel, *The Art of Fortification*, translated by Henry Hexham (Amsterdam: 1638)

Melzo, Ludovico, *Regole Militari del Cavalier Melzo sopra il governon e servitio della cavalleria* (1611)

Monro, Robert, *His Expedition with the Worthy Scots Regiment (Called Mac-Keyes Regiment) levied in August 1626* (London: William Jones, 1637), part II

Poyntz, Sydnam (ed. A. Goodrick), *The true relation of Sydnam Poyntz, 1624–1636* (London: Royal Historical Society, 1908)

Poyntz, Sydnam, *A True Relation of these German Warres From Mansfeld's Going out of England which was in the year (1624) untill this last yeare 1636 whereof my self was an eyewitness of most I have here related* (Tonbridge: Pallas Armata, 1992)

Praissac, Sieur Du, *The Arte of Warre, or military discourses, translated by John Cruso* (Cambridge: Roger Daniel, 1639)

Praissac, Sieur Du, *A short method for the easie resolving of any militarie question propounded, translated by John Cruso* (Cambridge: Roger Daniel, 1639)

Priorato, Count Galeazzo Gualdo, *An history of the late warres and other state affaires of the best part of Christendom beginning with the King of Swethlands entrance into Germany, and continuing in the yeare 1640.* Translated by Henry Carey Earl of Monmouth (London: W. Wilson, 1648)

Raymond, Thomas (ed. G. Davis), *Autobiography of Thomas Raymond* (London: Royal Historical Society, 1917)

Rhumelius, J. C., *Historia Morbi* (1621)

Ross, Alexander, *The History of the World the second part in six books being a continuation of famous history of Sir Walter Raleigh knight* (1640)

Smythe, Sir John, *Instructions, Observations and Orders Mylitarie* (London: 1595)

Turner, Sir James, *Pallas Armata* (London: 1683)

Vincent, Philip, *The Lamentations of Germany, Wherein, as in a Glasse, we may behold her miserable condition ... illustrated by pictures. Hereunto are added three Letters, one whereof was sent to the Dutch Consistory in London, under the hand ... of 14 distressed Ministers of Swyburggen in Germany* (London: J. Rothwell, 1638)

Wallhausen, Johann, *Art Militare a Cheval*, 1616

Wallhausen, Johann, *Kriegskunst zu Pferdt* (Frankfurt am Main: Iohann-Theodori de Bry, 1616)

Wallhausen, Johann, *Kriegskunst zu Fuss* (Oppenheim: Johann-Theod. de Bry, 1615)

Wallhausen, Johann, *L'Art militaire pour l'infanterie* (Franeker: Uldrick Balck, *c.*1625)

Ward, Robert, *Animadversions of Warre; or a Military magazine of the truest rules and ablest instructions for the managing of warre* (London: 2 vols., 1639).

Sardi, Pietro, *Corona imperiale dell'architettura militare divisa in due trattati. Il primo contiene la teorica. Il secondo contiene la pratica* (Venice: Barezzo Barezzi, 1618)

Smythe, Sir John, *Instructions, Observations and Orders Mylitarie* (1595)

Stevin, Symon, *Nieuwe maniere van sterctebow door spilsluysen* (Rotterdam: Ian van Waesberghe, 1617)

Watts, William, *The Swedish Intelligencer* (London, 1633). Three parts.

Watts, William, *A supplement to the sixth part of the Germane history* (London, 1634)

Secondary

17th Century War, Weaponry and Politics: 10th congress Stockholm 1984 (International Association of Museums of Arms and Military History)

Barker, Thomas, *The Military Intellectual and Battle; Raimondo Montecuccoli and the Thirty Years War* (Albany: State University of New York Press, 1975)

Bartz, Christian, *Köln im Dreissigjährigen Krieg: die Politik des Rates der Stadt (1618–1635); vorwiegend anhand der im Historischen Archiv der Stadt Köln* (Frankfurt am Main: P. Lang, 2005)

Bavarian Kriegsministerium Kriegsarchiv, *Geschichte des Bayerischen Heeres*. Im Auftrage des Kriegs-Ministeriums herausgegeben vom K. B. Kriegsarchiv (Munich, 1901)

Belaubre, Jean, *Troops of the Electoral Saxony during the Thirty Years War* (translated by Pat Condrey (Historical Products Company, 1982)

Bellander, Erik, *Dräkt och Uniform: den Svenska arméns beklädnad från 1500- talets början fram till våra dagar* (Stockholm: Norstedt, 1973)

Benecke, Gerhard, *Germany in the Thirty Years War* (London: Edward Arnold, 1978)

Berenger, *Jean Turenne* (Paris: Fayard, 1987)

Berg, Holger, *Military Occupation under the Eyes of the Lord* (Gottingen: Vandenboeck & Ruprecht, 2010)

Blackmore, David, *Arms and Armour of the English Civil Wars* (London: The Trustees of the Royal Armouries, 1990)

Brezezinski, Richard and Hook, Richard, *The Army of Gustavus Adolphus, 1: Infantry* (Oxford: Osprey, 1991)

Brezezinski, Richard and Hook, Richard, *The Army of Gustavus Adolphus, 2: Cavalry* (Oxford: Osprey, 1993)

Brezezinski, Richard Lutzen, *Climax of the Thirty Years War* (Oxford: Osprey, 2001)

Bruardic, Vladimir, *Imperial Armies of the Thirty Years War, 1: Infantry* (Oxford: Osprey, 2009)

Bruardic, Vladimir, *Imperial Armies of the Thirty Years War, 2: Cavalry* (Oxford: Osprey, 2010)

Bruce, John (ed.), *Calendar of State Papers, Domestic Series. Charles I. 1628–1629* (London: Longman, 1859)

Buchner, Alex and Volker, *Bayern im Dreissigjährigen Krieg* (Dachau: Bayerland, 2002)

Burckhardt, Carl J., *Richelieu and his Age* (London: George Allen and Unwin Ltd, 1965)

Bussmann, K. and Schilling, H. (eds.), *1648 War and Peace in Europe* (Munich: Westfalisches Landesmuseum für Kunst und Kulturgeschichte, cop, 1999)

Carman, W. Y., *British Uniforms* (London: Hill, 1957)

Chaboche, Robert, 'Les Militaires et la societe', in *Revue D'Historie moderne et contemporaraine*, no. 20 (1973) pp.10–24

Croxton, Derek, *Peacemaking in Early Modern Europe: Cardinal Mazarin and the Congress of Westphalia, 1643–648* (Selinsgrove, NJ: Susquehanna University Press, 1999)

Dahlgren, Erik W., *Louis de Geer, 1587-1652: hans lif und verk* (Uppsala: Almqvist och Wicksell, 1923)

Danner, Dr Adolf, 'Der Kommierzienrat in Bayern im 17 Jah,ert', part 1, Under Maximilian I', in *Oberbayerisches Archiv fur Vaterlandische Geschichte* (Munich 1910)

Davies, Steffan, *The Wallenstein Figure in German Literature and Historiography, 1790–192*0 (London: Maney Publishing, 2010)

Duch, Arno, *Die Politik Maximilians I von Bayern und seiner Verbündeten, 1618–1651* (Munich: R. Oldenbourg, 1970), vol. 1, part II

Duch, Arno et al., *Briefe und Acten zur Geschichte des Dreissigjährigen Krieges in den Zeiten des vorwaltenden Einflusses der Wittelsbacher... Neue Folge. Die Politik Maximilians I. von Bayern und seiner Verbündeten 1618–1651* (Munich, 1966)

Ebner, H. et al, *Festschrift Othmar Pickl zum 60. Geburtstag* (Graz: Leykam Verlag, 1987)

Eickhoff, Sabine, 'Das Massengrab der Schlacht von Wittstock', in *Militargeschichte* (February 2013)

Eickhoff, Sabine, et al., *1636, Ihre Letzte Schlacht, leben im Dreissigjährigen Kreig* (Brandenburg: Archaeologisches Landesmuseum, 2013)

Engerisser, Peter, *Von Lützen Nach Nördlingen* (Weissenstadt: Späthling, 2004)

Engerisser, Peter, *Nördlingen 1634: Die Schlacht bei Nördlingen – Wendepunkt des Dreißigjährigen Krieges* (Wissensdadt: H. Späthling, 2009)

Ergang, Robert, *The Myth of the all-destructive fury of the Thirty Years' War* (Pocono Pines, Pa.: The Craftsmen, 1956)

Ernstberger, Anton, *Wallenstein als Volkswirt im Herzogtum Friedland* (Reichenberg i.B.: F. Kraus, 1929)

Ernstberger, Anton, *Hans de Witte, Finanzmann Wallensteins* (Wiesbaden: Steiner Verlag, 1954)

Elster, O., *Geschichte der Stehenden Truppen in Herzogum Braunschweig-Wolfenbüttel von 1600–1714* (Leipzig, 1899)

Ferguson, James, *Papers illustrating the History of the Scots Brigade in the Service of the United Netherlands 1572–1782* (Edinburgh: Scottish History Society, 1899–1901)

Fortescue, John, et al. (eds.), *Calendar of State Papers Colonial*, vol. 8, 1630–1634 (London: HMSO, 1892)

Frauenholz, Eugene von, *Das Heerwesen in der Zeit des Dreissigjahrigen Krieges* (Munich, 1938–39), vol. 2

Friedrichs, Christopher R., *Urban Society in an Age of War: Nördlingen, 1580–1720* (Princeton: Princeton University Press, 1979)

Gindely, Anton, *History of the Thirty Years War*, transl. Andrew Ten Brook (London: Bentley and Sons, 1885)

Goetz, Walter 'Die Kriegskosten Bayerns und der Ligastände im Dreissigjährigen Kriege', in *Forschungen zur Geschichte Bayerns*, vol. 12 (Munich and Berlin: R. Oldenbourg, 1904)

Goetz, Walter, *Die Politik Maximilians I von Bayiern und seiner Verbündeten, 1618–1651*, vol. 2, part I (Leipzig: B. G. Teubner, 1907)

Grunzel, Joseph, 'Die Reichenberger Tuchindustrie in ihrer Entwickelung vom zünftigen Handwerk zur modernen Grossindustrie', in *Verein für Geschichte der Deutschen in Böhmen. Beiträge zur Geschichte der deutschen Industrie in Böhmen*, no. 5. (Prague, 1893)

Guthrie, William P., *The Thirty Years War, from White Mountain to Nördlingen, 1618–1635* (London: Greenwood Press, 2002)

Guthrie, William P., *The Later Thirty Years War, from the battle of Wittstock to the Treaty of Westphalia* (London: Greenwood Press, 2003)

Haberer, Stephanie, *Otto Heinrich Fugger (1592–1644): biographische Analyse typologischer Handlungsfelder in der Epoche des Dreissigjährigen Krieges* (Augsburg: Wissner, 2004)

Hanlon, Gregory, *The Hero of Italy, Odoardo Farnese, Duke of Parma, his soldiers, and his subjects in the Thirty Years' War* (Oxford: Oxford University Press, 2014)

Harte, Walter, *The History of the Life of Gustavus Adolphus* (London: G. Hawkins, 1759)

de Haynin, Louis, seigneur du Cornet, *Histoire Générale des guerres de Savoie, de Bohême, du Palatinat & des Pays-Bas, 1616–1627* (Brussels: C. Muquardt, 1868)

Hays, J. N., *Epidemics and Pandemics: their impact on human history* (Santa Barbara, Calif.: ABC-CLIO, 2005)

Heberle, Hans, *Der Dreissigjährige Krieg in zeitgenössischer Darstellung: Hans Heberles "Zeytregister" (1618–1672)* (Stuttgart: Kommissionsverlag Kohlhammer, 1975)

Heilmann, Johann, *Kriegsgeschichte von Bayern, Franken, Pfalz und Schwaben von 1506–1651* (Munich: I. G. Cottaschen, 1868), 4 vols

Heilmann, Johann, *Der Feldzüge der Bayern in den Jahren 1643, 1644 & 1645* (Leipzig: Goedsche, 1851)
Heilingsetzer, George, *Der Oberösterreichische Bauernkrieg, 1626* (Vienna: Militarhistorische Schriftenreihe, 1976)
Helfferich, Tryntje (ed., transl.), *The Thirty Years War, a Documentary History* (Cambridge, Mass.: Hackett Publishing Company, 2009)
Helml, Stefan, *Die Oberpfalz im 30jähriger Krieg, der Deutschland und Europa in seinen Bann zog* (Amberg: Scherer, 1990)
Hoeven, Marco van der, *Exercise of Arms , Warfare in the Netherlands* (Leiden: Brill, 1997)
Higham, Robin, 'Some Thoughts on the 30 Years War', in Jan Vilím, *Bellum Tricennale* (Prague: Historical Institute of the Army of Czech Republic, 1997)
Hilkhuijsen, Jos W. L. et al., *Beelden van een strijd: oorlog en kunst vóór de Vrede van Munster, 1621–1648* (Zwolle:Waanders, 1998)
Hinds, Allen B. (ed.), *Calendar of State Papers Relating to the English Affairs in the Archives and Collections of Venice*, vol. 18, 1623–1624 (London: HMSO, 1912)
Hinds, Allen B. (ed.) *Calendar of State Papers Relating To English Affairs in the Archives and Collections of Venice*, vol. 24, 1636–1639 (London: HMSO, 1923)
HMC Coke ms Report 12 app. 1
Huf, Hans-Christian, *Mit Gottes Segen in die Holle, Der Dreissigjahrige Krieg* (List Taschenbuch, no date)
Hoffmann, Friedrich, *Geschichte der Stadt Magdeburg* (Magdeburg, 1885)
Hopkins, David and Hillary, *The Tale of a Soldier's Coat: The Story of the Experimental Reconstruction of a 1643 Oxford Royalist Soldier's Coat* (Stuart Press, 2000)
Howard, Daniel (ed.), *Callot's Etchings: 338 Prints* (New York: Dover Publications, 1974)
Jacob, Carl, *Von Lützen nach Nördlingen: Ein Beitrag zur Geschichte des Dreissigjährigen Kriegs in Süddeutschland in den Jahren 1633 und 1634* (Strassburg i.E: Ed. van Hauten, 1904)
Jany, Curt, *Geschichte der Königlich Preussischen Armee bis zum 1807*(Berlin: K. Siegismund, 1928–37), 5 vols.
Jordan, Reinhard, *Chronik der Stadt Mülhausen im Thüringen* (Mülhausen; Danner, 1906), vol. 3
Kasper, Cordula, *Die Bayerische Kriegsorganisation in der zweiten Hälfte des Dreissigjährigen Krieges* (Aschendorff: Münster, 1997)
Kouril, *Milos et al Documenta Bohemica Bellum Tricennale Illustrantia* (Prague: Academia, nakladatelství Československé akademie věd, 1971-1977)
Kraus, Andreas, *Geschichte Bayerns: von den Anfängen bis zur Gegenwart* (München: C. H. Beck, 1983)
Kraus, Andreas, *Maximilian I: Bayerns Grosser Kurfürst* (Graz: Styria, 1990)
Krebs, Julius, *Die Schlact am Weissen Berge bei Prag* (Breslau: Wilhelm Koebner, 1879)
Krenn, Peter and Karcheski, Walter J., *Imperial Austria, treasures of Art, Arms and Armour from the State of Styria* (Australia: Art Exhibitions Australia Ltd, 1998)
Kasper, Cordula, *Die Bayerische Kriegsorganisation in der zweiten Hälfte des Dreissigjährigen Krieges, 1635-1648/49* (Aschendorff: Münster, 1997)
Langer, Herbert, *The Thirty Years' War* (Poole: Blandford Press, 1978)
Lindegren, Jan, *Utskrivning och Utsugning Production och reproduction i Bygdeå, 1620–1640* (Stockholm: Almqvist & Wiksell international, 1980)

Lugs, Jaroslav, *Firearms Past and Present: a complete review of firearm systems and their histories* (London: Greville, 1973)
Lyle, J. V. (ed.), *Acts of the Privy Council of England, 1623–1628* (London, 1932–1940), vols. 39–43.
Lynn, John, *Giant of the Grand Siècle: The French Army, 1610–1715* (Cambridge University Press, 2006)
Lynn, John, *Women, Armies and Warfare in Early Modern Europe* (Cambridge: Cambridge University Press, 2008)
Matthiae, Guglielmo, *Santa Maria Della Vittoria* (Rome: Ats Italia Editrice, 1999)
Mayr-Deisinger, Karl and George Franz, *Die Politik Maximilians I von Bayern und Seiner Verbündeten, 1618–1651* (Munich: R. Oldenbourg, 1966)
McNair, Don, *The Struggle for Stralsund, 1627–1630* (Farnham: Pike & Shot Society, 2012)
Mankell, J., *Arkiv Till Upplysing On Svenska Krigens Och Krigsinrättningarnes Historia* (Stockholm: P. A. Norsstedt and Soner, 1860)
Mann, Sir James, *Wallace Collection Catalogue, European Arms and Armour* (London: William Clowes and Son Ltd, 1962)
Matousek, Vaclav, 'Archaeological Erforschung der Schlachtfelder des Dreissigsjährigen Krieges', in Janos Stekovics, *Die Blut'ge Affair bei Lützen: Wallensteins Wende* (Wettin-Löbejün Stekovics, 2012)
Mazumder, R. N. et al., 'Typhus Fever; an overlooked diagnosis' in *Journal of Health, Population and nutrition*, vol. 27, no. 3, 2009
Medick, Hans, 'The Destruction of Magdeburg', in *Historical Workshop Journal* (Oxford University Press, Autumn 2000)
Meier, Franz, *Die bayerische Unterpfalz im Dreißigjährigen Krieg: Besetzung, Verwaltung und Rekatholisierung der rechtsrheinischen Pfalz durch Bayern 1621 bis 1649* (Frankfurt am Main: P. Lang, *c.*1990)
Mortimer, Geoff, 'The Thirty Years War in Eyewitness Personal Accounts', in *German History*, vol. 20 no.2, (2002)
Mortimer, Geoff, *Eyewitness Accounts of the Thirty-Years War 1618–48* (Basingstoke: Palgrave, 2002)
Mortimer, Geoff, *Wallenstein: the enigma of the Thirty Years War* (New York: Palgrave Macmillan, 2010)
Mortimer, Geoff, *The origins of the Thirty Years War and the revolt in Bohemia, 1618* (Basingstoke: Palgrave Macmillan, 2015)
Moxey, Keith, *Peasants, Warriors and Wives: popular imagery in the Reformation* (Chicago: University of Chicago Press, 2004)
Mungeam, Gerald, 'Contracts for the Supply of equipment to the New Model Army', in *The Journal of the Arms and Armour Society*, 1968, vol. 6, no. 3
Munich, Friedrich, *Geschichte der Entwickelung der bayerischen Armee seit zwei Jahrhunderten* (Munich: Lindauer, 1864)
Oelsnitz, A. C. von der, *Geschichte des Königlich Preussische Ersten Infanterie-Regiments* (Berlin: E. S. Mittler and Son, 1855)
Parker, Geoffrey, *Europe in Crisis: 1598–1648* (Glasgow: Fontana, 1987)
Parker, Geoffrey, *The Thirty Years' War* (London: Routledge, 1997)

Peters, Jan, *Ein Soldnerleben im Dreissigjährigen Krieg* (Berlin: Akadamie Verlag, 1993)
Petrelli, T. J. and Liljedahl, E. S., 'Standar och dragonfanor' in *Antiqvarisk Tidskrift for Sverige* Vol 14 nr 3 (1895)
Polisensky, J. V., *War and Society in Europe, 1618–1648* (London: Cambridge University Press, 1978)
Prinzing, F., *Epidemics Resulting from Wars* (Oxford: 1916)
Puhle, Matthais, *'Gantz verheeret!', Magdeburg und der Dreißigjährige Krieg* (Magdeburg: Mitteldeutscher 1998)
Venturini, Dr Carl von, *Amriss einer pragmatischen Geschichte des Kriegswesen im Herzogthume Braunschweig* (Magdeburg: Eduard Buhler, 1837)
Redlich, Fritz, *The Germany Military Enterpriser and his Work force: A Study in European Economic and Social History* (Wiesbaden: Franz Steiner, 2 vols., 1964)
Roberts, Michael, *Gustavus Adolphus, a History of Sweden 1611–1632* (London: Longmans, Green and Co., 1958), vol. 2
Reitzenstein, Karl Freiherr von, *Der Feldzug des Jahres 1621 mit der Besitzergreifung der Oberpfalz* (Munich: F. Straub, 1887)
Reitzengen, *Amtman von Der Feldzug 1622* (Munich: P. Zipperer, 1890)
Richardson, Thom and Rimer, Graeme, *Littlecote, The English Civil War Armoury* (Leeds: Royal Armouries, 2012)
Samsoen, Guillaume de Gerard, *The Comte de Tilly, General de la Guerre de Trente Ans* (Paris: OEIL, 1992)
Sandstedt, Fred and Sandstedt, Lena, 'Proud Symbols of Victory and mute witnesses of bygone Glories', in *Hoc Signo Vinces* (Stockholm: National Swedish Museums of Military History, 2006)
Sandstedt, Fred, *In Hoc Signo Vinces, A Presentation of The Swedish State Trophy Collection* (Stockholm: The National Swedish Museums of Military History, 2006)
Schlecht, Joseph, *Tagebuch Der Augustinernonne Klara Staiger* (Eichstätt, 1889)
Schroder, Peter and Asbach, Olaf (eds.), *The Ashgate Research Companion to the Thirty Years War* (Farnham: Ashgate, 2014)
Sennawald, Ronald, *Das Kursächsische Heer im Dreissigjährigen Krieg* (Berlin: Zeughaus, 2013)
Sommeregger, 'Savelli, Herzog Friedrich von', in *General German Biography 53* (1907)
Soden, Franz Freiheer von, *Gustav Adolph und Sein Heer in Süddeutschland von 1631 bis 1635* (Erlangen: Deichert, 1865)
Stadler, Barbara, *Pappenheim und die Zeit des Dreissigjährigen Krieges* (Winterthur: Gemsberg-Verl., 1991)
Swedish Army Staff, *Sveriges Krieg, 1611–1632* (Stockholm, 1936–1939)
Swedish Army Staff, *Sveriges Krieg Supplementary, 1611–1632*, Bilagsband vol. 1 (Stockholm: V. Pettersons Bokindustriaktiebolag, 1936)
Terry, Charles S., *The Life and Campaigns of Alexander Leslie, First Earl of Leven* (London: Longman, 1899)
Theibault, J. C., *German Villages in Crisis: rural life in Hesse-Kassel and the Thirty Years' War, 1580–1720* (Atlantic Highlands, New Jersey: Humanities Press, 1995)

Turek, Eva, *Under False Colours: A case of mistaken identity – are the colours those of Wallenstein or Liechtenstein?* (Stockholm: Armémuseum, 1996)

Venable, Mary Noll, 'Evenius and the Siege of Magdeburg', in Emily Nicholson et al. (eds.), *Linking of Heaven and Earth* (Farnham: Ashgate, 2012)

Villermont, Antonie Charles Hennequin, *Tilly: oder Dreissigjährige Kreig von 1618 bis 1632* (Schaffhausen: Fr Hurterschen, 1860)

Vogel, Hans, 'Arms Production and exports in the Dutch Republic, 1600-1650', in Marco van der Hoeven, *Exercise of Arms: Warfare in the Netherlands, 1568–1648* (Leiden: Brill, 1997)

Volkholz, Robert, *Juergen Ackermann, Kapitaen Beim Regiment Alt Pappenheim, 1631* (Halberstadt: Schimmellburg, 1895)

Watson, Francis, *Wallenstein, Soldier under Saturn* (London: Chatto & Windus, 1938)

Weber, Franz 'Gliederung und Einsatz des bayerischen Heeres im Dreissigjahrigen Krieg', in Hubert Glaser, *Um Glauben und Reich, Kurfürst Maximilian I* (Munich: R Piper & Co., 1980)

Wertheim, Dr Hans, *Der Tolle Halberstädter: Herzog Christian von Braunschweig im Pfälzischen Kriege 1621–1622* (Berlin: Internationale Bibliothek, 2 vols., 1929)

White, Lorraine, 'The Experience of Spain's Early Modern Soldiers', in *War in History* (2002), vol. 9, no. 1, pp.23–24.

Wilson, Peter, *Europe's Tragedy: A New History of the Thirty Years War* (London: Penguin, 2010)

Wilson, Peter, *The Thirty Years War: A Sourcebook* (Basingstoke: Palgrave Macmillan, 2010)

Wrede, Alphons von, *Geschichte der k. und k. Wehrmacht: die Regimenter, Corps, Branchen und Anstalten von 1618 bis Ende des XIX. Jahrhunderts* (Vienna: L. W. Seidel and Son, 1898–1905)

Websites

Der Dreißigjährige Krieg in Selbstzeugnissen, Chroniken und Berichten by Dr Bernd Warlich: <http://www.30jaehrigerkrieg.de/>

Peter Engerisser, website: <http://www.engerisser.de/>

Peter Engerisser, 'Matchlock Musket, Suhl approx, 1630' <http://www.engerisser.de/Bewaffnung/weapons/Matchlockmusket.html> (accessed 8 May 2015)

Thirty Years War blog by Daniel S: <http://kriegsbuch.blogspot.co.uk/>

Swedish Museums website: <http://digitaltmuseum.se>

Swedish Documentary on the battle of Lützen:
<https://www.youtube.com/watch?v=MCJNsEDjxSI>

Index

INDEX OF PLACES

INDEX OF PEOPLE

INDEX OF GENERAL SUBJECTS

The Century of the Soldier series – Warfare c 1618-1721

www.helion.co.uk/centuryofthesoldier

'This is the Century of the Soldier', Falvio Testir, Poet, 1641

The 'Century of the Soldier' series will cover the period of military history c. 1618–1721, the 'golden era' of Pike and Shot warfare. This time frame has been seen by many historians as a period of not only great social change, but of fundamental developments within military matters. This is the period of the 'military revolution', the development of standing armies, the widespread introduction of black powder weapons and a greater professionalism within the culture of military personnel.

The series will examine the period in a greater degree of detail than has hitherto been attempted, and has a very wide brief, with the intention of covering all aspects of the period from the battles, campaigns, logistics and tactics, to the personalities, armies, uniforms and equipment.

Submissions

The publishers would be pleased to receive submissions for this series. Please contact us via email (info@helion.co.uk), or in writing to Helion & Company Limited, 26 Willow Road, Solihull, West Midlands, B91 1UE.

Titles

No 1 *'Famous by my Sword'. The Army of Montrose and the Military Revolution* Charles Singleton (ISBN 978-1-909384-97-2)*

No 2 *Marlborough's Other Army. The British Army and the Campaigns of the First Peninsular War, 1702–1712* Nick Dorrell (ISBN 978-1-910294-63-5)

No 3 *Cavalier Capital. Oxford in the English Civil War 1642–1646* John Barratt (ISBN 978-1-910294-58-1)

No 4 *Reconstructing the New Model Army Volume 1. Regimental Lists April 1645 to May 1649* Malcolm Wanklyn (ISBN 978-1-910777-10-7)*

No 5 *To Settle The Crown – Waging Civil War in Shropshire, 1642–1648* Jonathan Worton (ISBN 978-1-910777-98-5)

No 6 *The First British Army, 1624-1628. The Army of the Duke of Buckingham* Laurence Spring (ISBN 978-1-910777-95-4)

No 7 *'Better Begging Than Fighting'. The Royalist Army in Exile in the War against Cromwell 1656–1660* John Barratt (ISBN 978-1-910777-71-8)*

No 8 *Reconstructing the New Model Army Volume 2. Regimental Lists April 1649 to May 1663.* Malcolm Wanklyn (ISBN 978-1-910777-88-6)*

No 9 *The Battle of Montgomery 1644. The English Civil War in the Welsh Borderlands.* Jonathan Worton (ISBN 978-1-911096-23-8)*

No 10 *The Arte Militaire. The Application of 17th Century Military Manuals to Conflict Archaeology* Warwick Louth (ISBN 978-1-911096-22-1)*

No 11 *No Armour But Courage: Colonel Sir George Lisle, 1615–1648* Serena Jones (ISBN 978-1-911096-47-4)

No 12 *Cromwell's Buffoon: The Life and Career of the Regicide, Thomas Pride* Robert Hodkinson (ISBN 978-1-911512-11-0)

No 14 *Hey for Old Robin! The Campaigns and Armies of the Earl of Essex During the First Civil War, 1642–44* Chris Scott & Alan Turton (ISBN 978-1-911512-21-9)*

No 15 *The Bavarian Army during the Thirty Years War* Laurence Spring (ISBN 978-1-911512-39-4)

No 16 *The Army of James II, 1685–1688: The Birth of the British Army* Stephen Ede-Borrett (ISBN 978-1-911512-39-4)*

Books within the series are published in two formats: 'Falconets' are paperbacks, page size 248mm x 180mm, with high visual content including colour plates; 'Culverins' are hardback monographs, page size 234mm x 156mm. Books marked with * in the list above are Falconets, all others are Culverins.